Coming Clean

COMING CLEAN

Overcoming Addiction without Treatment

Robert Granfield and William Cloud

Foreword by Stanton Peele

NEW YORK UNIVERSITY PRESS

New York and London

NEW YORK UNIVERSITY PRESS

New York and London

Library of Congress Cataloging-in-Publication Data

Granfield, Robert, 1955–

Coming clean : overcoming addiction without treatment /
Robert Granfield and William Cloud.

p.   cm.

Includes bibliographical references and index.

ISBN 0-8147-1581-8 (cloth : alk. paper)

ISBN 0-8147-1582-6 (pbk. : alk. paper)

1. Recovering addicts. 2. Self-care, Health. 3. Self-management
(Psychology) 4. Alcoholics—Rehabilitation. 5. Narcotic
addicts—Rehabilitation.   I. Cloud, William, 1947–   II. Title.

HV4998 .G73 1999

616.86'06—dc21   99-6526

CIP

Manufactured in the United States of America

10 9 8 7 6 5 4 3 2

For Midge, Karen, and Allison

CONTENTS

Appendix

FOREWORD

Writing a foreword to *Coming Clean* is a bit like being the best man at a wedding between two people you introduced—Bob Granfield (in the sociology department) and William Cloud (in the social work school) were both teaching courses at the University of Denver on drugs. Both were using my book *Diseasing of America*. When William learned this, he immediately contacted Bob—and one of the results is the volume that follows (as well as a strong friendship between the two men and their families).

Both Bob and William recognized that, as *Diseasing* and another of my books, *The Truth about Addiction and Recovery*, maintain, the disease theory of alcoholism and addiction does more harm than good. This approach is inaccurate and also self-defeating—how many people reckon they can improve their lives when they decide they are stricken with an "incurable" disease?

One proof that the disease theory is inaccurate comes from contemplating the words of such prominent disease theory advocates as Robert Dupont, former director of the National Institute on Drug Abuse. Dupont expressed the conventional disease wisdom when he wrote, "Addiction is not self-curing. Left alone addiction only gets worse, leading to total degradation, to prison, and ultimately to death."

But on what do Dupont and others of his persuasion base their view that addiction is incurable without their help? On the minority of patients who come to such professionals for treatment, the smaller minority who find such treatment helpful, and the finally tiny minority who maintain whatever benefits they acquire from stays in treatment programs or membership in AA and similar groups.

Yet, there is a large mass of people out there who refuse, reject, or fail at treatment. And this group is not helpless. Many of them, more in absolute terms and possibly a higher percentage of them than those who succeed at treatment, do get better. How would we hear about them? Some of the reasons they may have rejected treatment are that they don't like to call attention to themselves, or perhaps they refuse to acknowledge they are addicts, as treatment centers and AA and NA insist they must. And there certainly is no group to promote their success at self-cure.

But where is it written that the only route out of addiction is through attending group sessions and announcing you were born and will die an addict—one whose only salvation is the 12-step group or philosophy, acknowledgment of powerlessness, and submission to a higher power? Was this on the tablet Moses forgot to deliver to the children of Israel?

Forgive my sarcasm, but often the bromides of the 12-step movement are presented with exactly this degree of religious self-assuredness. And we know that nothing about humans is this cut and dried. Bob and William set about proving this in a way that confronts the disease theory at its most vulnerable point—all those individuals who succeeded without accepting its principles. As researchers, they identified self-curing addicts, ones who felt they were better off going it on their own, and who proved it.

Ask anyone you know in AA or NA or a treatment center about the people you will read about in this book. These professionals' reactions will be informative. They will speak of the denial of those who don't enter treatment or a 12-step group. You, in turn, must wonder about their own peculiar brand of denial—one that prevents them from recognizing the most common form of remission from addiction. This path, self-cure, is described in *Coming Clean*.

Here's a trick you can attempt at home—ask any 12-step counselor or group member what the hardest addiction is to quit. Inevitably, the person will indicate smoking. Then ask the person if he or she or a family member ever smoked and quit. If so, ask how he or she or the family member accomplished this—only one person in twenty will say it was due to therapy or a support group. Muse with this person over how, while believing all addiction requires treatment and group assistance to overcome, this person or those closest to him or her beat the hardest addiction on their own.

And so too is it with heroin, cocaine, and alcohol. While individuals who solve their problems with these substances on their own are often reluctant to come forward, theirs is the standard path to remission, not the one advertised by grateful 12-step program attendees. This startling conclusion—as driven home in this book—should cause us all to revise our notions of drugs, of addiction, of drug policy and treatment, and of our views on what people are capable of. Robert Granfield and William Cloud are to be commended, first for their strength of mind in determining the truths of addiction, and second for forcing Americans to confront their views on these topics. Even I, who played some role in directing the authors toward their recognition of the frequency and importance of natural remission in addiction, was forced to remind myself of the potency of human resolve and self-preservation by the remarkable stories told in *Coming Clean*.

Stanton Peele
Morristown
April 1999

PREFACE

This book is about overcoming addiction to intoxicating substances unaided by treatment or participation in self-help
groups. The title, *Coming Clean*, denotes two distinct meanings.
First, we use it as a way of invoking the popular metaphor for the
process of terminating addictions. However, we also use this
phrase as a metaphor for lifting the veil of secrecy surrounding
the fact that most people overcome their addictions without ever
entering formal treatment or participating in 12-step groups
such as Alcoholics Anonymous, Narcotics Anonymous, or Cocaine Anonymous. Recovery without treatment or natural recovery, as it is perhaps more widely characterized, has been virtually ignored by all but a small cadre of researchers and practitioners. Our purpose in writing this book is to help break the
silence about recovery without treatment by "coming clean"
about its occurrence.

The book draws heavily on in-depth interviews with forty-six former addicts who overcame their addictions to alcohol, cocaine, heroin, barbiturates, or amphetamines or some combination of these drugs without entering treatment or attending self-help groups. While our book is an exploration of the processes of how the drug addicts and alcoholics we interviewed overcame their addictions without treatment, we are in no way suggesting that treatment is unnecessary. The arguments we set forth in this book regarding the implications of natural recovery for treatment and public policy will make this clear. Suffice it to say here that the experience of natural recovery does not imply that addiction is overcome by nothing more than personal willpower. Our analysis will make it readily apparent that the termination of addiction must be understood within a complex set of social conditions and forces that surround an individual. As we demonstrate in the following pages, the reality of natural recovery, far from suggesting that supportive social policies are superfluous in helping troubled individuals overcome their problems, actually reveals their necessity. Ironically, a medicalized view of addiction as a disease requiring treatment may conceal a great deal of the valuable social support that is evident among those who experience natural recovery. Thus, an understanding of the processes of natural recovery can say more about the utility of progressive social reform in improving the lives of troubled individuals than the traditional disease narrative of addiction can. We wish to be emphatic so as not to be misunderstood or misrepresented: the reality of natural recovery from addiction calls for an expansion rather than a contraction of social policies aimed at providing individuals with the opportunities and resources necessary for establishing personal well-being. It also calls for a reappraisal of current U.S. drug war strategies that often hamper and undermine natural recovery efforts.

Because of the important implications that emerge from this exploration of natural recovery, we have labored to make this book accessible to a wide range of potential readers. It is our hope that scholars, students, mental health practitioners, criminal justice professionals, alcohol and drug policy makers, alcohol and drug counselors, and even people who suffer from alcohol and drug problems and their families will find this book valuable and enlightening. We can think of no greater reward for our efforts than to prompt our readers to question conventional thinking about addiction, recovery, and drug policy and to stimulate increased dialogue about the phenomenon of natural recovery.

Throughout the writing of this book, we struggled with our ability to communicate our ideas about natural recovery to the reader. To do this we felt compelled to use the conventional language of addiction. We are aware of the power of language and its ability to create meaning, to distort, and to perpetuate unfounded images that may be harmful. In our need to communicate to each other we sometimes take for granted the words we employ and the power that such words can have. The language that we use to discuss the world of alcohol and drug problems and the specific elements within it are particularly problematic. While it is beyond the scope of this book to propose a new, more conceptually nuanced vocabulary to describe this world, we enter below several caveats about some of the terms that we employ.

Alcohol and Drugs: We are cognizant of the fact that pharmacologically alcohol is a drug just as cocaine and nicotine are drugs. From a purely conceptual perspective, use of the term drugs throughout this book to refer to all mind-altering pharmacological substances would have sufficed. However, the social and legal status as well as the cultural meanings of alcohol distinguishes it from other drugs. Although we use this conceptual distinction throughout the book we in no way wish to imply that alcohol is not a drug. The terms intoxicants, substances, and mind-altering substances are also employed periodically throughout the book to refer to these drugs.

Treatment: We use the term treatment in this book to refer not only to conventional alcohol- and drug-treatment services provided by an agency or a professional, but also to participation in self-help groups. For the purposes of our discussion of natural recovery, we view participation in 12-step groups such as Alcoholic Anonymous, Narcotics Anonymous, and Cocaine Anonymous as a form of treatment for alcohol and drug dependency. In fact, participation in such groups and related activities are often an integral component of day-to-day activities in many professional treatment programs across the United States. While participation in other self-help groups such as Rational Recovery and Women for Sobriety is less frequent, such participation would also be viewed as alcohol and drug treatment.

Alcoholics, addicts, alcoholism, addiction: Throughout the writing of this book we had grave reservations and constant discussions about using these "loaded" terms in a book about natural recovery. The last thing we want to do is to contribute to further reification of constructs that are often as destructive for those experiencing alcohol and drug problems as they are useful. While people can experience profound habituation to alcohol and drugs, these terms and the images they connote run counter to many of our findings. Although all the people we interviewed experienced severe dependencies on these substances for lengthy periods of time, most of them no longer saw themselves as alcoholics or addicts after overcoming their habits. The conventional imagery associated with these terms evokes a fixed, and often self-defeating, identity of an alcohol- and drug-dependent person rather than the kind of fluid identity that often characterizes self-remitters. Our respondents challenged the "once an addict/alcoholic always an addict/alcoholic" imagery commonly associated with addiction. Nevertheless, we felt that we could not avoid using such terms to communicate our findings.

Recovery: Recovery in the alcohol and drug field is commonly thought of as a dormant state of addiction where habituation to these substances is seen as a permanent state from which one never recovers, rather than a temporary one. Therefore, the expression "in recovery" rather than "recovered" is typically used in the treatment industry to denote the recovery phase of one's addiction. While addiction can be a lifelong struggle for many, innumerable others who have been substance dependent do not endure the same kind of compulsive urge. In fact, many alcohol- and drug-dependent people reduce their intake of alcohol and drugs to nonproblematic levels without achieving abstinence. We seek to avoid the ideological basis of the conventional understanding of recovery by using it to refer to the behavioral cessation of the habitual or destructive use of intoxicating substances.

Self-remitters, Self-healers: We use these terms to refer to persons who employ a strategy of natural recovery to overcome their addictions. By using these clinical-sounding terms we do not wish to assign medical interpretations to them. These terms are used interchangeably throughout the book to refer to those who have overcome severe alcohol and drug problems unaided by treatment, including participation in self-help groups.

ACKNOWLEDGMENTS

Whether it's "coming clean" from addiction or writing a book, few people accomplish much without the assistance of others. Through the past several years of working on this project we have been fortunate enough to be surrounded by a supportive network of friends and colleagues who have contributed to our thoughts and perspectives on natural recovery. First, we would like to express our sincere appreciation to the individuals whose voices are heard in this study. Their willingness to talk openly about their alcohol- and drug-addicted pasts made this book possible. We hope that they found some intrinsic reward in the opportunity to tell their stories and have their stories heard by others. We also wish to thank the University of Denver's Faculty Research Fund that provided financial support in the early stages of this research.

There are a number of people without whom this project might never have been completed. There were several students who assisted us with data collection and the transcription of interviews, most notably Kristina Mathews, Lori Oswald, Kate West, and Lori Wingerter. Neysa Folmer of the Graduate School of Social Work provided essential administrative support. We benefited from the insights of many friends and colleagues who read earlier drafts of our work. These people took time out of their busy schedules to discuss and comment on our work and helped us refine our arguments. The contributions of the following people listed in alphabetical order are greatly appreciated: Augie Diana, Mike Faragher, Jim Granfield, David Hester, Tom Koenig, Jim Moran, Patricia Morgan, Maureen Norton-Hawk, Stanton Peele, Craig Reinarman, Burke Rochford, Linda Sobell, and Glenn Walters.

In addition, two individuals must be singled out for their notable contributions. Peter Adler, our friend and colleague at the University of Denver, gave us the kind of encouraging and insightful comments that every writer desires. Not only did we find Pete's own ethnographic work inspiring but his critical reflections on both the empirical and theoretical dimensions of our work significantly improved the final product. Sandy Schwartz at Virginia Commonwealth University was nothing short of exemplary in his editing and analysis of our work. Sandy provided an unselfish line-by-line editing that pushed us to further clarify our arguments. Together, the two of them epitomize what is meant by the phrase a "community of scholars."

We also wish to thank Jennifer Hammer at New York University Press for her support and encouragement, as well as for her skills in helping us craft our final product. Additionally, we wish to acknowledge the fine editorial contributions of Usha Sanyal. Portions of this book were previously published in professional journals. We would like to thank the editorial boards of the *Journal of Drug Issues,* the *Clinical Sociological Review,* and *Addictions Nursing* for providing us with a forum to work out some of our ideas.

Writing on this manuscript began while Bob was a visiting professor at Middlebury College. He would like to thank the Sociology/Anthropology faculty of Middlebury College and the students in his Drugs and Society class for providing him the opportunity and intellectual freedom to develop many of the ideas articulated in this book. He wishes also to thank Cindy Smith and Dale Goddard, owners of the "Painter House" located in Middlebury, Vermont, who made available accommodations that were ideal for contemplation and writing. Finally, he wishes to express his deepest appreciation to his wife, Marian, his closest friend and lifelong soul mate. Her contributions to this book were many throughout its various stages. Not only did she read and edit each successive draft of this book, but she also challenged us, told us when she thought our writing was unclear, and offered valuable suggestions for improvement. Her most overt contribution is noted in the book's title, a masterful solution to a question that had plagued us for several months.

William wishes to thank the two most important people in his life, his wife Karen and their daughter, Allison, without whose support this book could not have been completed. Also, he would like to acknowledge the inspiration provided to him through the years by Bill Linkens.

Chapter One

RECOVERY WITHOUT TREATMENT

An Introduction

"Addiction is just an opinion to me!" These were the words John used to describe his ten-year bout with alcohol dependency. Having consumed alcohol excessively on a daily basis for this decade-long period, John had become fed up with the constant hangovers, blackouts, fist fights, and other problems that resulted from his alcohol-induced anger. The child of an alcoholic father who had died of an alcohol-related illness, John was being counseled by his friends to admit that he was an alcoholic. Realizing he was desperately out of control, John concluded that he needed to take charge of his life. On New Year's Day in 1982, he made a monumental decision that significantly transformed his life. That morning, he stopped drinking and embarked on what he called a new "adventure" of abstinence from alcohol. When we interviewed John more than ten years after his New Year's resolution, he was reaping the benefits of that "adventure," having reestablished himself financially, socially, and spiritually.

On the surface, John's experiences with alcohol, his decision to quit, and his success at overcoming dependency would appear rather prosaic. Each year, thousands of people like him reach a point in their substance-abusing careers where they enter treatment facilities for addiction and set out on the road to recovery. John's case would be considered rather routine were it not for one exception: he never sought professional assistance for his ten-year alcohol problem, nor did he affiliate with the most common 12-step group, Alcoholics Anonymous. After resolving to stop drinking, John did so—on his own. Now, more than ten years later, his alcohol dependency is merely a period of his past life from which he feels removed. When asked about his erstwhile dependency, John replies dispassionately, "I used to drink a lot, now I don't."

This book is about John and numerous others like him who overcame serious dependencies on alcohol and drugs without recourse to formal addiction treatment or 12-step group involvement. Our study closely explores the social lives of untreated former alcoholics and former addicts who have "spontaneously" or "naturally" recovered from a lifestyle of addicted and compulsive substance use. The stories of these untreated individuals and the legions of other self-remitters have remained relatively obscure to all but a small group of researchers who have studied the phenomenon of untreated recovery for more than twenty years. While these researchers have elucidated the multiple pathways or routes to recovery, including recovery without treatment, their writings have been limited to scholarly journals for a specialist audience; in general, little attention has been paid to individuals like John who overcome their addictions without treatment.[1] Despite this relative disregard, however, we cannot deny the existence of recovery without treatment, for as David Lewis of the Brown University Center for Alcohol and Addiction Studies has declared, "[T]here can be no doubt that spontaneous remission occurs."[2]

Because individuals like John are successful in overcoming their addictions without treatment they represent an important subject of study. By closely examining their social lives this book seeks to expand the discourse on natural recovery. We wish to uncover the social dynamics within these individuals' lives that facilitated their triumph over addiction. We intentionally adopt a sociological perspective because we firmly believe that natural recovery can be best understood through a close inspection of the social lives of self-remitters. In being mindful of their social lives we hope to breathe life into the stories of those who overcome addiction without treatment. Not only will we thereby enhance the understanding of natural recovery, but we will also have provided a sound basis from which to consider the implications of natural recovery for treatment, prevention, and drug policy.

Currently, there is an enormous literature that describes how addiction can be overcome through treatment or participation in 12-step groups. The essential problem with much of this recovery literature is that we are exposed to a battalion of voices which, almost without exception, offers recovery narratives that mirror the reigning disease model of addiction. All too often this literature takes for granted a set conception of the multiple and variegated pathways into and out of addiction. In an almost mantralike cadence, we read that people are hopelessly and permanently addicted, that they are powerless over the substances they use, that they must "hit bottom," and that their sanity is restored only through formal treatment interventions or 12-step group involvement. This literature, much of which is promoted by the addiction industry itself, would have us believe that treatment and 12-step groups are a necessary prelude to meaningful recovery and that anything short of this is a prescription for self-delusion, continued dependency, further deterioration, and possibly even death. This potent ideology not only dominates the health and wellness sections of our bookstores but has also influenced Hollywood films and television programs, which typically portray addicts as transforming their lives only after they have entered treatment. Even the recent PBS special on addiction hosted by Bill Moyers made strong, passionate claims about the imperative of treatment and 12-step groups in overcoming dependencies on alcohol and drugs.[3]

The popularity of this disease-oriented view must not be underestimated. Ninety percent of the American public accept the view that addiction is a disease that must be treated.[4] However, this widely-held view of addiction, with its associated intervention mandates and disease-based ideology, does not comport with the experiences of those who discontinue their dependencies without treatment. Although it is impossible to estimate the size of the self-remitter population, the available research as well as the interviews conducted for this book, convince us that such individuals are ubiquitous in our society. Researchers have maintained that their numbers are large and even assert that they substantially outnumber those choosing treatment facilities or 12-step programs.[5] Some have estimated that as many as 80 percent of problem drinkers never enter treatment and suspend problematic use without it.[6] Untreated remitters are our next-door neighbors, our colleagues at work, and our relatives. They are our teachers, our doctors, our lawyers, and our social workers. They build our houses and they figure our taxes. They sell us commodities, teach us to ski, write the software we use, and wait on tables. We are convinced that such people are pervasive throughout society, and yet for the most part their success in overcoming their addictions has gone largely unnoticed. In a very real sense, they are hidden from our view.[7] They appear neither at Alcoholics or Narcotics Anonymous groups, nor on treatment rosters. They have not enrolled in therapeutic communities or outpatient counseling programs. They generally do not present themselves to others as being addicted, in recovery, or in any way diseased. In effect, they are the proverbial elephants in the room that no one sees.[8] They are hidden from our gaze because they do not fit into commonly accepted definitions of what it means to be addicted and "in recovery," and, as we shall see, most prefer to remain in the shadows.

While stalwart advocates of the disease concept consider the thought of natural recovery from addiction heretical, the general concept of natural or spontaneous recovery is well known in the medical literature. People who have been diagnosed with terminal conditions or who have been severely disabled have sometimes experienced complete reversals, referred to by Caryle Hirshberg and Marc Ian Barasch as "remarkable recoveries."[9] Such recoveries have bewildered the medical community for years. Although they are treated "like orphans in the annals of medical investigation," they nonetheless call into question the limits of Western medicine.[10] In their work on remarkable recoveries, Hirshberg and Barasch "discovered people who had the unyielding courage to confront multifarious demons, the strength to transform their lives in the face of wearying and terrifying circumstances, the conviction that doctors often sought to undermine, and the spirit to cherish loved ones as they never had before."[11]

Consistent with Hirshberg and Barasch's narratives of remarkable recoveries, Norman Cousins, in his widely acclaimed book *Anatomy of an Illness*, found that laughter was indeed the best medicine in overcoming a life-threatening disease.[12] Diagnosed with a terminal condition known as *ankylosing spondylitis,* a degenerative spinal disease, Cousins placed himself on a strict regime of laughter during which he read joke books and watched film comedies such as the Marx Brothers that left him roaring with laughter. While the medical reasons for his "natural" recovery remain unclear, Cousins adamantly maintained that his participation and belief in his own treatment plan were integral to his recovery.

Experiences such as these lend support to Andrew Weil's provocative observations concerning natural recovery in his best-selling book *Spontaneous Healing.*[13] Weil, who trained at Harvard Medical School, became profoundly disenchanted with conventional medicine's methodology of healing. In his numerous books and lectures, Weil maintains that Western medical wisdom posits that illness and its treatment originate outside the body. From this perspective, the human body is seen as being under attack by external disease agents that require chemical, surgical, or other therapeutic weapons to be brought to bear in the fight to restore health. For Weil, however, this implies a dangerous passivity on the part of the patient that potentially increases the chances of illness and may delay or even inhibit the body's natural healing processes. Rather than rely solely on the external sources of healing associated with medical interventions, Weil proposes that people have the innate and intrinsic capacity within themselves to experience spontaneous healing. By documenting the spontaneous recoveries of people with an assortment of medical conditions, Weil reaches the provocative conclusion that "spontaneous healing is a common occurrence, not a rare event." In our book, we shall present and analyze the social lives of individuals who recovered from their addictions to alcohol and drugs without treatment. In so doing, we shall demonstrate that such "recoveries" are anything but remarkable. Rather, they are, as Weil suggests, commonplace.

Recovery from Addiction without Treatment

The resolution of alcohol and drug addiction without formal treatment has been referred to as natural recovery,[14] maturing out,[15] autoremission,[16] spontaneous remission,[17] and spontaneous recovery.[18] Although a number of different terms are prevalent in the literature, they all subscribe to the basic principle that people overcome substance-abuse problems without recourse to treatment.[19] In this book we use these terms interchangeably.

While researchers have explored the dynamics of recovery without treatment for quite some time, the concepts they have developed and the implications associated with them have been largely ignored by professionals and the general public. This is not because knowledge of such recoveries is recent. Indeed, the evidence of such recoveries is more than two hundred years old. Recovery without treatment was first documented by Dr. Benjamin Rush—the only physician to sign the Declaration of Independence—who is often credited with developing an early understanding of alcoholism as a disease and who wrote extensively about such recoveries. In one of his reported cases, Rush cited the profound effect that a child's observation could have on an alcoholic parent:

> A farmer in England, who had been many years in the practice of coming home intoxicated, from a market town, one day observed appearances of rain, while he was in market. His hay was cut, and ready to be housed. To save it, he returned in haste to his farm, before he had taken his customary dose of grog. Upon coming into his house, one of his children, a boy of six years old, ran to his mother, and cried out, "O mother, father is come home, and he is not drunk." The father, who heard this exclamation, was so severely rebuked by it, that he suddenly became a sober man.[20]

The fact that Rush documented many such cases long before the emergence of addiction treatment and self-help suggests that natural recovery has had a lengthy history.

Natural Recovery: A Disregarded Perspective

While evidence of natural recovery from addictions has existed for years, it has been ignored by most. There are several reasons for the lack of attention accorded to natural recovery, particularly among clinicians. One reason for this is that clinicians, like most people in society, have been socialized into the dominant disease-based theory of addiction. Moreover, clinicians' training programs seldom discuss alternative approaches to understanding and responding to addiction. Addiction professionals are generally socialized into what Anthony Giddens calls a "practical consciousness," that is, a tacit or taken-for-granted assumption of the presumed naturalness of everyday life.[21] As a nonconscious activity, this practical consciousness marginalizes and censors alternative realities. It separates the thinkable from the unthinkable. It simultaneously creates the possibility of awareness and restricts the development of alternative insights. Practical consciousness acts as a kind of "working consensus" that embodies the socialized mind, or what the French sociologist Pierre Bourdieu has characterized as the "habitus," namely, the largely unreflective set of dispositions, values, and beliefs that individuals willingly accept.[22] This marginalization of alternative perspectives associated with the habitus of addiction is further exacerbated by the fact that a high percentage of addiction clinicians are themselves "in recovery." It has been estimated that over 70 percent of professional counselors working in substance abuse treatment centers across the country have personally experienced substance abuse problems.[23] Most of them have been presocialized into their occupational roles through their participation in formal treatment programs, self-help groups, or both. Consequently, they are frequently reluctant to entertain the possibility of untreated recovery.

A second reason for the paucity of attention accorded to natural recovery has to do with the lack of organized efforts to see untreated recovery as a viable recovery option. Concepts such as addiction, alcoholism, and treatment do not emerge full-blown in the public consciousness. Rather, they are constructed by individuals and groups who lobby in their favor.[24] Sometimes such classifications are based more on historical circumstance than on scientific credibility. Enoch Gordis, Director of the National Institute on Alcohol Abuse and Alcoholism, acknowledged this point a number of years ago. According to Gordis,

> [I]n the case of alcoholism, our whole treatment system, with its innumerable therapies, armies of therapists, large and expensive programs, endless conferences and public relations activities is founded on hunch, not evidence, and not on science. . . . Contemporary treatment for alcoholism owes its existence more to historical processes than to science.[25]

Linguistic categories like treatment occupy a sociohistorical and political realm in that people struggle for ownership of public issues. This is particularly the case with conditions and behaviors that are classified as social problems.[26] Concepts such as alcoholism, addiction, or treatment represent claims advanced by individuals and groups over other possible conceptualizations of the same behavior. For instance, drunk driving can be seen as a problem of sick, or as in the late 1990s, immoral individuals who are in need of change. Such a perspective would suggest the need to transform individual behavior through education, treatment, or through punitive sanctions. However, the problem of drunk driving could also be classified as an environmental one associated with poorly designed safety features on cars, lack of public transit, or the almost unlimited availability of alcohol. As we have seen over the years, the modal way of classifying the drunk driving problem has been to individualize the problem and work toward changing the errant driver. However, such a formulation of the problem of drunk driving emerged out of the lobbying efforts of groups like Mothers against Drunk Driving (MADD) that engaged in a national campaign to "problematize" drunk drivers.[27] This group gained considered legitimacy from the alcohol beverage industries as well as from politicians and government actors. Thus, regulations pertaining to issues such as drunk driving do not simply emerge unmediated by human activity. Instead, regulations contain a logic that represents the prerogatives of interested parties and dominant ideas.

This analysis can be applied to the concepts of addiction and alcoholism. The disease concept of alcoholism grew out of the efforts of Alcoholics Anonymous and the National Council on Alcoholism (NCA).[28] The NCA, an influential private alcoholism group supporting the disease concept, has reacted sharply to alternatives to abstinence-based approaches such as "controlled drinking," and has lobbied to raise money for medical studies of alcoholism.[29] As a public relations arm of the alcoholism-as-disease movement, the NCA enlisted "well-placed scientists and physicians to promote the disease model of alcoholism."[30] These organizations, along with the work of E. M. Jellinek and the Yale Center for Studies on Alcohol, popularized the modern disease theory of alcoholism despite limited scientific support.[31] This view became institutionalized during the Nixon Administration with the founding of the National Institute of Alcohol Abuse and Alcoholism (NIAAA) that awarded federal grants for the treatment and prevention of alcoholism. More recently, organizations such as the Hazelden Foundation have produced and circulated a prodigious amount of material that advances a disease concept of addiction, requiring treatment. In addition to their intense marketing of alcoholism as a disease and the related treatment imperative, this organization has been extremely successful over the years at promulgating disease models for an ever-expanding range of behaviors including sexual practices, obesity, and drug use.

Advocates for untreated recovery, on the other hand, have not achieved the organizational power and influence needed to shape policy. There is no lobby for untreated addicts, nor, as we shall see shortly, do such people wish to be identified as addicts or former addicts. Given the stigma associated with addiction, it is not surprising that self-remitters would wish to keep their former addictions concealed. There are no national celebrities speaking out about their own natural recovery, nor are government agencies pouring large sums of research money into studying this population. Consequently, untreated recovery does not possess the political force needed to constitute a social movement which could pose a significant challenge to the dominant disease-based perspectives. In fact, members of the antitraditional lobby who speak out in favor of such options are frequently held in contempt and vilified by those who support traditional views.

A third reason for the reluctance to accept untreated recovery as a viable option for overcoming dependencies on alcohol and drugs is related to the general climate of temperance that pervades American society. In his insightful historical analysis of the concept of addiction, Harry Levine described how addiction was "discovered."[32] For Levine, the idea that alcoholism is a progressive disease whose chief symptom is loss of control emerged out of the moralistic climate that pervaded the nineteenth-century Temperance movement. This climate, much of which remains today, promoted the view that it is an addict's moral responsibility to abstain from use. The power of substances over humans became reified as people were increasingly seen as victims of demon alcohol. The "science" of modern-day addiction carries with it much of the moralism associated with this previous historical period. As Stanton Peele has pointed out, "the idea of progressive, irreversible, inevitable exacerbation of the habit, causing loss of control of personal behavior and of the ability to make moral discriminations, actually retains strong elements of both colonial and temperance moralism."[33] The persistence of this moralism, with the attendant necessity of being "saved," makes the concept of untreated recovery seem dubious.

A final reason for the unfavorable reception of untreated recovery is related to the perceived impact such an option might have on the market for addiction services. The addiction industry is an immensely profitable one. In the minds of many, it would be severely compromised if natural recovery were to become a viable option for alcoholics and drug addicts.[34] The profit-based incentives of treatment services cannot be denied. A number of years ago researchers at the Alcohol Research Group, a prestigious research institute at the University of California, Berkeley, published a compelling article that highlighted the profit incentives associated with the addiction industry.[35] These authors found that traditional treatment paradigms had changed significantly in the 1970s in the wake of third-party insurance coverage for addiction treatment. As a result of this expanded coverage, more and more professionals and private hospitals had entered the addiction treatment field. As this occurred, the definitions of addiction, the timing of intervention, and who was best suited for treatment also changed dramatically. Intervention was expanded to include families and children, as competition for a decreasing supply of dependent persons became more intense. Alcoholics were treated at earlier stages, suggesting that intervention can occur at different periods and not simply when a person "hits bottom," as was previously thought.

In this ever-expanding marketplace of social problems, new "addictions" emerged that were subject to the same treatment protocols as alcohol and drug dependency. Indeed, part of the reason for the turn toward managed care in addiction treatment has been the runaway costs associated with substance abuse treatment services. Ironically, even with the initiation of "cut-rate" interventions, the cost of addiction services continues to escalate out of control in several states. While this is not to say that there is a conspiracy of silence about untreated recovery by those professionals who are able to create a need for their services, it is unlikely that such professionals would actively encourage options that could undermine their livelihood.

Whatever the reasons for the lack of public attention accorded to recovery without treatment, closing one's eyes to it will not make it disappear. All too often, opposition to the idea of untreated recovery takes on ideological dimensions. Such ideological opposition frequently results in beliefs about addiction and recovery that are "data proof"; that is, no amount of empirical support or verification of alternative recovery realities can dissuade opponents from their rejection of any notion of untreated recovery.[36]

However, despite the rejection of natural recovery as a viable option, several studies have documented its existence. Exploration into the phenomenon of natural recovery has generally addressed three particular areas of concern; the prevalence and rate of untreated recovery, the factors responsible for initiating and maintaining spontaneous remission, and the reasons for not seeking out traditional recovery options. We shall consider each of these topics separately.

Prevalence

A significant number of people with alcohol- and drug-related problems have recovered independently of treatment or self-help.[37] In their report on addiction treatment, researchers at the Harvard Medical School presented findings from a study indicating that 80 percent of all alcohol-dependent people who recover for a year or more do so on their own, some after being unsuccessfully treated.[38] In a series of studies conducted in Canada to determine the prevalence rate of recovery without treatment, seasoned researchers Linda and Mark Sobell found an impressive incidence of natural recovery.[39] In their studies, data from two general population telephone surveys that passed the rigorous standard of random sampling, that is, a sample of people who had an equal probability of selection as everyone else, were analyzed. Both surveys found that over 77 percent of those who had overcome an alcohol problem had done so without treatment. In an earlier study the Sobells and their colleagues reported that a sizable majority of alcohol abusers, 82 percent, recovered on their own. In his highly acclaimed work *The Natural History of Alcoholism,* noted Harvard researcher George Vaillant, also reported that an impressive number of those he had followed over an extensive period of time overcame their alcohol problems without recourse to treatment or 12-step programs.[40]

The prevalence of untreated recovery among illicit drug addicts is no less significant. In their study of 106 problem cocaine users who quit, Dan Waldorf and his colleagues found that just over 71 percent stopped drug use without treatment.[41] Interestingly, more untreated quitters were able to successfully stop on their initial attempt than treated ones. Among those who are involved in a criminal subculture, however, such untreated success may occur less often. One study of 343 male inmates in a medium-security prison found that 25 percent of incarcerated offenders with a drug problem had stopped using drugs on their own before reaching prison.[42] Although the rate of untreated recovery in this group is lower than in the previously cited study, the author nonetheless maintains that the natural remission of dependency occurred twice as often among the prisoners he studied than did treatment-based remission. While the drug users in each of these studies reported extensive involvement with drugs, the lower rate among the incarcerated may suggest that the life circumstances that led them into prison posed greater barriers to effective self-change. As we will illustrate later in this book, a person's status in society significantly affects the ability to engage in the kind of self-change associated with natural recovery.[43]

Initiation of Untreated Recovery

Just as there are multiple pathways into addiction, so too are there divergent avenues out of intoxicant dependency. The process of untreated recovery is often precipitated by a combination of "avoidance-oriented" and "approach-oriented" conditions.[44] Avoidance-initiated recovery occurs when people experience negative consequences as a result of their substance abuse and consequently discontinue their habit. For instance, the experience of "hitting bottom," as described in the 12-step literature, has been commonly considered a necessary precondition for recovery.[45] Among the untreated cocaine quitters studied by Waldorf and his colleagues, between 23 percent and 46 percent experienced work, financial, or health problems.[46] Similarly, in their comparative study of treated and untreated alcoholics, the Sobells found negative consequences to be a common theme among both groups.[47] Each group reported high levels of physical, social, legal, work, and financial problems. These problems often act as catalysts to change.

However, a number of drug addicts, including those who undergo untreated recovery, report approach-oriented reasons for discontinuing their use. For instance, some heroin addicts have discontinued use as a result of the "pulls" of the good life exemplified by the dominant value system of work and stable living rather than from the "pushes" associated with hitting bottom.[48] Many of these addicts "drift out" of addiction in order to salvage and enhance their stake in a conventional life as represented by jobs, families, and friends.[49] In some cases, approach-oriented explanations of change such as an increasing sense of responsibility, the preservation of social relationships, experiencing a religious conversion, having a child,[50] getting married,[51] establishing new relationships, and forging new identities[52] outnumber avoidance-oriented reasons for cessation.[53]

In general, the research on untreated recovery generally supports both avenues of cessation. This is particularly true among untreated remitters who engage in ongoing cognitive evaluations of the positive "pulls" and negative "pushes" associated with recovery. As previous researchers have pointed out, self-change is strongly associated with the ability to reflect on the costs and benefits of continued use.[54] One study, for instance, found that cognitive appraisals had powerful transformative effects. For almost half of the respondents in that study of alcohol-dependent people who discontinued use without treatment, "the very notion or idea of consuming an alcoholic beverage automatically and instantaneously evoked powerful negative thoughts or feelings such as disgust, embarrassment, physical discomfort, or even nausea."[55]

Where reflected appraisals of use occur, both avoidance-oriented and approach-oriented strategies seem to be equally effective pathways out of addiction. In fact, one pair of researchers proposed a three-stage model of spontaneous remission that combined both the avoidance and approach orientations.[56] The initial stage in their model involved finding the resolve to terminate the use of substances. They found that in most cases such resolve was precipitated by avoidance experiences such as medical, financial, and work-related problems, as well as "bottom-hitting" events. The second stage consisted of making a public pronouncement to quit that demonstrated one's resolve. Finally, their third or maintenance stage involved the development of approach-oriented assets such as social support, new relationships, increasing self-confidence, identity changes, and increased involvement in institutions like the family, religion, and education.

Reasons for Avoiding Treatment

Untreated remitters share one trait in common: all have circumvented treatment. However, their reasons for doing so vary widely. In general, self-healers have an aversion to traditional forms of intervention.[57] Many avoid addiction treatment because they fear embarrassment and stigmatization. Others are uncomfortable about self-disclosure. Unlike natural remitters, those who affiliate with Alcoholics Anonymous may be more open to the requisite "emotion work" surrounding self-disclosure that defines their meetings.[58] Still other self-remitters maintain that they can change without assistance, believing they are able to take care of themselves and that treatment would not help them, or possessing negative images of treatment.[59] While advocates of the disease model of addiction often see such people as being in denial, these studies demonstrate that drug- and alcohol-dependent people base their rejection of treatment on reasons they consider rational.

Overview of Book

We have written this book with several objectives in mind. As academics engaged in teaching and research, we are guided by general theoretical interests. Our thinking on natural recovery has been influenced by the sociological principles associated with "symbolic interactionism." The central insight of interactionist theory is that all behaviors, emotions, beliefs, rules, and objects become meaningful within the broader social context of interaction with others. Thoughts and actions are neither determined nor fixed. Rather, they are mediated by the social contexts in which an individual is embedded and possess a fluidity of meaning that is open to change and shifting perspectives. This general theoretical perspective allows us to explore the *processes* through which people give meaning to the substances they use, and to examine how these meanings and their situated contexts shape use. It also facilitates an exploration of the process of self-change, the antecedents of this change, and the avenues to meaningful identity construction.

Through the years a wealth of sociological analyses of alcohol and drug use have underscored the importance of understanding the interaction between the individual and society. These studies have avoided both a "pathology paradigm"[60] that depicts individuals as sick, and a "moralistic paradigm" that characterizes drug users as depraved, morally irresponsible deviants. Instead, they have taken people for what they are in order better to understand their thoughts, actions, dispositions, struggles, and vocabularies of motive.[61] As a result, these studies have paid close attention to the social lives of drug-involved individuals, whether they be crack users in the barrios, women who exchange sex for drugs, or high-level drug dealers.[62]

We adopt this "qualitative" perspective because it gives voice to addicts who all too often have been subject to disparaging observations by journalists and politicians, or to overly-medicalized accounts by clinicians and physicians. It is our hope that by listening closely to these formerly alcohol- and drug-dependent people who recovered without treatment, we will come to a better understanding of the social basis of self-change and be able to raise important and searching questions about treatment, prevention, and drug policy in America. We agree with the Sobells who have argued that since our understanding of alcohol and drug problems is usually based on the accounts of treated individuals, those who have recovered on their own can tell us much about the process of self-healing, and by extension about broader policies regarding alcohol and drug use. Additionally since significant numbers of people experiencing alcohol and/or drug problems never seek treatment, like the Sobells we hope our book will provide such people real-life lessons and illustrations from those who have succeeded in overcoming their addictions without treatment.

While our interests in addiction and untreated recovery emerge out of sociological theory and past research studies, we have also been influenced by our personal experiences over the years. For Bob, the experience of being a professional musician helped foster an interest in untreated recovery. Alcohol and drug dependency is a well-known occupational hazard among musicians. The biographies of popular and unknown jazz and rock musicians are filled with references to alcohol, drugs, and addiction. The tragic and premature deaths of jazz greats Billy Holiday and Charlie Parker, of rock legends Janice Joplin, Jimi Hendrix, and Jim Morrison, and of iconoclastic artists such as the Sex Pistol's Sid Vicious and Nirvana guitarist Kurt Cobain, were all related to drug abuse. Countless others, however, experienced problems with alcohol and drugs but overcame them, often without treatment. At least in one case, a self-avowed heroin-addicted percussionist, Ron Santiago, overcame his drug problem by tuning into the ritual and traditional dimensions associated with diasporic drumming.[63] For Santiago, heroin use became incompatible with his growing ritualistic connection to drumming. Thus, the music world is rife with tragedies involving alcohol and drug addiction but also with the untreated victories of those who were unwilling to let themselves and their careers be destroyed.

William, who is of African-American ancestry, spent his youth as well as young adulthood in the inner cities, where he personally witnessed a wide array of tragic social problems in his own neighborhood, including serious drug problems among his acquaintances, friends, and even relatives. While his overall interest in drug dependency was influenced by firsthand exposure to this problem, his specific interest in recovery without treatment was inspired by his personal knowledge of numerous people who had had severe drug dependencies but managed to overcome them, with and without treatment. This interest was further fueled by his observation that while there appeared to be similarities between the two groups, there also seemed to be striking dissimilarities. For his part, this book is a tribute to both groups of acquaintances, friends, and relatives whose suffering and victories are the seeds from which it grew.

This book is based on in-depth interviews with forty-six formally alcohol- and drug-dependent individuals who overcame their addictions without treatment. Twenty-five of these people reported having alcohol problems, while the remaining twenty-one experienced problems from the use of illicit substances, most notably powder cocaine, "crack" cocaine, and heroin.

For the purposes of this book, we used three criteria for untreated recovery. First, respondents had to have been drug- or alcohol-dependent for at least one year. As Table 1 indicates, on average our respondents reported being dependent for approximately eleven years. In our sample, only one person reported being addicted for one year. The remaining people in the sample were addicted for two or more years. Determination of dependency was made only after careful consideration; each respondent had to have experienced frequent cravings,

Table 1
Reported Years of Addiction and Years since Addiction

| | Years of Addiction | | | Years since Addiction | | |
	Alcohol	Drug	Total	Alcohol	Drug	Total
1–2	0	3	3	3	2	5
3–5	5	8	13	10	9	19
6–8	1	6	7	3	7	10
9–11	4	1	5	4	1	5
12–15	4	3	7	3	0	3
16–20	4	0	4	2	2	4
21+	7	0	7	0	0	0
Total	25	21	46	25	21	46
Average	14.7	5.9	10.9	6.8	5.9	6.5

extended periods of daily use, and serious consequences resulting from such use.

Second, to be eligible, our respondents had to have resolved their dependency for at least one continuous year. The average length of termination for the entire group was six and a half years. For several reasons we chose not to equate recovery with abstinence. Because those who recover without treatment typically do not subscribe to a rigorous norm of abstinence, we decided to include people who continued to use small to moderate amounts of substances.[64] Also, evaluations of treatment protocols have found that many formerly addicted people significantly decrease the amount of intoxicants they consume without necessarily achieving abstinence. The recently completed Project MATCH, an eight-year, 27 million dollar investigation of treatment effectiveness funded by the National Institute of Alcohol Abuse and Alcoholism, found that subjects across three distinct treatment settings substantially reduced their drinking intensity and frequency without necessarily achieving abstinence.[65] It should be pointed out, however, that all but two of our respondents practiced abstinence.

The final selection criterion we used was that respondents had to have received no treatment at all, including participation in 12-step groups, or have participated only minimally in treatment and not attribute recovery to their treatment. In fact, about 90 percent of our subjects fit into the first category of never having undergone treatment at all. The remaining 10 percent had very limited contact with treatment but unequivocally maintained that they did not recover because of this experience.

We employed a technique known as "snowball sampling" to select these men and women. This sampling strategy uses referral chains and media advertisements to identify appropriate study participants. Such samples are not random and therefore cannot be considered representative reflections of the population of self-remitters. However, such sampling strategies are necessary because self-remitters are often hidden. Although this method can carry a risk of sampling error, studies of natural recovery using such samples have found little evidence of selection bias.[66]

Our initial step was to use referral chains developed through the chance meeting of an untreated remitter by one of the authors. This person put us in contact with two others who gave us the names of other untreated remitters they knew and so on. About half the individuals we interviewed were contacted through this method. In order to solicit additional interviews, we placed advertisements in local newspapers. We interviewed fifty people using these combined approaches. However, four people were eliminated from the sample either because they had spent a considerable length of time in treatment which they believed had helped them overcome their dependencies, or because reported patterns of drug use were not indicative of dependency.

The respondents we recruited for this study reported having middle-class and stable working-class backgrounds.

Table 2

Age, Education, Gender, and Occupation of Sample

	Number	Percent
Age		
20–29	7	15
30–39	13	28
40–49	18	39
50+	8	17
Education		
Less than 12	2	4
High School	11	24
Some College	14	30
College	13	28
Postgraduate	6	13
Gender		
Male	28	60
Female	18	40
Occupation		
Professional	12	26
Business (Owner or Administrator)	13	28
Skilled/Semi-Skilled	8	17
Service Employee	2	4
No Occupation (Student, Homemaker, Retired)	11	24

As Table 2 indicates, most of the people we interviewed had completed high school or held GEDs, most had been to college, and several respondents held graduate degrees. Most were employed in professional occupations, including law, engineering, and health care, held managerial positions, or operated their own businesses. Three-fifths of the group were male (28) and two-fifths were women (18). The age range in the sample was twenty-five to sixty, with an average age of thirty-eight years.

The interviews we conducted lasted between two and three hours each and, with the consent of each interviewee, were tape-recorded for subsequent analysis. Unlike many previous studies of untreated recovery that primarily seek to quantify the experiences of self-healers, we sought to collect rich textured data that would offer a "thick description" of the process of untreated recovery.[67] We used no standardized instruments, nor did we conduct any statistical testing. Rather, we treated our interviews as "guided conversations" during which we asked our subjects probing questions about their experiences with untreated recovery.[68] Thus, the approach we take in this book is strictly qualitative in that we explore the meaning and the meaning-making activities of our respondents with regard to their use of intoxicants and their natural recovery. Ours is a "naturalistic inquiry" that seeks not to test theories or hypotheses about use and natural recovery, but that strives to inductively identify patterns within the data in order to develop a better understanding of the social lives of untreated remitters and to learn from their experiences.[69] In so doing, we hope not only to offer additional insight into the phenomenon of natural recovery, but to raise questions regarding implications for treatment, prevention, and drug policy as well.

This book is divided into two sections. The first and larger part explores natural recovery from the perspective of those who have experienced it. Throughout this book we remain close to the data by allowing our respondents to speak at great length. Chapter 2 introduces the reader to the self-healers we interviewed. Instead of presenting pathology-based narratives of these individuals, we focus on the meaning and purpose substances had for them. In this chapter we explore our respondents' everyday narratives of alcohol and drug use by examining the process of initiation into drug use, their escalation of use, and the problems they confronted during their dependencies. Our main purpose in this chapter is to demonstrate that people find the use of substances meaningful. Rather than offering a medicalized account of their emerging dependencies that reduces excess to biology or pharmacology, this chapter explores how our respondents perceived their heavy use of intoxicants as having several social and psychological benefits.

Chapter 3 explores the processes of natural recovery used by our respondents. This chapter focuses on the various strategies they employed to break away from their addictions to alcohol and drugs. We argue that self-remitters become engulfed in roles and activities that are incompatible with heavy intoxicant use. For most, this process is akin to a conversion experience, although, as our respondents reveal, one that reflects a growing connection to society rather than a specific spiritual dimension. We conclude this chapter with a discussion of how people's emerging stake in conventional life facilitates their recovery.

Chapter 4 undertakes a close analysis of the reasons respondents gave for circumventing treatment. We employ the postmodernist insights of Michel Foucault as a way of understanding the processes through which treatment creates identities, and also to understand how treatment ideology and the professionals who carry it out reflect a form of power. In addition, we explore the implications that rejecting treatment had for our respondents' identities. Although there were some exceptions, the majority rejected the imagery of the addict, preferring to normalize their dependency by integrating it into their lives instead.

Chapter 5 moves the level of analysis from a "micro" perspective to a "macro" one. Using the insights of structurally oriented sociologists such as Anthony Giddens, we explore how our respondents' situated contexts affected their ability to engage in natural recovery. Drawing upon the general concept of "social capital" (i.e., the social relations within which individuals are embedded and the resources that potentially flow from these re-lations), we examine how our respondents benefited from their associations with others. Although our respondents almost uni-formly believed that it was their own "intestinal fortitude" that allowed them to quit using drugs or alcohol, it will be clear from this chapter that much of their determination and ability to transform their lives occurred within a larger social context.

Part 2 of this book explores the implications that recovery without treatment has for treatment professionals as well as for prevention work and drug policy. Chapter 6 explores the advan-tages of recovery without treatment and the implications of nat-ural recovery for practitioners. It introduces the concept of re-covery capital to conceptualize the structural and personal re-sources that can be used to overcome alcohol and drug dependencies. It concludes with a discussion of the threats to re-covery capital, the conditions that impinge on recovery capital, and the relevance of recovery capital for treatment practitioners.

In Chapter 7, we broaden the perspective of this book by dis-cussing the implications of our study of natural recovery for prevention and drug policy. In addition to examining these is-sues, we explore what the experiences of our respondents tell us about social and cultural life more generally. Finally, we have also included an appendix in which we provide suggestions for recovery without treatment. Based on the lessons from our re-spondents and from the extant literature, we discuss specific hands-on strategies that people can use if they wish to attempt the process of recovery without treatment.

A Final Note

We conclude the current chapter with some general comments on formal treatment as well as self-help groups such as Alcoholics Anonymous. While the success of treatment has been heralded for years by therapists and members of self-help groups, questions about treatment efficacy remain. What can reasonably be said about treatment and 12-step groups is that they have moderate success rates. Research studies on the impact of treatment and self-help groups suggest that the outcomes of such interventions are fairly modest.[70] In one longitudinal study of 4,500 subjects whose drinking qualified them as alcoholics, 70 percent who had received some form of treatment drank alcoholically during a five-year follow-up. Ironically, only 53 percent of those alcoholics who had not received any treatment continued to be addicted to alcohol.[71]

Even the most recent, high-profile Project MATCH findings report only moderate success within the three treatment types they compared: 12-step facilitation programs, cognitive therapy, and motivational enhancement counseling.[72] Unfortunately, no untreated control group was included in the study. The findings of this massive study on the relationship between treatment matching and successful clinical outcomes raise serious questions about the efficacy and necessity of lengthy interventions. While only a minority of individuals achieved abstinence, a significant number did experience a decrease in the percentage of days they drank in a month. Quite unexpectedly, however, no differences were noted across the treatment groups studied, suggesting that the gains from long-term efforts like 12-step groups are no different from minimal forms of intervention. The briefest treatment worked just as well as the most extensive ones, which challenges the conventional wisdom regarding the need for protracted treatment. Additionally, this study found that few of the matched client characteristics such as severity of alcohol involvement, a client's conceptual level, cognitive impairment, or gender had any relevant impact on the outcomes. Only a client's psychiatric severity, motivation level, and aspiration to experience greater meaning in life affected success rates. Thus, "the largest statistically most powerful, psychotherapy trial ever conducted" found that alcoholics who are motivated and who are psychologically stable can experience substantial and enduring drinking reductions with relatively modest treatment contact.[73]

Some readers of this book will probably take exception to our focus on natural recovery from addictions because of its implicit challenge to the disease concept of addiction. For many people the disease concept is indisputable, as is belief in its inexorability and permanency. Given that many of these people may have successfully overcome addictions of their own through treatment or 12-step groups and may believe that such interventions saved their lives, their discomfort with our focus and analysis is understandable. Some might believe that we are dismissing the value of any treatment altogether. However, readers would be ill-advised to view our work as a universal rejection of treatment. Some treatment approaches are effective and, as we shall demonstrate later in this book, may be critical for those alcohol- and drug-addicted people whose use of intoxicants and social circumstances do not afford them the incentives, much less the opportunity to stop. For such people, treatment of one sort or another may be essential. While the concept of untreated recovery challenges much of the dogma associated with the dominant disease-based treatment ideology, we are not suggesting that formal treatment programs are unnecessary.

As we will demonstrate later in this book, many of our untreated remitters engaged in activities that are functionally equivalent to effective treatment or 12-step group participation. However, despite some similarities between untreated and treated remitters, there are, as we shall see, critical differences. Overall, we seek to raise questions about the reified concept of addiction, to challenge the presuppositions regarding the necessity of extensive long-term treatment, and to demonstrate the power that people have over the substances they consume. Ultimately, we seek to show that the frequently traveled road of untreated recovery is paved with considerable success.

PART ONE

PERSPECTIVES ON NATURAL RECOVERY

Chapter Two

SLIPPIN' INTO DARKNESS

Narratives of Use and Addiction

The addiction literature typically portrays drug and alcohol addicts as possessing distinct physiological and psychological characteristics that distinguish them from the nonaddicted world. The view of addiction as a disease tends to marginalize addicts and separate them from society. Those who are addicted and dependent on substances such as heroin, crack cocaine, and even alcohol are classified and treated as "other" by nonaddicts and by powerful social institutions. As Waterston has argued, the deviant image of drug addicts has contributed to a "ghettoization" of users and to the "construction of a false separation between them and us."[1] This removal of heavy use from the context of everyday life contributes to the view that drug addicts and alcoholics are uniquely different from the "normal" population and thus legitimizes their differentiated treatment by those who aspire to treat or punish them for their excesses.

This chapter undertakes a close analysis of the meaning our respondents ascribe to their use of drugs like alcohol, cocaine, and heroin. It also focuses on the variegated problems they experience when they become dependent. We examine the processes that led our respondents into their drug use and abuse, processes that principally involve a search for meaning and social relevance. Additionally we explore their related financial, employment, legal, and relational problems. We begin with a discussion of the disease concept of addiction and illustrate how this perspective ignores the multitextured meaningfulness that individuals derive from the substances they use. Following the insights of Finnish sociologist Pertti Alasuutari, we explore what he refers to as the "everyday-life" narratives of alcohol- and drug-dependent people.[2] Unlike the metanarrative of addiction, an everyday-life view of addiction focuses attention on the importance of social context and meaning as influencing use. From this perspective, abuse is not seen as aberrant but as a person's means of creating meaning and of establishing identity.

Classifying Problems with Intoxicants

Over the past two centuries, the marginalization of drug and alcohol-dependent people has led to various types of sanctions designed to punish those who stray from the accepted norms of use. Inspired by the Temperance ideology of self-control and sobriety that emerged in the seventeenth and eighteenth centuries, recalcitrant inebriates were previously subjected to public humiliation, physical torture including whipping and branding, and in some cases slavery, as with American Indians.[3] Justifications for such treatment lay in the dominant religious frameworks that were used to construct moral order. Puritan ideology tended to view excessive alcohol consumption as a sin and the excessive consumer as a moral degenerate. In the eyes of the leading Puritan clergy of the time such people had allowed the devil to intrude upon and corrupt their souls. Thus, in Puritan society deviant drinkers experienced what anthropologists refer to as "liminality" and were regarded as dangerous, inauspicious, and polluting.[4] Because their practices were considered profane, they were considered to be outside the normative boundaries of social life and were subject to various forms of social control designed to interdict their desire and excess.

In the modern era, the punitive and often draconian sanctions associated with traditional forms of religious control evolved into strictly legal-rational forms of punishment.[5] In America, the major drug laws of the twentieth century—the Harrison Narcotics Act (1914), Prohibition (1920), and the Marijuana Tax Act (1937)—led to the utilization of law-enforcement measures that punished users and removed them from society. In most cases, these control efforts were directed at those too powerless to escape the claws of an ever-encroaching state-supported moral campaign to rid society of addictive substances. As in Puritan America, the treatment of deviant alcohol and drug users during this period was inspired by a Temperance culture that marginalized deviant users. Use was not seen within its everyday-life context of cultural practice or as a rational response to the emergent pressures of modern society, but rather within an individualized context of self-control, restraint, and obedience to the rule of law. In most cases, the liminality imposed upon users of these forbidden substances was enacted primarily upon members of the lower classes who were considered inferior to the higher social classes.

The first and most significant legislative effort to control drugs in the twentieth century focused on alcohol. The Temperance movement during the late eighteenth and nineteenth centuries was principally a moral crusade aimed at controlling

working-class immigrants.[6] Alcohol came to be seen as a "proletarian" substance and was reproved for what many considered
its contribution to social decadence and moral decay.[7] However,
as Reinarman and Levine write, "the period between 1900 and
1920 was riddled with class, racial, cultural, and political conflict
having little to do with drinking problems."[8] Nevertheless, alcohol was held responsible for the major social problems of the
time. The lower-class masses that consumed alcohol would be
saved through the constitutional amendment banning the substance. However, as several analysts of drug policy have pointed
out, at the federal and state levels Prohibition had less to do with
"saving" the great unwashed masses than with controlling and
limiting their activities.

Much of the early Temperance movement was directed at
controlling working-class laborers, particularly during the har-
vesting season.[9] The elite and middle-class reformers saw a connection between labor, productivity, industry, and the church.
Most of the earliest Temperance leaders were wealthy Protes-
tants who felt that the barroom was promoting immorality, in-
dolence, and political subversiveness. As a type of coercive reform movement designed to impose an arbitrary social order,
Temperance reflected the bourgeois interests of self-control and
sobriety over the interests of the working class. Temperance represented a celebration of prosperity and capitalism and a rejection of the way of life of the working class. Intemperance among
the working class was "typified" as excessive and immoral, and
considered to be responsible for the major social problems of the
times, including delinquency, broken families, crime, violence,
mental illness, and moral degeneracy.[10] Although the working
class resisted the moral entrepreneurship and restrictive laws associated with capitalist expansion, they were unable to prevent
the all-out war against alcohol that coalesced in the form of national Prohibition. Ironically, the working class regained the

right to consume alcohol only after the success of working-class mobilization efforts designed to "meet the challenge of sustained, repressive corporate anti-unionism."[11] By the early 1930s capitalists who were once in favor of Prohibition as a way of controlling the working class were calling for its repeal in order to mollify working-class interests that posed a significant challenge to capitalist hegemony.

Like the movement against alcohol, control efforts in the late nineteenth and early twentieth centuries directed at narcotics were also aimed at controlling marginalized groups in society. The passage of the Harrison Narcotics Act in 1914, although originally a tax revenue law that required users to obtain a prescription for use, was principally aimed at controlling the "dangerous classes," namely, lower-class minorities who were seen as posing a threat to the middle-class way of life. These racist fears resulted in overreaction on the part of some law enforcement agents who, in the case of cocaine, switched from a .32 to .38 caliber pistol, believing, as they claimed, that a lower caliber was unable to stop a "cocainized" black man.[12] Similarly, the Opium Smoking Ban of 1875, the precursor to the Harrison Narcotics Act, focused on the so-called nefarious activities of Chinese immigrants who were accused of selling narcotics to white women and children in order to turn them into slaves.[13] Such irrational racial fears led to the prosecution of immigrants who had struggled shoulder to shoulder with whites to build the American West.

With the passage of these laws, alcohol, narcotics, and marijuana ceased to be socially approved intoxicants, and came to be seen as dangerous substances capable of unleashing various forms of moral destructiveness upon society. Individual users were placed in liminal categories as criminal and moral degenerates and treated accordingly, with prosecution and incarceration. In the wake of these law enforcement efforts treatment programs were closed and even physicians who continued to prescribe narcotics to addicts were prosecuted and often imprisoned.[14]

The modern disease concept of addiction continued the practice of placing deviant users in liminal categories that separated them from "normal" others. The disease framework of alcoholism, developed during the 1930s and 1940s, advanced an individualized perspective that removed the act of drinking from its functional everyday context. Drinking was subsequently medicalized and pathologized. The alcoholism framework, as articulated by the founders of AA as well as by E. M. Jellinek, considered the father of the modern-day disease concept, constructed the abuser as being out of control, as having unrestrained cravings and urges, and as possessing an illness that has an associated symptomology and etiology.[15] Under such a designation alcoholics became the objects of efforts by experts to transform them, and to restore their humanity and civility.

Sociologists who have studied addiction are inclined to see it as a social construction. A constructivist view of addiction posits that while some individuals have problems with alcohol and drugs, the designation and experience of this problem behavior as a disease is socially generated. In this sense, addiction is a social accomplishment that attributes meaning and moralities to those assigned to the category of drug addict or alcoholic.[16] The construction of alcohol- and drug-dependent people as diseased is not unlike the arbitrary labeling of someone as mentally ill.[17] This is not to suggest that people do not experience problems associated with their use of intoxicants, but that the articulation of the problem as an illness requiring therapeutic intervention is based more on politics and culture than upon medical science. Constructing alcohol and drug addiction as an illness has significant implications for the way troubled individuals conceptualize their experience and for how they are treated.

Addiction: A Cultural Perspective

While the disease concept of addiction has reigned supreme over the years to the point that it is now hegemonic, that is, it possesses its own self-legitimating ideology, alternative conceptions of addiction that focus on the broader social context of use have also been advanced.[18] For instance, Alasuutari uses the concept of the "everyday-life frame" to explore the meaning and function of intoxicant use in a particular social and cultural context.[19] In the absence of an everyday-life framework, the concept of addiction becomes medically reductionist. The addict is simply seen as flawed and in need of repair. Unlike the overtly medicalized disease framework of addiction, an everyday-life framework transcends the individualist metaphor of disease and repositions the analysis of addiction and dependence in the realm of contextualized normality, that is, use that "reflects social organization and people's way of life."[20] For instance, using heroin or crack cocaine for the purpose of gaining respect or drinking heavily as a sign of working-class solidarity and masculine pride are not flawed within the context of their use.[21] In such cases, people are controlled less by the substances they use than by the circumstances surrounding this use.

This fundamental insight was most eloquently articulated by the late Norman Zinberg who argued that intoxicant use and abuse are intimately related to the social context in which they are embedded.[22] For instance, heroin addiction among American soldiers fighting in Vietnam was not such an inexplicable activity given the uncertainty about life they confronted each day during the course of duty. Large numbers of enlisted men in Vietnam reported having used and becoming addicted to heroin. However, as Lee Robins and her colleagues found, once they had returned from Vietnam and were outside the abhorrent war setting, few of these veterans became readdicted.[23] We see alcohol and drug use as reflective of the various ways in which people seek and often find personal meaningfulness, comfort, and security in a social setting that may be incapable of providing these basic needs. Addiction may thus have its roots in prevailing social and cultural conditions. In the words of Richard Klein, drugs of all kinds, including even tobacco, constitute effective instruments "for mediating social interaction." They are weapons "against the intrusion of other subjectivities and a sort of magic wand that seductively invites intrusion."[24]

Such a cultural view of use and addiction circumvents the placement of alcohol and drug abusers in liminal categories to be transformed by a well-intentioned, medically articulated rite of passage. The everyday-life view refuses to see addiction as unusual and extraordinary. Rather, it sees addiction as a way of being in a world that offers few other sources of meaning, or, as Peele contends, a "way of coping with life, artificially attaining feelings and rewards people feel they cannot achieve in any other way."[25] Addiction to alcohol and drugs follows from a felt need to transcend one's normal state.[26] It results from an insatiable consumption of substances for the sake of the meaning found in the experience of using those substances. Thus, recourse to addiction is recourse to meaning and personal significance artificially produced.

It is difficult to find alcohol- and drug-addicted people who have not been socialized into disease-based categories. Even if people do not believe they have a disease when they enter treatment or self-help programs, they generally do so after they have affiliated for a period of time. Those who do not adopt the disease narrative of addiction are frequently pressured into accepting its medicalized imagery. In fact, failure to convert to the addiction-as-disease metaphor is considered to be proof positive of addiction. Indeed, one principal goal of treatment is to inculcate in alcohol and drug abusers an acceptance of the disease ideology of addiction, complete with its medicalized reinterpretation of personal biography. The past is reconstituted to reflect a pattern of behavior consistent with the symptomology of addiction. A person is said to have consumed substances excessively not by choice but out of a compulsion brought on by a disease. The person is said to have been unable to witness the turmoil caused by substance abuse not because use was satisfying, but because he or she was in denial. The person is seen not simply as having transitory problems with substances, but as an addict who will never fully recover and who must be ruthlessly vigilant lest he or she cascades further down the slippery slope of addiction.

Given the predominance of this disease narrative it is difficult to find alcohol- and drug-addicted people who possess normalized narratives of their use. Such nonpathologized and nonmedicalized narratives, although perhaps heretical to the dominant disease view of addiction, are nonetheless important to illustrate the fact that significant numbers of people discontinue their addiction to alcohol and drugs without treatment. In the remainder of this chapter, we examine how our addicted respondents found meaning in their use and abuse of intoxicants. In short, we seek to illustrate the everyday, nondiseased narratives of formerly dependent individuals who terminated their dependencies on alcohol and drugs without the assistance of formal treatment or self-help protocols.

Everyday-Life Narratives of Intoxicant Use

Dennis began using alcohol and illicit drugs when he was thirteen years old. As he remembers it, "I wanted to be cool, so I started drinking and using marijuana." The son of a college professor, Dennis drank alcohol and smoked marijuana throughout the next several years. By the time he graduated from high school, he was a daily user of marijuana. Choosing not to follow in his father's footsteps, Dennis drifted around and eventually became involved in selling PCP. "It was nasty, nasty stuff," he remembered. In his early twenties, his consumption escalated to using cocaine primarily as a "social thing," not unlike the majority of cocaine users studied by others.[27] His use of cocaine was initiated through friends. Eventually, through his associates, he began dealing cocaine "because there was money to be made in it."

Dennis's cocaine use escalated further after some of his friends began to inject cocaine. "I watched them do it and rush out and breathe real hard. It appeared they were quite enjoying it." Although slightly reticent about using needles, he decided to try a little "taste." As he described the experience, injecting cocaine produces a powerful physical sensation: "It is like the biggest wall of euphoria I've ever experienced. It's like your whole body is a sex organ and you, your whole body is orgasming, including your head." Despite the pleasurable affects he derived from injecting cocaine, Dennis only "mainlined" for a short while. As he explained:

> I have no [needle] marks and I wanted to stop before I had any. That was my biggest fear, that I would be discovered as an IV drug user and the shame that would be surrounding it. It's OK, it's socially acceptable to snort cocaine but, it is not to inject it. . . . I knew that it [injecting] was gonna kill me if I kept doing it.

Although Dennis discontinued his intravenous use, he nevertheless continued to snort cocaine heavily.

Dennis's pattern of drug use shifted again after a friend taught him how to free-base. In a short time he became a heavy "baser" which caused him to become more involved in selling cocaine to support his growing habit. His life became increas-

ingly frantic as his use escalated. As he describes this episode of
his life:

> I was always able to maintain my own use by selling cocaine.
> One day I would be scraping to put ten thousand dollars to-
> gether to pay "the man." But then the next day I would have
> another quarter pound of cocaine in my hand and I would be
> off for another week.

Contrary to enslavement metaphors of dependency that see people as being at the mercy of the drugs they use, Dennis was able
to maintain a stable job at a tractor trailer company earning fif-
teen dollars per hour in 1980. Financially, Dennis was doing very
well. With his steady legitimate job and his dealing business
"growing like mad" he was experiencing the "good life." He
owned a home, dressed well, and attracted women, including the
woman, a "100 percent innocent person," who would become his
wife. Through his earnings from his day job and drug dealing,
Dennis appeared quite affluent, a fact that concerned his wife's
parents:

> I was always taking her to fancy dinners and bought her nice
> clothes. I wasn't flashy, but I spent a lot. They [her parents]
> just couldn't figure out how I was doing it. Her dad swore up
> and down that I was in the Mafia and he wasn't far off base.

They were soon married and, as he recalls, "I thoroughly cor-
rupted her before long. Not only did she start basing, she managed the drug money for me."

Eventually Dennis was fired from his job at the trailer company because of excessive tardiness and absenteeism resulting
from his daily use of cocaine. Later he was reinstated because a
legal technicality in his union contract had been violated. However, after a short period of time, Dennis decided to leave the
company on his own and he and his wife moved to Denver.

Although strangers in Denver, they soon became involved in Denver's drug-using networks. As he describes his initial experiences in Denver, "I ran into and became friends with one of the biggest cocaine importers in Colorado. I ended up working for him for three years." Although Dennis no longer free-based, his daily use of snorting cocaine continued.

Dennis purchased an aquarium business with some excess money he had accumulated from drug dealing. However, he eventually lost this enterprise as a result of his heavy drug use. A friend introduced him to crack cocaine and according to Dennis, "that became the worst year of my life." He began smoking crack daily, even at work while he could hear customers "five feet outside my door." Although Dennis's business was initially successful, he began having serious cash flow problems because he was skimming hundreds of dollars off from his sales per week to purchase drugs. As a result, he declared bankruptcy and lost his business. In addition, he nearly lost his wife and almost became a physical wreck. After this series of avoidance-oriented experiences, Dennis made the decision to stop using drugs for good.

Surprisingly, throughout his extensive history of drug use, Dennis retained his connection to his family members, which he believed was important to his eventual recovery. Reflecting on his family, Dennis asserted that "my parents raised me with good morals and values. The person I am today is because of them." Also, although he lost his business, he had a remarkably stable employment history throughout his period of abuse. In addition, Dennis "never did any immoral acts." It never "dragged down" any of his other "standards" nor, contrary to popular images, did he commit any crimes other than using and selling drugs. All in all, for his more than ten-year history of heavy drug consumption, Dennis fared well. He remained relatively stable, maintained his family relationships, and emerged from the experience with an intact family, a new and prospering business, and a positive outlook on life.

Dennis's dependence, while not characteristic of all drug users or even of those in this study, is nonetheless typical in its form. Each of our respondents began using alcohol and drugs within the larger context of friendship networks. Like Dennis, each of our respondents used and abused intoxicating substances for the meaning and value they derived from them. Whether it was for social acceptance and connections, physical pleasure, status and respect, or personal enhancement, all our respondents found significance and meaning within the social context of alcohol and drug use. None of them suffered from any psychological pathology, nor were any of them members of the urban underclass. Despite their heavy involvement with alcohol and drugs, all our respondents possessed relatively stable backgrounds. With the exception of two, all had completed their high school degree, and several had college and graduate degrees. Most were employed, both during and after their period of dependency in well-paying working-class trades or in professional occupations including law, engineering, and the health-related field. Some, like Dennis, held managerial positions or operated their own businesses. All our respondents had similar demographic characteristics as Dennis in that none were enmeshed in a web of impoverishment and violence, contrary to what is commonly associated with alcohol and drug abuse in the urban landscape.[28] All our respondents began their using careers in economically viable settings and possessed a variety of resources including friends, family members, an education, job connections, and material possessions. They all had a large degree of what sociologists and political scientists refer to as social capital.[29]

For the most part, our respondents became involved in using and even abusing substances because of the meaning they derived from the experience. Howard Becker and other researchers have found that drug users learn to perceive drug-related experiences as valuable. Aside from learning the techniques associated with use, Becker found that users also learn to perceive and appreciate the effects of a drug. In short, drug users find meaning in the experience of using. Similarly, seasoned drug researchers Dan Waldorf and his colleagues found that most persons who used cocaine failed to perceive any mind-altering effects the first time they used it; they had to learn the effects.[30] Even the eventual dependency and status of being an addict, as Waldorf found, provided a passage into a respected identity. This identity can express itself as cultural resistance against having to accept demeaning social and occupational roles associated with being poor.[31] In fact, addiction itself is related to the meaning substances have for users. In his pathbreaking sociological work on narcotic addiction Alfred Lindesmith recognized the importance that cultural meanings have for drug users.[32] He found that users become addicted to heroin when they learn to associate the taking of the drug with feeling "normal." The effects and experience of drugs are thus never separated from the social context in which they are used and given meaning.

Most of our respondents began to use of alcohol and drugs during their early teens and escalated their use principally because they found a number of benefits associated with these substances. For some, these benefits were related to the growing pains of their adolescent years. As one forty-four-year-old woman explained, "I started in 1968 when I was fourteen. I was a rebellious teen who had no self-esteem. I was always told I was no good." Alcohol and drugs provided an escape from the tensions she faced during these difficult years. These substances were particularly attractive not only because of the physiological effects they produced, but also for the community and acceptance she felt when with other users.

For some, the strong social networks formed with other drug users became a potent force. For instance, Daria, a twenty-five-year-old former addict, explained her attraction to heroin as follows:

> I started when a boyfriend that I had but didn't really like introduced me to heroin. I was seventeen and I knew he did heroin but it was mysterious and attracted me to the guy. I eventually stopped seeing him, but I continued to use. I was modeling and everybody was doing it. It was really expensive, it looked really good, and it didn't look bad. It didn't look like junkies strung out on the street. It was fun. I loved it. I was friends with really hip people from famous rock bands. We just did it and did it and did it.

For people like Daria, drugs provided an opportunity to become integrated into a world of meaningful relationships, relationships that eluded them in the "straight world."

Contrary to popular opinion on addiction, few of our respondents reported becoming immediately dependent on substances, including narcotics. Rather, dependency occurred over a significant period of time, usually taking years to develop. Respondents generally attributed many benefits to their incipient and even dependent periods of drug use. For instance, Betsy, a former cocaine addict and speed freak, identified her early drug-taking experiences with the political and cultural resistance of the 1960s and 1970s. At that point in her life, drugs were consumed ritualistically for the purposes of mind expansion and cultural protest. As she reflected:

> I started using drugs when I was fourteen years old. I didn't really like pot because it slowed me down. I liked speed and psychedelics. When I originally started I was part of that culture that believed in the mind-expanding experience. We were political. We were activists. We did things. We didn't sit

around and smoke pot and talk about how high we were or how high we were going to get. It was a real incredible time of learning and change. We wanted to stop the [Vietnam] war, and we wanted equality and civil rights.

Interestingly, Betsy did not feel she was dependent on drugs during this politically active period in her life even though she considered herself a heavy user. Nor did she, at the time of the interview, have a pathologized reinterpretation of her past experience as being dependent but in denial. In fact, she had friends during this early period who were consuming cocaine and narcotics "for the wrong reasons," as she described it, and who eventually died. At least at this point in her life, Betsy's consumption of drugs was not unlike those Navajo who practice peyotism. For the Navajo, the consumption of drugs represents a tool with which to experience revelatory visions.[33] Similarly Betsy chose the road of intoxication in her quest to gain insight into the troubled world in which she lived. She believed that the road to wisdom and personal growth was available through the use of intoxicants. During this period in her drug-using career, her consumption was limited by the introspective and political journey she had undertaken. Her drug use was part of a larger collective, almost sacred, movement to transform the world. This higher calling created rituals that served to restrict the amount she used.

Betsy's problem with drugs and her ensuing dependency occurred primarily as a result of drug use removed from the ritualized context of political experience. Over time and with her declining activism, her drug use deteriorated into a mere consumerist practice and she fell into a pattern of dependent drug use. Indeed, what had protected her from dependency earlier on was not the property of the substances she was consuming, but rather the ritualization of drug use itself. Now that her drug use was divorced from this sacred realm, she began experiencing severe problems. She eventually met and married a man who dealt crack cocaine and, as she explained, "it ended up just a real strange life style for several years." Betsy explained her descent into dependency in the following way:

> By the end of the first year I was probably doing a gram a day, every day. . . . We partied a lot. We did a lot. We were always out in the clubs and stuff. I was working and I would be up for days and then I got to where I had to keep doing it so that I could work. It went on like this for several years.

For this respondent, drug use was no longer associated with a deeper political meaning. Rather, the experience of the drug had itself become meaningful, gratifying, and self-reinforcing.

Like Betsy, other respondents identified benefits associated with their years of drug use, seeing it as a way to experience the world differently from what they believed was otherwise possible. Carl, a forty-year-old male respondent who had been dependent on cocaine and crack for six years, reported that he started using marijuana at the age of twenty. Shortly after this period, Carl stopped using marijuana because he no longer enjoyed the effects. As he explained it, "I like to feel energized, actually in control and up instead of down. Pot brought me down." Carl soon entered into a relationship with a woman who was a heavy cocaine user. Though he began using cocaine heavily, on the average of a gram per day, he nonetheless experienced it as meaningful and beneficial. As he recalled: "I like to write poetry. I would stay up until 4 A.M. and would say that my best poetry came from my drug-using sessions." Carl believed that his creative and expressive talents resided in cocaine rather than in himself. Like our other respondents, he soon began using drugs as his primary way of experiencing and relating to the world around him. In short, Carl had developed what Andrew Weil refers to as a bad relationship with the drug.[34] For Carl, drugs mediated relationships, work, and even recreation, as his consumption became increasingly central to his life.

Some respondents used drugs to relieve the private troubles they were experiencing in their lives. Some began abusing these substances due to problems of abuse and alcohol dependency in their families. The pharmacological effects of intoxicating substances allowed them to temporarily escape from their personal and emotional difficulties. One respondent explained that she had grown up with alcoholic parents who made her feel insignificant. She found self-confidence and self-esteem through her drug use and her participation in a subculture of drug users. Another respondent, a forty-six-year-old engineer who consumed a quart of gin each night for several years, explained that he "became more and more reliant on it [alcohol] to fulfill personal needs and to overcome depression." Having grown up in an abusive family with alcohol problems, he turned to alcohol as a form of self-medication and to help him perform "certain roles" that made him uncomfortable unless he was intoxicated.

In other cases, abuse was a way of life growing up. Ralph, a businessman with a twenty-year history of alcohol dependency, commented:

> The alcohol started in high school and my mother was an alcoholic. All the guys I ran around with were pretty affluent. Our parents were members of the country club. All the fellas, we all drank heavily in high school. It was the thing to do. Then in college, in the fraternity, alcohol was plentiful and encouraged. . . . We were all nice, up and coming young men. But in fact, we were all drinking heavily. . . . For me drinking was a way to kind of disassociate myself from my problems. I felt terribly inadequate and my self-esteem was very low. I think a lot of this stemmed from the fact my mother was an alcoholic and died when I graduated from high school. There was

a lot of turmoil in our house. Before she died I was charged
with taking care of her because my father traveled quite a bit.
It was a pretty dysfunctional environment.

These respondents found that alcohol and other drugs initially
provided them with effective solutions to their private troubles.
Unfortunately, as with many people who become dependent on
these substances, what initially appeared to be a solution soon itself became a source of significant disruption.

In addition to seeking solutions to long-standing problems
through drugs and alcohol, our respondents also sought out solutions to more immediate troubles. As one thirty-six-year-old
graduate student explained: "I don't think I ever had sex without
drugs." For her, her dependency grew out of using cocaine to
overcome her deep-seated insecurities, including her sexual insecurity. Similarly, another respondent, a forty-four-year-old
systems analyst, reported that alcohol served as a way of dealing
with her sexual conflict. In her words, she was afraid to "open
the door" to explore her sexual desires and feelings for other
women: "I think the reasons for my drinking were to keep me
from seeing behind the door." For each of these individuals, intoxicants served as attempted solutions to personal problems.
However, the more they looked for chemically induced solutions
to their problems, the more they slipped into the darkness of dependency.

Slippin' into Darkness

In the 1970s, the Los Angeles-based funk band, WAR, wrote and
performed a song entitled "Slippin' into Darkness." While many
of their recordings were about America's deteriorating social
conditions, this song's title captures the experience with dependence reported by our respondents. Rather than waking up one

day to find themselves hopelessly dependent on intoxicants, their dependency and related problems were an ongoing process of personal deterioration that was not immediately apparent to them. Traditional views of addiction would characterize this failure to perceive their condition as "denial" and evidence of their disease. Indeed, drug- and alcohol-treatment programs expend significant amounts of energy convincing addicted people of their denial in order to move them forward in their recovery.

However, from an "everyday-life" perspective denial is nothing short of a different definition of the situation.[35] People who are alcohol- and drug-addicted are not necessarily "denying" their problems; rather, they simply do not subjectively define their experiences as overtly problematic. For all our respondents, recognition that something was wrong and required their attention involved a transformative process during which their perception of substance use as enjoyable, beneficial, and necessary changed to a definition that associated use with pain and suffering. This transformation is a social one and occurs over a lengthy period of time.

Part of the explanation for our respondents' failure to recognize their need to change despite their everyday private troubles, is that substance use is culture-bound. Substances and their use, even their heavy use, do not possess singular and unified meanings. Rather, they embody multiple and often contradictory meanings that affect people's consumption patterns and experiences. Alcohol and drugs serve multiple utilitarian, convivial, as well as hedonistic purposes. This is particularly the case in a capitalist society that has generated great affluence. Such affluence produces cultural contradictions by increasing the desire to pursue pleasure.[36] Advanced capitalism depends on mass consumption for its survival and has increasingly marketed commodities of pleasure, indulgence, and desire to consumers who are no longer bound by the ascetic norm of self-sacrifice once associ-

WOW

ated with the spirit of capitalism.[37] Witness the dramatic growth in the leisure industry and in extreme sports that market intense feelings of pleasure, thrill, and release from everyday concerns. Indeed, mass consumption for image and pleasure has become intrinsic to modernity.

Given the cultural emphasis on pursuing pleasure, it is not surprising that our respondents continued to use intoxicating substances despite the problems they experienced. They were not necessarily "in denial," rather, they simply preferred to pursue a life of excessive substance use and live with the consequences. Warren, a fifty-three-year-old master plumber who had formerly been addicted to cocaine for five years, told us, "At some point I realized it was a dependency thing, but by then I didn't mind, I liked the risk." Until an individual reaches a point where problems come to be defined as intolerable, he or she sees them merely as collateral damage in the pursuit of pleasure. For our respondents, these problems—or externalities, as economists might call them—continued to grow over a lengthy period before they perceived them as painful and problematic enough to warrant change. While this transformation process is explored in the next chapter, here we wish to highlight the many problems our respondents experienced during their active periods of dependency.

These problems typically involved multiple dimensions of their lives including the occupational, financial, and relational, and to some extent the legal and medical. Our respondents experienced several of the symptoms associated with dependence, such as preoccupation with alcohol or drugs, increasing tolerance, onset of withdrawal, blackouts, relational conflicts and family turmoil, occupational and money problems, depression and anxiety, physical deterioration, surreptitious use, craving, and the feeling of being out of control. According to any standardized criteria, our respondents would have been considered dependent and eligible for treatment. Indeed, the most widely used authority for determining dependence, *the Diagnostic and Statistical Manual of Mental Disorders* (DSM IV), the "'bible' of psychiatric disorders,"[38] uses distinct criteria such as loss of control, continuation despite adverse consequences, preoccupation, development of tolerance, and withdrawal when rendering a diagnosis of substance abuse.[39] All our respondents reported having experienced increasing tolerance as well as signs of withdrawal, including cravings and the inability to discontinue their use.

Our respondents were particularly vivid in their recollections of these cravings. A thirty-six-year-old graduate student who was dependent on cocaine for five years and had not used it for seven years, explained her cravings as follows:

> I started using just on weekends but I soon got into the pattern of using every day. If I was out [of cocaine] I would find myself going through the house looking for any crumb, anywhere. I would send my kids outside and play so I could indulge without them seeing me. I became frantic if I didn't have any coke.

Another respondent, a twenty-six-year-old assistant manager, explained that her "whole life revolved around getting the next hit. I couldn't imagine life without it." A third explained the withdrawal she went through when she stopped her daily consumption of cocaine: "I got very irritated because I needed it. My body wanted it. I would lock myself up in a room and punch the walls and the dresser. . . . I couldn't sleep. I was afraid I was losing my mind." Similarly, the few individuals we interviewed who were dependent on opiates reported experiencing powerful cravings associated with withdrawal. As one young woman with a heroin addiction recalled, "I knew that I was doing it every day but I didn't care what addicted meant. I was bringing it to work because I was getting sick at work without it." Thus, our respondents experienced the physical and psychological signs of dependency.

In addition, they reported experiencing a wide range of personal problems that were exacerbated by their excessive use of substances. These problems will be explored in greater detail in the next chapter in relation to respondents' decisions to transform their lives. Here we simply wish to document the most salient problems they were experiencing, in order to illustrate the extent of their dependencies. Their financial problems were quite pronounced. Most reported spending inordinate sums of money on drugs to support their consumption habits. They drained savings accounts, exhausted paychecks, and pawned personal effects such as jewelry, tools, and stolen merchandise in order to purchase substances and maintain their use. Some, like Dennis whom we discussed earlier, lost businesses they had begun years earlier.

Related to these financial problems were difficulties maintaining employment. While most held jobs at various points during their dependent careers, they did experience employment problems. Several respondents reported losing jobs or not being able to maintain one. As one respondent commented: "I started having a lot of problems keeping a job. I couldn't get to work because I was up all night." As respondents began having employment troubles, the financial problems soon mounted, frequently resulting in difficulty paying bills. As a twenty-seven-year-old contractor explained:

> I was staying up all night and all morning. We would do it [use cocaine] in the office. The sun would come up and people would start coming to work. So my performance went downhill which meant the income went downhill. So with less money, I wasn't going to slack up on the cocaine, so I slacked up on paying the bills.

These and related financial problems were typical of all our respondents, regardless of the substances they used.

In addition to occupational and financial problems, troubled
and tormented relationships were common among our respondents. Many of the relationships they entered into were based on
a common interest in heavy drug and alcohol use, and were
therefore often doomed from the beginning. As one respondent,
a thirty-six-year-old switchboard operator who began getting
high because it allowed her not "to feel all the sad stuff" in her
life, reflected: "I moved in with a man who turned out to be my
first husband. We didn't really have that much in common, except drugs. He was an alcoholic and drug addict. . . . He was always mean to me and we would fight all the time." Another
woman who "married real young" explains the physical violence
that was inflicted upon her by her abusive husband:

> I married someone older than me who dealt drugs during col-
> lege and probably still does. We did it together. That's what
> the relationship was built on. . . . It was starting to affect me
> physically and my appetite was horrible and the relationship
> with my husband was just unbelievably awful. . . . I wound up
> in a battered women's shelter. . . . There was no argument that
> didn't end in some kind of physical hitting.

Our respondents' relationships were frequently conflict-ridden.
For instance, a forty-five-year-old lawyer explained that he had
continuous problems with relationships: "My first wife left me
because of my drinking. After I married a second time, we soon
got a divorce because of my drinking. My second wife also had a
drinking problem and we eventually got divorced." Almost the
same story was told by a sixty-year-old salesperson:

> I was dysfunctional in that I needed to drink to get through
> the day. In 1974, my wife and I separated and eventually got

divorced. . . . I was dating this other lady and eventually moved in with her. She was an alcoholic too. We got married but it didn't last too long.

While many went through a process of what sociologist Diane Vaughan refers to as "uncoupling," that is, the process through which individuals slowly disengage from a marriage, others were able to weather the frequent storms despite their marital conflicts.[40] A twenty-six-year-old registered nurse commented that his significant other of about two years at the time was "fed up" with his drinking and threatened to leave, although she had never followed through on her threat. Relationships such as this that survived are important to the natural recovery process and will be explored in a later chapter.

Given the frequency and intensity of their relational conflicts, it is not surprising that the children of our respondents were adversely affected. As sociologists have frequently pointed out, witnessing such discord can have severely detrimental effects on a child's social and psychological development, including subsequent alcohol and drug abuse. Family researchers make all too clear that:

> Children from violent homes are more likely to have personal trouble—temper tantrums, trouble making friends, school problems—failing grades, discipline problems, and aggressive and violent flare-ups with family members and people outside the home. These children are three to four times more likely than children from nonviolent homes to engage in illegal acts—vandalism, stealing, alcohol, drugs—and to be arrested.[41]

For many of our respondents their marital conflict spilled over onto their children. One respondent recalled how a family conflict escalated to the point where his daughter called for assistance: "My wife and I, now my ex-wife, would fight all the time. It got so bad that my daughter phoned the police and turned me in and my ex-wife because we were doing so many drugs." Another respondent reported fighting incessantly with her husband who was also drinking heavily, becoming violent, and physically abusing her children.

Less frequently, our respondents also experienced an assortment of other troubles such as dropping out of school at an early age, having health complications, and assorted legal problems stemming from criminal offenses ranging from DUIs to property crimes. With regard to the latter, it should be pointed out that none of our respondents fit the category of users that Charles Faupel identifies as being most prone to criminal behavior.[42] For Faupel, the relationship between drugs and crime involves a complex interaction between the availability of drugs and the degree of stability in a person's life. Drug addicts most prone to criminal activities generally lack access to drugs and experience significant disruptions in conventional roles that would serve to regulate use.[43] While all of our respondents experienced significant disruption in their lives, with the exception of a very few, most were able to acquire substances and maintain some stake in conventional roles. As we shall demonstrate in a later chapter, the ability to maintain a stake in conventional life not only prevented them from becoming deeply enmeshed in a subculture of drug addiction where crime might have been more prevalent, but it also helped them in their attempts at personal transformation. *Foundation of RC..*

Conclusion

In modern society people are constantly in search of meaning. Sociologists and social psychologists have long been interested in understanding how people make their lives meaningful. A central insight in sociology is that people actively construct their social worlds by making meaning. Human behavior is not merely a passive reaction to genetically scripted messages, but is an active process of interpretation and negotiation in which meanings are created and attached to the objects, situations, and events occurring in our social environments. Meanings are neither universally held nor permanently fixed. They are properties conferred upon the world by individuals in the process of social interaction. Thus, how people define their social situations and give meaning to them is sociologically important.

By utilizing an everyday-life framework of addiction, we have explored how our respondents gave meaning to their heavy use of alcohol and drugs. Rather than adopting a disease narrative of dependency that defines away the social meanings of these substances for users, we have sought to understand and articulate the subjective meanings they, and the associated intoxication experiences, had for our respondents. The use of substances is never independent of the complex web of meaning within which they are embedded. Instead, these substances are symbolic representations of various dialectical facets of being. Alcohol and drugs represent sources of distinction as well as sources of condemnation. They embody elements of community and individualism. They are religious and sacred as well as secular and profane. They medicate through numbing and promote pleasure through emotional release. They are both the path to knowledge and the escape from knowledge. To paraphrase Freud, they are both eros and thanatos, that is, they are both life desiring and death desiring. Indeed, they are many things to many people and understanding these meanings is critical to understanding dependency.

While all our respondents began their use in a controlled fashion, their search for meaning through alcohol and drugs eventually led them to their addictions. Our respondents sought many things in the substances they used that they were unable to find elsewhere. They found relationships, status, relief, acceptance, and pleasure. Unfortunately, they found a host of financial, employment, relational, legal, and health problems as well. Each user developed different levels of dependency on the substance of his or her choice and lived in a contradictory existence of ecstasy and agony. How they reached the decision to terminate their dependency and the process through which this occurred is explored in the next chapter.

Chapter Three

THE PROCESS OF RECOVERY
WITHOUT TREATMENT

The present chapter illustrates that our respondents' decisions to end their addictions to intoxicating substances occurred through a process in which they redefined their experience of drug use. Although they gave no one reason for quitting, most users who discontinued their addictive use had ceased to enjoy the effects of these substances and now directly associated drug taking with unpleasant physical and emotional sensations.[1] Whether overcoming addiction as a response to "avoidance" conditions such as the experience of "hitting bottom," or to "approach" factors, including the desire to maintain employment or form a new identity, all our respondents developed a firm resolve to transform their lives. However, having made this resolve, they were confronted with the problem of accomplishing their goal. This chapter focuses on the stages and associated strategies they used to break their cycles of dependency on alcohol and drugs without treatment. In it we explore how our respondents moved from active use to cessation of addiction.

There are several characteristics commonly associated with the cessation of addiction on alcohol and drugs without treatment. Previous research on the topic of recovery without treatment has found three overlapping characteristics related to cessation.[2] First, most individuals who manage to end their addictions without treatment engage in behavioral or psychic avoidance of these substances and the related social cues that stimulate the desire to use. Many drug addicts abandon the geographical areas in which they reside to physically extricate themselves from networks of drug users and dealers. Users actively avoid substances altogether, or, in some cases, "symbolically" avoid substances and related cues by constructing and presenting the image of a nonuser.[3] While this symbolic avoidance is not always successful, it often helps addicts remove themselves from the social and psychological pressures to use.[4]

A second common strategy among self-remitters is the building of structure. As Harvard Medical School researchers Shaffer and Jones point out, structure builders often develop alternatives to drug use.[5] Since the subculture of drug addiction can be intensely engulfing, alternative activities must be pursued to substitute for the jettisoned lifestyle.[6] As Patrick Biernacki has written: "[T]he cessation of the addiction is the result of their becoming more immersed in the activities of the non-addictive world and less involved in activities related to the world of addiction."[7] Whether these structure-building activities are deliberate pursuits or fortuitous encounters, they help the addict establish a nondependent existence.

Finally, self-remitters establish or reestablish meaningful relationships with individuals whose lives are organized around sobriety.[8] In this way, recovery from dependency is a group phenomenon in which addicts develop new relationships that "they do not want to risk losing by using drugs again."[9] These relationships help addicts forge new or residual roles that are crucial to the process of identity transformation.[10] Such transformations can be understood as an ongoing process of interaction through which people adopt new meanings and new self-images.[11]

As we will demonstrate in this chapter, these meanings and related processes of self-change occur interactionally within a complex web of social relations. For instance, Biernacki asserts that addicts develop "stakes in conventional life" that "function as strong symbolic wedges and work to continue the separation of the ex-addict from the world of addiction."[12] While increasing the stakes in conformity are often seen in any recovery process, the concept of stakes leaves much unanswered. For instance, what particular self-change experiences are related to strategies facilitating increased stakes? Are certain strategies particularly effective in producing a radical change in the self? What are the experiences associated with developing a stake in conventional life? Are there similarities in the recovery strategies of different people, or are these strategies distinct for different people and different substances? Such questions draw our attention to the broader social processes that inform the untreated recovery experiences of our respondents.

Dependency, Recovery, and Conversion

Gregory Bateson, the cognitive anthropologist, presents a view of addiction that is particularly useful to the present analysis.[13] In his ethnographic work with alcoholics in AA, Bateson reached the provocative conclusion that dependency represents a form of knowledge that is replete with error. For Bateson, dependency remains until the experience of tension or panic provides a favorable moment for self-transformation. While Bateson believes that this point is reached when an alcoholic "hits bottom," a point at which the alcoholic has bankrupted his or her values of self-control, others maintain that such transformations occur through the desire to preserve social connectivity.[14] According to Bateson, at such critical moments in an alcoholic's life, possibilities appear which open the way to new images of the self. These new images are built upon what Bateson refers to as a "complementarity" that is aimed at establishing a collaborative relationship with the world. This move to complementarity represents a revision of meaning, or as O'Reilly writes, an "epistemological reorientation" that promises a resolution to various subjectively felt tensions.[15]

This new framework, one that Bateson believes is promoted through self-help groups like Alcoholics Anonymous, binds alcoholics to conventional norms in society by helping them to see that they are connected to something that transcends themselves. In the parlance of AA, this typically involves believing in a "higher power." Thus, for Bateson complementarity is the cognitive state in which an alcoholic develops a "stake" in society, thereby allowing him or her to live with the social world rather than living in opposition to it. Through complementarity, the alcoholic experiences a cognitive restructuring that replaces a logic of individualism with a logic that is lodged in community.[16] This communitarian moment associated with affiliation to AA facilitates embracing a world in which the alcoholic was previously lost. It is this embrace of the world that empowers the transformative capabilities of alcoholics, thereby permitting them to find existential meaningfulness in recovery.

For Bateson, as well as for sociologist Norman Denzin, the function of treatment and self-help groups is to rebuild the self in relation to society by providing alcoholics with a ready-made network of associates and instilling in them a rigid belief system and a normative set of values proscribing use. Such a rebuilding proceeds through a ritual sanctification of the collective life that engulfs the individual. This engulfed self "denotes a constellation of roles all organized around and through one salient identity."[17] Such a self is typified by a large degree of identification with activities and epistemologies that make up that central identity. The engulfed self of the recovering alcoholic is enveloped by the collective life of AA within which he participates. Whether engulfment involves recovery from dependency,[18] the adoption of a deviant identity,[19] role exits,[20] or specialized roles like athletes,[21] the engulfed self represents a significant transformation of identity in which new meanings, practices, and associations achieve saliency over less valued ones.

Such intense identification with a particular role, and with its related identity features, is frequently associated with experiences that produce dramatic shifts in an individual's perception of the world, and in his or her fundamental definition of the situation. As many sociologists have pointed out, occasions of epistemological transformation often occur through powerful conversion experiences. Not surprisingly, the recovery literature is replete with conversion narratives. References to conversion are widespread in the accounts offered by many recovering alcoholics and drug addicts.[22] In his symbolic interactionist account of Alcoholics Anonymous, David Ruby describes the appeal of AA groups as follows:

> Telling one's "story" or "giving testimonial" is perhaps the best known aspect of AA's organization dynamics. . . . The testimonial is made up of two parts: a story about how bad it was before AA and a story about how good it is now. AA members frequently refer to the drinking part of the testimonial as a "drunkalogue" and to the second part as a "sobriety story."

Students of conversion and commitment have sometimes pointed out the importance, for the commitment process, of a "commitment act" which symbolizes the initiate's incorporation into the group. . . . Speaking in tongues or receiving baptism of the holy spirit may serve for members of the Pentecostal movement as the "bridge-burning act" that separates their old identity from the new; in AA, one acknowledges one's embracement of the alcoholic identity by telling one's story.[23]

The ritual storytelling in AA creates a powerful interactional context for conversion experiences to occur. Through such storytelling people acquire new languages, new epistemologies, new associations, and ultimately new narrative structures regarding alcoholism.

Among sociologists, the experience of conversion is typically described as "a radical reorganization of identity, meaning, life."[24] It is the process "of changing a sense of root reality."[25] Typically, a conversion is an active process through which people give up one way of life for another.[26] In their classic model of conversion, Lofland and Stark identify the predisposing conditions and situational contingencies associated with a conversion experience.[27] These conditions and contingencies include: (1) a felt personal tension in which the individual experiences doubts about life and the circumstances within which they are presently embedded; (2) a selection of problem-solving approaches; (3) activation of problem-solving activities, frequently those that are spiritually based; (4) a disruption of identity associated with experiences like traumatic events or the culmination of unpleasant events that function as turning points where "old lines of obligations and lines of action were diminished and new involvements became desirable and possible";[28] (5) the creation of affective bonds with members of a group that offer a solution to a person's quest for meaning; (6) a severing or neutralization of ties with those who may challenge the convert's new epistemological orientation; and (7) intensive interaction through which a person becomes a "deployable agent" or total convert.

It is not surprising that much of the alcohol- and drug-abuse recovery literature employs the metaphor of conversion. Even Bateson's cybernetic theory of alcoholism refers to the dramatic identity transformation in self-help groups as conversion. Interestingly, however, much of the natural-recovery literature describes the process of identity transformation among alcohol and drug addicts as being akin to a conversion. For instance, in his description of how heroin addicts break away from addiction without treatment, Biernacki attributed a conversion-like process to most of those he interviewed:

> The void created when people stop using addictive drugs and separate themselves from other users commonly is filled by a round of activities that have a single focus. For example, if part of the strategy to establish some distance from the drug corresponds with the ex-addict's becoming a member of a religious group, then the daily-life activities focus on religious matters—praying, reading the bible, attending church services, and the like. If the initial move away from the drug scene happens to correspond with the ex-addict's becoming involved in a political group, then each day centers on political and related activities—a sort of focused immersion. *In many instances, the intensity of the involvements and the exclusiveness of them resemble missionary zeal.* The all-encompassing nature of the activity is reminiscent of the ex-addict's past behavior with drugs. (Emphasis added)[29]

Even alcoholics who reject the religious and philosophical tenets of self-help groups as being too heavy-handed and cultlike, nevertheless experience a "conversion" to a new identity devoid of the mysticism that surrounds AA. For instance, many people in secular sobriety organizations like Rational Recovery or Secular

Organizations for Sobriety report having adopted personal religious orientations without the disease narrative of addiction associated with AA.[30] Though such individuals reject the meta-
physics of AA, many have nonetheless experienced conversion-
type transformations of the self.

   The metaphor of conversion is a useful means of understanding natural recovery from alcohol and drug addiction. While the
process of change experienced by our respondents was not iden-
tical to other religious conversion experiences, it was nonetheless similar in some respects. Whether a set of experiences con-
forms to a theoretical model of conversion or not is not paramount to an analysis of our respondents' lives. What matters
here is that the extrapolation from their accounts can be used to
build an explanatory model of recovery without treatment. Respondents in this study experienced only some of the stages
identified in the conversion model discussed above. This does not
suggest that the original models of conversion are incorrect, or
that the model presented here is superior. It simply reflects sub-
tle variations in the "conversion motifs" of our respondents that
appeared in our data.[31] The stages of our respondents' conversion and the strategies they used are outlined below.

Strain

None of our respondents set out to become dependent upon alcohol and/or drugs when they began using; rather, their addiction took place over an extended period of time. All of them described being introduced to substances through intimate social
networks. As one thirty-four-year-old self-employed businessman recalled:

> I was thirteen years old, at my buddy's house. He had just got-
> ten a little bit of marijuana from his older brother. I can re-

member fumbling around in his bedroom where I sat at the top of the stairs watching for his mother to come in while he started to fit it [marijuana] into the [rolling] paper. There were three of us there and I wasn't going to smoke. The other guy had gotten high occasionally with his brother over the previous year. My best friend had only gotten high one previous time, and I wasn't going to get high. But, you know, I was going to be cool about it and see what went on. I watched them get high and thought it was no different than smoking cigarettes. So I decided to try it.

Following Becker's study of marijuana users, all our respondents began using alcohol and drugs in social settings in which they learned the techniques and motivations associated with use, acquired an understanding of their effects, and developed an appreciation of the effects produced through intoxication.[32]

While none of our respondents began careers as full-blown alcohol and drug abusers, as we pointed out in the previous chapter they all eventually reached a point where their level of use had escalated to the problem stage. Concern about the use of substances was typically triggered by the problems they were experiencing. This concern, or first doubts as Ebaugh calls them, produced significant tensions and strains in our respondents.[33] Strain occurred on a variety of different levels and was typically followed by the desire to take some kind of action to reduce the tension.

For our respondents, alienation and feelings of social disconnection were typical forms of strain. As several social scientists have pointed out, the experience of alienation is associated with a sense of social isolation and estrangement from self and others.[34] One woman, a thirty-three-year-old paralegal whose husband was dealing heavy "weight," explained the personal strain she eventually came to experience:

> My life was deteriorating quickly. I was not creative. I wasn't
> happy. I wasn't producing what I was capable of. . . . I was
> lonely. I was sad. I had a little one and another on the way. I
> think during the whole drug scene I just wasn't able to do and
> be who I was to the level of satisfaction that I would want to
> perform at.

For this respondent, the collapse of her sense of self as an effective and creative human being initiated the process of identity
transformation that she would eventually experience.

A second type of strain common among our respondents occurred through social interaction with others. The importance of
others early on in the identity transformation process has been
documented in several studies of recovery, religious conversions,
and role exits more generally. For instance, in her work on former alcoholics, Ebaugh found that doubts about drinking begin
to emerge when family or friends become aware of a problem.[35]
Under such conditions, the alcoholic must either work harder to
rationalize his or her activities, or is challenged to reconsider
prior excuses. Not unlike Ebaugh's role exiters, our respondents
experienced strain when intimates and friends raised the specter
of concern about their abuse. For instance, one twenty-seven-
year-old woman who had been an active cocaine "free-baser" for
more than four years explained that "my parents couldn't trust
me. They didn't like me. My friends were the same way. They
were seeing a different person." Several respondents commented that their friends confronted them and told them they
were using alcohol and drugs in excess, and that they were ruin-
ing their lives. Consistent with Ebaugh's findings, significant
others, friends, and parents had a great impact on our respondents, triggering their doubts about the use of intoxicants.

In addition to these interactional difficulties, many respondents complained about domestic violence. This was particularly the case with female respondents who reported numer-

ous instances of physical violence directed at them by husbands or boyfriends who were themselves dependent on alcohol and/or drugs. In addition to the fear and brutality associated with living with violent men, many of our female respondents also complained about the generalized fear of male drug users. This fear was most pronounced among women who were in relationships with men who were dealing drugs. As one respondent explained:

> I remember a guy coming over at 2:30 in the morning. Terri, my husband, wasn't there and I was home by myself and I was scared. This guy really scared me. He walked right into the house and I had a hard time getting him out of the house. I was really afraid that he was going to hurt me or rob me or rape me.

Given the hierarchical gender relations that frequently exist in heavy drug-using circles, such fears are well justified.

For other respondents, the strain from excessive use of substances was related to more dramatic occurrences. Some ran afoul of the law, being arrested for DUIs or for participation in criminal activities. Other respondents were associating with people who were involved in criminal activities. Many of them felt disconnected from these people, as they themselves did not have a history of criminal involvement. Others recounted having serious financial difficulties that forced them to sell their assets in order to purchase drugs. One self-employed carpenter who had used cocaine and crack for five years explained that he had lost a considerable amount of money through his years of abuse:

> I bought a townhouse that I ended up losing. I pawned my toolbox, which was probably worth $15,000, I hocked it for $800 to buy a quarter ounce of coke. I ended up putting all my money into coke.

As illustrated in the previous chapter, respondents also experienced difficulties in locating and holding onto jobs, which caused great financial strain, particularly when it came to purchasing drugs. As one respondent reported, "I was in debt for thousands of dollars and there was a lot of financial pressure. My landlord put me out of business because I hadn't paid rent for a year."

Finally, several respondents complained of health consequences as a result of their extensive use of substances. Frequently, these health consequences were a direct reaction to the side effects of the substances they were using. While not all respondents experienced health problems as a result of their use, many did. In this respect, they were not unlike the drug users reported in other studies.[36] Many of our respondents complained of the ill-effects associated with the use of substances, such as nose sores and abscesses from extensive cocaine use, chronic insomnia, withdrawal symptoms, digestive tract problems, infections from needles, and a general sense of being sick all the time. One respondent, a twenty-five-year-old woman who had been a heroin addict for five years, complained that her health problems interfered with her career in fashion modeling. As she explained, "I was getting sick all the time at work and I had to eventually stop working. . . . It fucked up my teeth, it fucked up my skin, and I just looked like shit." Another respondent reported that she lost a great deal of weight and developed a painful ulcer that contributed to chronic nausea that eventually required surgery.

These multiple degradations served to promote in our respondents a reappraisal of their commitment to substance use. Such events initiated the process of disengagement from alcohol and drug addiction by providing "concrete evidence of how stressful or unpleasant role demands are and of the misfit between these role expectations and his or her ability or desire to meet them."[37] Frustrated aspirations, traumatic life experiences, feelings of alienation, and a general existential angst frequently acted as catalysts to powerful conversion experiences that radically restructured and reorganized our respondents' identities and meaning systems. Such existential crisis occurs through the process of engulfment in dependency roles. Despite the painful nature of these events, most of our respondents continued their active heavy use until they experienced a dramatic turning point in their lives that fostered in them a desire to change.

Turning Points

The actions of all our respondents had persisted for quite some time before they became aware that their lives were in need of a change. For most, a turning point occurred that sharply and dramatically disrupted their lives to the extent that they recognized that they were no longer "themselves." As Lofland and Stark write, turning points occur at the "moment when old lines of action were complete, had failed or been disrupted, or were about to be so, and when they faced the opportunity (or necessity), and possibly the burden, of doing something different with their lives."[38] Such turning points represent "cultural dislocations" in which the previous patterns on which their lives have been constructed become increasingly unworkable.[39] These epiphanies either lead to the resurrection of residual roles or to the adoption of new roles and practices that are associated with a radically transformed identity. In order to experience this mutability of self, the individual must often first experience a dramatic dislocation of self that signifies the emotional and physical dis-ease from which he or she suffers.[40] Such turning points, while different for different people, are critical for those who undergo an eventual identity transformation.

The turning points identified by our respondents were both approach-oriented and avoidance-oriented. Frequently they were related to experiences involving other people, particularly intimates. For instance, one respondent explained that his resolve to stop using occurred when his father passed away. As he described his turning point:

> My father was an alcoholic. He would come home from work and would drink several quarts of beer and watch TV and go to bed. He finally died from a tumor that doctors said came from his heavy alcohol use. I decided to quit that day.

The painful experience of losing a parent contributed to a cultural dislocation of meaning for this respondent. The death of loved ones can often rupture the manner in which individuals compose their lives. At such moments, they are often ripe for personal transformation. Referring to the power of death to increase his awareness of the need for personal change, another respondent explained:

> The biggest reason I decided to quit using was that I lost my brother at forty-one in 1989. He died on the same day my father died, exactly twenty years prior. They both drank themselves to death. I had become keenly aware a few years earlier that my father died from alcohol. It came to the surface because I saw my brother doing the same things. Eventually, my brother died. When I first got the news I thought he'd put a bullet in his head. Actually, he died from pancreatitis. To me that was the final straw. That was enough loss. I told myself that I would put all my drinking behind me and I did.

For this respondent, the proverbial "straw that broke the camel's back" was not only the loss of loved ones, but the recognition that he could experience a similar fate if he persisted in his heavy use of alcohol. In fact, the ability to identify with others, particularly those who had experienced pain and suffering, helped him reach this turning point. This complementarity and identification with a "generalized other" fractured his working consensus of intoxicant use by leading him to a profound awareness of his connection to a larger world outside his own immediate experience.[41]

For many respondents the experience of complementarity, and with it the turning point in their lives, was facilitated by responsibilities for children. The innocence of children and the need to nurture them provided a powerful motivation to terminate an addiction. This was particularly so for our women respondents, several of whom experienced the turning point in their dependency careers either when giving birth or during some egregious incident involving their children. For instance, one woman, presently a patient advocate in a large metropolitan hospital, explained:

> I became pregnant and I decided I was going to change my life and be a wonderful mom. I occasionally used pot when I was pregnant, but I stopped using coke and crack. After my child was born, I never went back.

Having a child, however, is not always a predictor of who will terminate their dependency on alcohol and/or drugs. Some did not experience a turning point until a later child was born. One woman, who already had a young child at home, recognized that she needed to change her life when having her second child. As she explained:

> I think during my nine-month period during my second child, I realized that the quality of my life was so poor because of drugs and alcohol. . . . I realized week after week how badly I felt and needed to change. So I threw out all the scales [to weigh drugs] and it scared the hell out of my husband. I just told him that I was afraid of losing my kids. I wasn't a good mother, but I wanted to be.

In addition to giving birth, egregious episodes involving children created the motivation to change. One twenty-four-year-old African-American male described an event involving his child that he found particularly disturbing:

> I remember coming home one morning and my son was sleeping. I went into the living room, sat down and just started having the urge. I got my pipe and I scraped the [crack] residue off. It was just enough for one hit. When I released it, I blew the smoke into my son's room. That was a slap in the face! I felt like the devil on earth.

Similarly, another respondent recounted a transformative story involving her child:

> I went with this other couple and my kid and we all got loaded. I drove the car going around mountain passes. I remember thinking I'm going to get into an accident. I pulled over because I didn't want to have an accident and kill my kid.

A third respondent reported an egregious incident she found quite disconcerting:

> We had gone out for Mother's Day to a bowling banquet and I started drinking. I went home, changed and went out again and continued drinking. I didn't get home until 2:30 in the morning. John, my husband, was waiting and started getting angry with me and I just went off. I started demolishing the house. I ripped the door off the frame. I had this big gash in my hand. He called the cops and they came and put handcuffs on me. My kids were standing there, in the doorway. This was Mother's Day and they were watching their mom being carted off in a police car. I decided at that point that that was the lowest I had ever gotten and I wasn't doing anything for my kids. It was just enough.

As these respondents suggest, having and caring for children can provide the turning point that radically changes people's lives. Despite their heavy alcohol and drug use, these men and women demonstrated remarkable responsibility when attending to the interests of their children.

Turning points also occurred through "bottom-hitting" events that were so far outside the realm of normalcy that they produced profound awareness of a problem. Such events signaled that an individual had transcended the boundaries of controllable drug use. A thirty-four-year-old businessman who was dependent on cocaine and crack explained one such event in gripping detail:

> My final binge was the day of the big hailstorm. It was the worst binge ever and thank God it was my last. Most of my other binges had always been on a daily basis. . . . This time I started in the morning and I drove to my friend's house and we were off on a three-day binge. We sat up all night long. My wife was calling frantically to all the people at the store. I just blew off my business, I just blew off my family. And we were just there sucking the pipe. I ended up getting so paranoid I asked him to move my car down the street. For a day and a half, we were sitting there smoking, smoking every five minutes, just torching up a big ol' hit. The next day he took off for work and I stayed. I smoked more and that night we free-based all night. I'd been up now for about three days. In the morning, we're free-basing as he's putting a suit and tie on. . . . Meanwhile, when he's at work, I'm down in the basement because I keep hearing noises. . . . I was down in the laundry room that didn't have any windows so nobody could see in. When the hailstorm came, I freaked. . . . It was such a horrible sound. It hit so fast and I thought the SWAT team was breaking down the front door. . . . I flushed a quarter ounce into the drain. I then snuck out in the other room and I looked out and there was all these hail things and I was just, I just shit my

pants. I couldn't believe it. Then I went back down stairs and remembered I had dumped it [crack] down the floor drain.... I was able to recover part of it. It was disgusting. Right then and there I knew I had to deal with this thing. I ate a couple of Valiums and called my wife. I came clean with her and I never used again.

Many of those who "came clean" believed they had become someone else. Several came to realize they were not themselves and that, as one respondent commented, "this wasn't me." What is truly remarkable about their narratives is that they had the presence of mind to identify residuals in their identities that produced a profound dissonance that called out for resolution.

Cessation

Once our respondents experienced turning points in their lives they faced the dilemma of implementing some means of personal transformation. Therapeutic regimes and 12-step groups typically instruct people who have reached this point in how to stop using drugs and alcohol and rebuild their lives. Self-help groups, for instance, teach new converts the dynamics of alcoholism and drug addiction and attempt to forge in them an identity that relabels them as sick.[42] Self-help groups like Alcoholics Anonymous dramatically reorient members' epistemologies of substance abuse and provide them with a ready-made alternative community that socializes them in the role of a recovering alcoholic.[43]

However, people who discontinue their dependencies on alcohol and drugs without the assistance of formal treatment or self-help choose not to participate in such resocializing communities where they might have learned cessation strategies. As a result, they have to develop their own cessation strategies. Termination of addiction typically requires that structural supports in people's lives such as job, family, and other involvements become salient. As Stanton Peele has written, "addicts improve when their relationships to work, family, and other aspects of their environment improve."[44] The social context of a dependent person's life significantly influences his or her ability to overcome alcohol and drug problems.

This point is consistent with Zinberg's now classic proposition, supported by a wealth of empirical research, that the social context in which an individual is embedded greatly influences the patterns and experiences associated with alcohol and drug use.[45] From this we might also conclude that the social context in which a dependent person is embedded similarly influences his or her ability to transform his or her life. Indeed, researchers have consistently found that nonpharmacological factors such as social class, gender, and race are critical to understanding how people develop drug problems as well as how they terminate their dependencies. These factors not only affect one's immersion in a drug subculture but also mediate the opportunities and incentives to change one's life. Sheigla Murphy and Marsha Rosenbaum, who have explored the relationship between drug use and social context, conclude that:

> Being a member of the middle class means having material possessions and/or the resources with which to acquire them (e.g., family help, education, job connections, etc.). Although virtually anyone from any background can get into trouble with drugs, individuals who possess life options or have a stake in conventional life tend to have a greater capacity for controlling their drug use or for getting out of trouble if they don't.[46]

Thus, social contexts are significantly related to the process of conversion to nondependent roles. We explore this in greater detail in a later chapter.

The strategies that our respondents used to initiate their cessation of dependencies can be clustered into three general areas. Their repertoire of cessation strategies included engaging in alternative activities, relying upon relationships with family and friends, and avoiding drugs, drug users, and the social cues associated with use. Of the forty-six respondents we interviewed, twenty-nine reported that engaging in alternative practices served to initiate cessation, while twenty-eight and twenty-three respectively cited the importance of personal relationships and the avoidance of drugs. We break these strategies down further into more specific cessation categories. Table 3 provides the frequency of specific strategies associated with each category. Most respondents used a combination of strategies.

Alternatives are those practices and activities that provide renewed structure in the drug-dependent person's life. As our data indicate, religious and educational activities constituted the primary means though which respondents built structure in their postaddicted lives. Relationships denote the old or new social interactions and relations that provided assistance and support during respondents' cessation efforts. Finally, avoidance strategies reflect the conscious activities which our respondents engaged in in order to break away from substance-using influences. These three general strategies and the social contexts in which respondents were embedded together created a dynamic of conversion that radically transformed personal identities and ultimately led to a cessation of intoxicant dependencies.

Theories of conversion typically hold that conversion experiences represent solutions to personal crises in an individual's life.[47] Such experiences can lead an individual to separate him or herself from the conventional norms and values of society.[48]

Table 3
Strategies Associated with Cessation of Dependency

Alternatives		Relationships		Avoidance	
Religion	15	Family	21	Drug/cues	12
Education	10	Friends	9	Friends/family	12
Physical	6	New Friends	7	Geographical	5
Read/Write	5				
Work	4				
Community	3				
Other	5				

Other conversion experiences, however, provide a "waystation to respectability" for individuals wishing to be reabsorbed into the dominant society.[49] This reintegrating function of conversion has been associated with groups such as Alcoholics Anonymous and other self-help groups that allow people to perform sick and repentant roles, thereby facilitating their reintegration into mainstream society.[50] The performance of such roles and the conversion to an AA epistemology subsequently reduces the stigma associated with being alcohol or drug dependent and facilitates reintegration into conventional life.[51]

Alternative Activities

Not unlike individuals who affiliate with 12-step groups, those who engage in natural recovery without treatment frequently experience conversion to a new way of life and a new epistemology of meaning. Our respondents spoke of becoming intensely involved in alternative pursuits that engulfed them and gave them new meaning. These pursuits led to a dramatic realignment of their relationship with the world and were incompatible with heavy alcohol and drug use. These pursuits were frequently religious in nature. For instance, one respondent, a thirty-six-year-old graduate student who had been an IV cocaine user for five years, discovered a sense of meaning and purpose through her participation in Buddhist rituals:

> I had to redo my life. I had to recreate who I was. You have to have something inside of you that says, "I need to be something different." I got involved in Buddhist religion through a friend and it changed my life. I felt that if I had some kind of spiritual faith, that would help, and it did. Through Buddhism I really discovered a respect for myself and found that I had the power to overcome obstacles.

Another respondent not only experienced new meaning through his participation in Buddhist cosmology, but even succeeded in dramatically reinterpreting the substance upon which he had previously been dependent. As he explained it, alcohol, the substance of his dependency, was transformed into a sacred substance through Buddhist ritual practice:

> I participate in Buddhist rituals and alcohol is a big deal. There's a ritual of about half an hour that involves alcohol and chanting. The ceremony helps us to understand that we all volunteered to have the problems we have so we can work through these problems to show other people how to do it. That's the answer to the question. In the ceremony there's wine on the table but nobody drinks it. It just sits there. The alcohol represents a contradiction.

Not unlike the peyote eaters of the southwestern United States who consume the drug for religious purposes only, for this respondent alcohol was now associated with a deity and had to be treated with respect. Such a new epistemology provided this former alcoholic with the cultural prescriptions and proscriptions to overcome his dependency. Not only had this forty-seven-year-old mechanical engineer derived new meaning in his life, but he had also "ritualized" alcohol in a way that made it incompatible with his previous drinking behaviors.

Other respondents had less structured religious experiences, but no less transformative. A sixty-two-year-old alcoholic of twenty-six years, who had stopped drinking sixteen years earlier, attributed his termination to a "spiritual awakening." He narrated a cessation story that, from his perspective, was nothing short of miraculous:

> I had a spiritual awakening. I was talking to God one night, sharing my thoughts. Then I heard a little voice in my mind saying, "Why don't you turn to me for help?" I said I don't know if you're God but I'm going to test you. I'll pray to you for one week, I'll give you seven days and if you don't do something after seven days, well, that's it. I prayed to him for those seven days nearly every moment and nothing happened. Then that little voice came back into my mind and asked, "How was your day today?" It wasn't too bad. "How was your day yesterday?" It went all the way back through the week. I said, you know, it's been a really good week. It just blew my mind. It was so powerful I can't explain it, even express it in words. I just fell to my knees and thanked him. That got me motivated to start practicing my faith again and I became really active. I started religious groups and devoted a lot of time to the church. Our priest one day asked people to write down names of persons who might have a calling for a deacon. The priest pulled me in a few days later and said that my name came up quite a bit. He said, "The people think you might have a calling." He asked me if I'd consider it and the next thing I knew I got a letter from the Archbishop saying "Congratulations, you've been accepted to the class for the deaconate." I've been a minister in the church for ten years now. Because of my religious convictions, I can say my desire for drinking has completely been eliminated.

Not unlike the two Buddhist respondents above, this former alcoholic found new meaning, purpose, and structure through his conversion to and immersion in Catholicism. Another respondent who described herself as having become a "personal growth freak" explained that not only had she become actively involved in her church, but she had mystical experiences that led to a spiritual transformation. She recounted these experiences in the following way:

> I took a lot of spiritual types of classes, self-image classes, fully alive and human classes. . . . I did a lot of reading about past life stuff and went to a spiritual counselor who told me some past life information about my ex-husband and that I was pretty preoccupied with suicide. She explained to me that in my past life with my husband we were pretty unhappy. I left him and he killed himself. The piece of my alcohol and drug abuse that really had me was this constant thinking about killing myself and I couldn't understand what it was. And now that I have that information, what it did was give me some reason, some karmic kind of reason as to what that was all about. Getting this information and becoming active in various spiritual activities made me realize I could survive.

She concluded her explanation of her spiritual conversion with reflections on the loss of spiritual significance and meaning in modern postindustrial society. Not unlike other religious converts who see a spiritual malaise in society, she commented: "We have so little talk of spirit in our culture. Spirit and spiritual growth traditionally get kicked out of our culture because of economics and politics and we need to have more spirit so that our children don't give into pressures of the whole [drug] scene." For many respondents, their conversion experiences had led to a total purification of the body. Many stated that they had given up a variety of other substances, including tobacco and coffee.

While religious conversion was the most common cessation strategy employed by our respondents, they reported other types of conversion as well. Their acceptance of nonreligious ideologies and their involvement in secular organizations were no less a conversion experience for them. Most of their conversions revolved around intense immersion in other institutionalized roles associated with education, work, and community life. Interestingly, the rhetoric they used when discussing these institutionalized roles was often as intense as those who spoke of experiencing religious conversions. For instance, a health care worker who years earlier had dropped out of school and sold cocaine to support her eight-year dependency described how important returning to school was for her:

> I started school immediately after I stopped using. This was a difficult time for me. I started a program at Metro State College and I started learning about things. I learned about why my body went through those changes and the mental part of it. I think I used schooling a lot as my recovery. I just threw myself into it. Metro is real conducive to personal inner growth because you take these great classes and you start to apply them to your life.

This respondent went from being drug dependent to becoming an addiction counselor. Likewise, another respondent experienced a conversion through education that eventually led her down a similar occupational path. This respondent, a forty-one-year-old woman formerly dependent on alcohol and cocaine, explained that when she quit using these substances after twenty years, she knew she needed to become involved in something that would provide her with a meaningful alternative to drug use. For her, education and particularly training in the social services seemed felicitous.

> Given all the problems I had had with alcohol, human service work seemed like a natural choice for me. I entered school in December of 1991 just shortly after I stopped using. School was really important to me. I was really doing it for a healing process of myself. I felt such a strong commitment to school, like I was on a mission.

In the words of J. David Brown, both these respondents had become "professional-exs" through their total immersion in higher education and their newly constituted occupational roles.[52] Not unlike those who had experienced a religious conversion, the new roles these respondents had forged in education and later through work allowed them to formulate and implement new epistemologies and meanings about the life they had composed and the one they were presently composing.

Other respondents immersed themselves in a variety of different activities. One woman with a long history of alcohol problems became actively involved in a women's group and participated in various feminist events. Another woman immersed herself in civic activities by vigorously taking up community service and volunteer work in homeless shelters and environmental organizations. Others resolved the difficulty of overcoming addiction by focusing on their own bodies. For instance, several discussed how they had changed their lives by becoming physically active and "getting into shape." Some reported becoming vegetarians or getting involved in holistic medicine. What characterized all these pursuits was that they inspired in our respondents a desire for focused immersion in which they could become engrossed.[53] Whatever activity they chose—whether it was religion, education, community, politics, work, or physical well-being—it typically became the focal point of their lives and was fervently performed. Interestingly, our respondents' stories suggest that they had become as deeply involved in these new activities as they had once been in alcohol and drug use during their periods of dependency. Such complete involvement in alternative activities suggests that these pursuits act not merely as substitutes and replacements for addiction, but that they represent avenues to new meaning and epistemologies through which an individual can compose a self in relation to collective life that is incompatible with excessive alcohol and drug use.

Relationships

Active involvement in these alternative pursuits allowed our respondents to enter into significant relationships with nondrug users and to avoid others who were connected to the drug scene, thereby making their conversion to a conventional life easier. They were not unlike religious converts who develop affective bonds with other converts and terminate their emotional attachments to others with discordant visions of reality.[54] For instance, our respondents highlighted the importance of residual relationships as well as new ones in accomplishing their personal transformations. Many of them had not yet "burned their bridges" and were able to rely on the support of family and friends. One respondent explained how an old college friend helped him get over his dependency on crack:

> My best friend from college made a surprise visit. I hadn't seen him in years. He walked in and I was all cracked out. It's like he walked into the twilight zone or something. He couldn't believe it. He smoked dope in college but he never had seen anything like this. When I saw him, I knew that my life was really screwed up and I needed to do something about

it. He stayed with me for the next two weeks and helped me
through it.

Several other respondents had good friends who stuck by them
during their efforts at personal transformation. One twenty-six-
year-old businesswoman who used cocaine daily for two years
explained, "I had some very dear friends that were very supportive and they helped me take a look internally as far as
pulling up my own willpower and making the decision to quit. I
owe them a lot." Another reported that she "couldn't have made
it without my friends."

Other respondents overcame their addictions with the help of
their families. As one respondent explained, "My wife and my
children were the most helpful in making the decision to quit. I
was able to draw upon their strength." Similarly, one woman,
who reported being abusive to her husband during her period of
dependency, spoke about receiving his support when she decided
to change her life. As she explained, "I'm getting a new identity
and I'm identifying who I am and John, my husband, despite all
we've been through, is right behind me. I look to John for support and he gives it to me." Another respondent was able to turn
his life around when he met and eventually married his wife:
"When I met my wife Patty, I made the decision to quit drinking. Meeting her helped a lot. It changed my life." Another respondent, a young woman with an extensive heroin addiction,
discussed how her husband stood by her:

> I think the main reason I'm clean today is because of my hus-
> band. One day we had a fight and he was ready to leave. He
> had had enough. I thought, well I'll just leave but I couldn't
> because I was chained to my drug dealer. My husband didn't
> end up leaving but everything was packed. We even fought
> about which dog we would take. I knew he felt sorry for me
> and he totally understood. He had done some heroin too and

had a brother die from it. My husband had been clean for quite a while now. I knew any day that he would leave and that if I didn't fucking stop I was going to lose him and I didn't want to lose him. I knew that I finally had a really good person and I should do everything I could to quit.

The existence of such natural communities made it less necessary for these people to seek out alternative communities such as those found in 12-step groups. Such groups may be considerably more attractive when a person's natural communities break down. Indeed, the fragmentation of communities in postmodern society may account for much of the popularity of self-help groups.[55] In the absence of strong personal networks, these programs give people a means to constitute new relationships that help construct a sense of purpose and meaning in life. However, for many of our respondents the conversion to a nondependent lifestyle was facilitated in part by the strong relationships they were able to salvage from their years of dependency. Their experiences are a testament to the reintegrating potential that close friends and loved ones can provide, particularly during times of personal crisis.[56] The importance of these relationships to natural recovery will be analyzed more fully in chapter 5.

Avoidance

In addition to establishing or reestablishing connections with family and friends, our respondents also severed their connections, either literally or symbolically, with the substance-using world. Many of them discontinued relationships that they believed had contributed to their desire to use. For women, this often meant terminating relationships with men who were not only alcohol and drug dependent, but frequently violent as well.

One woman explained how she left her husband after deciding to quit using cocaine and speed:

> The last time I got high was June 23, 1987. This was the last time. It was also the time I decided to leave my husband for good. I had left my husband once before but this time I knew I had to get out. We started to tweak on coke and he gets his gun and started to shoot the house up. I had to fight him over his rifle because he thought that the house was surrounded. I threw him out for good a week later. I was dealing for him and I knew that that was the only way to get away from the whole scene.

Another woman explained how ending an abusive marriage afforded her the path to personal transformation:

> When I stopped using crack and became affiliated with the Unitarian Church, I started to have some self-esteem and began to feel good about myself. I was trying to grasp a new life. To do that I had to leave my husband. He was very abusive, I was a battered wife for four years, and he was heavily into the drug scene. [After leaving him] it was just a rebirth into a much better lifestyle.

Exiting the drug scene was typically the reason given by women who ended relationships with men. For them the dynamic of their relationship with a man contributed directly to their addictions. One woman who was introduced to drugs by her husband, commented:

> At one point I saw that I was in an abusive relationship with my husband and that my cocaine use was directly related to the person I was having a relationship with. I realized that I could never stop while I was with Harry. I would make up my mind to stop, but he would do it and I would do it too. But when I left him and I wasn't living with people who did it or around people who did it very often, I was fine.

As is typical of drug use among women, our female respondents were introduced to drugs by men to whom they attributed their eventual dependencies.[57] This is not unusual given that women drug users are frequently enmeshed in a web of asymmetrical power relations. As Murphy and Rosenbaum have argued, men use their power over the supply of drugs to manipulate and control women.[58] For our female respondents, empowering themselves to overcome their gender subjugation in these relationships was a prerequisite to their independence from a lifestyle of excessive use.[59]

Severing one's connection with drugs and alcohol also meant avoiding other users, not only intimates. Although respondents who were dependent on alcohol reported changing their friends, it was more typical of the illicit drug users we interviewed to avoid contact with other drug users. As our respondents suggest, this is because networks and connections are more important for acquiring drugs than for acquiring alcohol. As a forty-eight-year-old engineer who used crack daily for three years explained: "The crack was easy to get. I cut my connections with people who could supply it to me. So my ability was cut, so that helped me quit." A twenty-six-year-old businesswoman who was a daily cocaine user employed a similar strategy:

> I basically took myself away from these people [other users], out of the situation to where it wasn't readily available. It really wasn't too difficult once I made the decision myself that this was what I chose for myself. I just didn't associate myself with anyone who used or dealt.

Avoiding friends who used drugs as well as areas where drugs were commonly available served to remove respondents from the drug scene in which they had been ensconced.

Breaking one's tie to the drug scene sometimes required one to physically relocate. In the drug rehabilitation field such physical relocation is referred to as a "geographic cure." Such cures

Table 4
Cessation Strategies by Substance Type

| | Type of Addiction | |
	Alcohol (N = 25)	Drug (N = 21)
Alternatives	23	18
Relationships	16	14
Avoidance	10	19

are often thought to be associated with the addictive syndrome and to be part of the addict's denial system. However, such "geographic cures" have been shown to be effective as a means of removing oneself from a network of drug users.[60] When we examined the extent to which our respondents had used a geographical cure we found some interesting differences between those who had alcohol problems and those who had problems with illicit drugs like cocaine, crack, and heroin. None of those with alcohol problems had employed a geographical cure. While they frequently severed their relationships with users, none had actually relocated to another geographical area. By contrast, one-quarter of the drug addicts we interviewed reported using a geographic cure. This difference speaks to differences in the salience of network structures between alcoholics and drug addicts. This suggests that drug-using networks are more engulfing than alcohol-using ones, thereby creating more of a felt need among drug addicts to place themselves at a distance from these networks. As Table 4 indicates, the use of avoidance strategies, including geographic cures, was more common among our drug-addicted respondents than among those with alcohol problems.

Overall, while there was great similarity between our respondents with respect to cessation strategies, those previously addicted to drugs were much more likely to employ avoidance strategies than were those with alcohol problems only. Each group typically adopted alternative activities at a similar rate, and, to a smaller extent, similarly relied on close relationships to help them end their addiction. As suggested above, the difference in the degree to which alcoholics and drug addicts utilize avoidance strategies no doubt indicates profound variations in the social context of use. These variations suggest that while cessation experiences among alcoholics and drug addicts are similar in many respects, there are some important distinctions as well.

Rewards

The final stage in the personal transformation of our respondents was the realization of the rewards associated with their new nondependent status. Not unlike religious converts who value the perceived changes in their lives that result from their conversion, our respondents viewed their cessation of addiction as beneficial. Perceiving the benefits associated with personal transformation is critical if self-change is to be lasting. Thus, once converts realize that their conversion to a metaphysical belief system does not result in the transcendence of earthly burdens they often abandon their religious commitments.[61] As with religious converts, drug and alcohol addicts must learn to perceive and value the benefits associated with nondependency. This is often problematic, as the rewards associated with the experience of using substances are many. They range from the tangible, such as sexual excitement, increased energy and self-confidence, and relaxation,[62] to the less tangible such as gaining respect, demonstrating cultural resistance, and experiencing community.[63]

There must be a set of rewards for alcoholics and drug addicts who discontinue their use of these substances. Acknowledgment of the rewards of cessation is typically part of the ritual experience of 12-step groups. For instance, AA has people recite their "drunkalogue" in which alcoholics narrate their "sad tales" of addiction as well as stories about their personal salvation through fellowship in self-help. These salvation tales typically demonstrate how their lives have improved dramatically since they became sober.

Not unlike those in 12-step groups, our respondents attributed a number of rewards and benefits to their new nonaddicted status. One area that improved was that of family and kinship relations. As pointed out earlier, many of our respondents had experienced significant marital and family turmoil during their period of active use, which had led to separation and family dissolution for some. As for those whose relations had been disrupted but did not end in separation, dramatic improvements occurred in their family lives. One respondent, an alcoholic for ten years, was thankful for the reprieve he received from his family. As he explained, he felt he had been given a new lease on life.

> What benefits are there to quitting? Well I have two healthy beautiful children who know the truth about their parents and their relationship and their use of drugs and alcohol. They are empowered to express their feelings about how they feel. I'm able to express who I am to my family, I have a passion for my life with them. . . . I'm even the PTA president at my kids' school.

Relationships with spouses were also seen as having improved. This was particularly important to respondents who felt they had violated the trust of their significant others. A forty-seven-year-old electrician who had engaged in a twenty-year struggle with alcohol dependency described his renewed relationship with his wife as follows:

I have a good marriage now. I have a good wife and at first she was leery when I told her I was quitting. At first she didn't trust me. What do you expect? But I've gained her trust and I'm able to enjoy the things with her that I never did.

Other respondents experienced improvements in their relations with siblings and parents. "I have my family back," one respondent exclaimed in an elated voice, "My parents are very proud of me and my brothers and sisters have a lot of respect for me. It just feels great."

In addition to renewed relations with family members and friends, respondents saw improvements in their level of attachment to and involvement in society. Most of them reveled in their new pursuits. One businesswoman saw a number of benefits to her transformation, particularly in the arena of civic engagements: "I'm now very active. I'm singing in two choruses. I'm on the Board of Directors of a non-profit agency. And I volunteer down at Channel Six [a local Public Broadcasting Station]." Other respondents found pleasure in a wide variety of other activities. One commented: "I write poetry, I journal, I listen to music, go to films, take walks with friends, just call friends and say I'm down. . . . I enjoy getting into conversations with people now."

For the most part, our respondents reported just feeling better. Upon reflection, they generally indicated that they had become more deeply satisfied with life and they had found happiness in their lives. One respondent referred to having returned to her "former self." As she explained, "I'm happier now. I'm not high strung. I'm back to the Amber that I remember. I'm relaxed and more easygoing." Several believed that their self-esteem had increased, while others reported that their financial status had improved. Still others reflected that they had become more honest and trustworthy. Overall, they attributed dramatic improvements in their lives to their cessation of dependencies.

Whether they had reestablished their connections with family and friends, become more active in their communities, or experienced greater satisfaction in their work, all our respondents found their personal transformations affirming and deeply rewarding. One respondent enthusiastically summarized her life now that she had quit using drugs in the following way: "It's really kind of fun because I'm getting to know me. It's kind of neat. I'm getting a whole bunch of outlooks. I think it's for the better. I'm turning into me. Look out!"

Conclusion

People who become dependent upon alcohol and drugs do so in large part because they define the excessive use of these substances as meaningful and valuable in their lives. As Stanton Peele has asserted, "[P]eople are susceptible to these addictive experiences to the extent that they occupy unsatisfying and stressful positions in society, to the extent that they feel concrete consensual social rewards are unobtainable or not worthwhile, and to the extent that they relate to the world through dependencies and believe in the efficacy of external forces."[64] As many seasoned researchers through the years have demonstrated, substance use and addiction are never independent of the complex web of social relations within which they are embedded. Addiction can never be reduced to a mere pharmacological determinism that reifies the power of chemistry over the human spirit.[65] Certainly, the pharmacological properties of substances like alcohol and drugs do matter to a degree, but by themselves they do not produce dependency. A more holistic conceptualization of dependency requires an understanding of the confluence between drug, set, and setting; that is, between the drug itself, an individual's expectations and personality, and "the situation of use, the social conditions that shape such situations, and the historically and culturally specific meanings and motives used to interpret drug effects."[66] Our findings demonstrate that an understanding of recovery, particularly recovery that does not involve traditional treatment approaches, requires an appreciation of this complex interaction.

Addiction to alcohol and drugs is a powerfully engulfing experience. Our respondents' sobering tales indicate that overcoming such problems without treatment typically involves becoming immersed in personal relationships and social activities that are equally rewarding and satisfying. Our analysis demonstrates that recovery from addiction without treatment occurs when individuals' relationships with family, work, and other aspects of their environment improve. Our respondents' recovery narratives demonstrate that the power that individuals have over intoxicants, even the addictive use of the substances, is often greater than the power these substances have over individuals. Ultimately, the people we interviewed experienced a conversion to conventional social life that allowed them to live with the world as opposed to against and above it. They all developed a renewed stake in conventional life and in their social relationships which enveloped them and gave them a sense of sacred, ritual selfhood.[67] In a very real sense, they converted to the spirit of collective life as represented by their investments in social relationships and existing social institutions.

For most of our respondents, the "complementarity" they experienced occurred over a period of time, reflecting a gradual process of identity transformation. The question of how our respondents reconstituted their new identities in light of this conversion experience naturally follows from this analysis. How they viewed themselves in relation to their previous dependencies, why they chose to circumvent treatment, and the implications of these choices for their self-identities are the subject of the next chapter.

Chapter Four

CIRCUMVENTING TREATMENT
AND SALVAGING THE SELF
Natural Recovery as Cultural Resistance

So far we have explored what sociologists refer to as the "careers" of our alcohol- and drug-dependent respondents. Like Goffman's classic treatment of the "moral career of mental patients," our respondents experienced a "regular sequence of changes" in the course of their use of intoxicants.[1] They did not remain static through this period; rather, they went through distinct stages from their initiation to their eventual exit. Along the way they attributed a variety of subjective meanings to the substances they were using. Although initially they experienced substance use as rewarding, they eventually came to associate excessive use with personal strain. These strains typically led to "turning points" associated with the desire to avoid further trouble or to salvage relationships and structures in their lives.

Such turning points were followed by intense participation in alternative activities that not only acted as functional substitutes for the intrinsic rewards of alcohol and drug use,[2] but were typically concurrent with the establishment of new or residual non-drug-using relations and the avoidance, particularly among drug addicts, of intoxicant users and social cues related to use. The final stage in their natural recovery process was the attribution of rewards to nonuse and/or nondependency. Such rewards often entailed the establishment of satisfying relations with nonusers.

The Social Construction of Addiction

As pointed out in chapter 2, the concepts of dependence and addiction can be viewed as a social construction. This does not imply, as is sometimes suggested, that people do not experience problems with these substances. Rather, the social constructionist argument posits that the concept of addiction itself is culture-bound.[3] This social constructionist perspective is largely concerned with the historical and interactional forces that led to the identification of excessive alcohol and drug use as addictive diseases. As pointed out earlier, the disease concept of addiction is a fairly recent invention, having emerged shortly after the turn of the century. Excessive intoxicant use can and has been thought of differently through the years and in other cultures. Addiction is simply one way of classifying excessive use. Thus, claiming that addiction is a social construction does not imply that drugs are good, or that people do not experience hardships, but rather that the classification of abuse as a medical problem or a disease is a matter of scholarly investigation.

There are generally two meanings associated with a constructivist perspective on addiction. One sees addiction as reflective of a culture that is based upon rationality and the control of spontaneity.[4] In such cultures, excessive consumption of mind-altering substances fails to comport with the dominant values. For instance, a capitalist society premised upon rationalized forms of labor, strict conceptions of time, and the value of productivity is incompatible with the Dionysian pursuit of pleasure and the abandonment of self-control.[5] The problem of addiction emerges out of the moral fabric of a changing society.

A second meaning of the constructedness of addiction, however, is associated with how individuals define, treat, and respond to the concept on a daily basis. This "micro-" sociological perspective posits that the subjective qualities of individuals are constituted by the terms used to describe them. For instance, people with physical or mental disabilities are typically thought to be impaired and thereby to have a limited capacity to function in society, as opposed to simply having different abilities.[6] Organizations that service people with disabilities often employ these definitions and treat the disabled accordingly. Hospitals imbue the behavior of mentally ill patients with the quality of illness, even when they are not actually ill.[7] Human service organizations classify the disabled in ways that isolate and separate them from "normal" society by characterizing their services as therapeutic and, at times, by forcing the disabled to accept a role of total dependency.[8] Thus, people become the objects of signification by signifiers that "describe a role, a relationship, and a location from which many connotations flow."[9]

Similarly the concept of addiction is an arbitrary label applied to those who consume intoxicants excessively. From this "symbolic interactionist" perspective, the meaning of addiction is wrapped up in society's reactions toward users.[10] Like disabled individuals, addicts are socialized into the addict role by a host of people including their families and various mediators such as therapists, judges, lawyers, employers, and friends who have sanctioning power over them. From this perspective, addicts become addicts not through their excessive use of substances alone but through a social process of degradations and mortifying experiences that assign a discredited moral status to them. Their moral lives are transformed within the institutional context of treatment and hospitalization. Following Goffman, the internalization of an addict identity represents a by-product of one's immersion in addiction treatment institutions which socialize one into the addict role.[11] In these facilities addicts learn to "walk the walk and talk the talk" of a person who has been assigned the moral status of addict.[12] As many sociologists have pointed out, their experiences in these powerful institutions "frame and shape people's changing conception of self."[13]

That the identity of an alcoholic or an addict is constructed through the social process of treatment is not some arcane sociological proposition relevant only to abstract academic discourse. Treatment professionals themselves readily admit that the goal of therapy is to teach substance abusers that they are "sick." While therapists would steadfastly object to the more radical assertion that addiction is largely an illusion or "myth"[14] possessing a reality merely in the social judgments of others, no doubt they would subscribe to the constructivist logic that maintains that treatment institutions impose, or attempt to impose, new conceptions of the self on substance abusers. For therapists, the adoption of a new conception of the self as "addicted" or "alcoholic" is the sine qua non of recovery and failure to do so is typically seen as evidence of a person's persisting sickness.

However, this begs the question of identity for untreated drug addicts and alcoholics. If sociologists are correct in assuming that the institutional context in which a person is embedded is largely responsible for emerging conceptions of the self, then one might hypothesize that individuals who recover without treatment resist disease classifications of their past, present, and future, and instead offer more normalized accounts of themselves. In this next section, we explore the vocabulary of motives our respondents gave for circumventing treatment. Each one offered a series of reasons, in most cases negatives ones, for why he or she chose to forgo the standard treatment options available to him or her. In short, we suggest that the meaning respondents gave to treatment accounted for their decision to eschew therapy and self-help.

Related to the question of why our respondents avoided and, in some cases, denounced treatment, we explore the implications the circumvention of treatment has for their self-conceptions. As we demonstrate in this chapter, despite the severity of their alcohol and drug problems they almost uniformly resisted disease-based significations of the self. Like many people with disabilities,[15] our respondents objected to and actively resisted the pejorative genealogies of the addicted self that are embedded in the broader constellation of power relations intended to control and discipline the body.[16] In a society that is "at war" with drugs—where users, and especially abusers, are vilified and demonized—our respondents exhibited a type of cultural resistance against the dominant addiction narrative that seeks to impugn and denigrate their character.

Treatment and Power

Understanding why our respondents circumvented treatment requires some conceptual exploration of the meaning that treatment and therapy had for them. No one has been more insightful about the social meaning of therapy and its implications for the self than Michel Foucault. Throughout his scholarly career, Foucault concerned himself with the regulation of the body through medical science and penology and with the internalization of discipline in human affairs. The institutions of the asylum and prison regulate the body, discipline the mind, and otherwise manage a broad range of human behaviors that are considered excessive and deviant.[17] For Foucault, forms of deviance like madness and insanity are judgments rather than facts and like all forms of official judgment represented though the law, medicine, and religion, they are imbued and inscribed with the power to subjugate the individuals so categorized.[18] In the words of British sociologist Nicholas Fox, medicine, education, the law and penology, psychiatry and social work, are *"disciplines* of the modern era, both a realm of expertise and a way of literally disciplining the bodies of those who are the subjects of these experts."[19]

Foucault's contribution to understanding the relationship between power and knowledge was not simply to demonstrate that these disciplines constitute powerful symbols and significations that construct, apply, and circulate arbitrary claims about health, legality, or morality. He was just as concerned with the self-internalization of these historically situated narratives as with the archeology of their formation. It was in the internalization of arbitrarily constructed boundaries that Foucault saw the invasiveness of power of these disciplines.

In one of the final essays written before his death in 1984, Foucault outlined the direction of his new research on the internalization of self-control, or "technologies of the self."[20] By this, Foucault meant those processes "which permit individuals to effect by their own means or with the help of others a certain number of operations on their bodies and souls, thoughts, conduct, and way of being, so as to transform themselves in order to attain a certain state of happiness, purity, wisdom, perfection, or immortality."[21] In this rather arcane essay Foucault explored the incoherence of the concept of self-care and personal transformation. His central point was that the methods or technologies of self-care adopted by individuals are historically situated in distinct cultural epochs. For instance, the ancient Greeks sought to "care for the soul" by "taking care of oneself." Caring for oneself in Athenian society meant searching for wisdom, truth, and perfection. Later, however, this maxim of self-care gave way to the Christian precept to "know thyself." Unlike the principle of "taking care of oneself," knowing thyself translated into a renunciation of the self; that is, it was associated with the moral principle of discovering one's faults and weakness so as to control and discipline them. In the Christian tradition, the self is renounced through the process of confession, whereby the individual declares his or her status as a repentant sinner. As Rose points out, the act of confession serves to constitute one's identity:

> In confessing, one is subjectified by another, for one confesses in the actual or imagined presence of a figure who prescribes the form of the confession.... But in confessing, one also constitutes oneself. In the act of speaking, through the obligation to produce words that are true to an inner reality, through the self-examination that precedes and accompanies speech, one becomes a subject of oneself. Confession, then, is the diagram of a certain form of subjectification that binds us to others at the very moment we affirm our identity.[22]

Thus, an ascetic Christian "technology of the self" is a self that is at once rejected and renewed.

Foucault's analysis of the "technology of the self" can be extended to the fields of health and treatment.[23] Like the examples given by Foucault, therapy and treatment, whether for depression,[24] disabilities,[25] physical fitness,[26] or addiction inscribe the body with the power of arbitrary symbols that regulate and discipline people. The power of these technologies resides not merely in the status differences between professionals and lay people. While the dominance of professionals over their clients or patients has been well documented by sociologists such as Eliot Freidson, professional power is also inextricably associated with the ways that professional caregivers ascribe meaning to the bodies of those considered to be in need of care.[27] Deficient biologies and flawed selves are ascribed to those deemed sick. It is through this constitutive process that the subjectivity of the patient or client takes shape. Such interactions, however, are infused with power in that the patient/client, through a kind of Foucauldian self-surveillance, often accepts the subjective construction of selfhood articulated through the professional work being delivered upon him or her.

While Foucault's position on the ability of language to inscribe power has been criticized, his poststructuralist analysis nonetheless helps us understand why some might reject treatment for addiction. If, as Foucault suggests, therapy and treatment constitute the subjectivity of the patient/client through the unique "technology" of locating the source of a person's problem within some genetic or psychological flaw, what of those who do not accept the "truths" ascribed to them by therapy? Students of medical sociology and disability studies have frequently pointed out that the meaning of illness is never universal and is almost always subject to contested battles between groups who seek to claim definitional ownership of the "problem." For instance, parents and physicians often struggle over whose definition of a child's disability will prevail.[28] Through a "politics of health-talk" which Nicholas Fox describes as medical "discourse and its consequences for power, control and knowledgeability," the assignment of an individual to particular classifications does not occur without struggle.[29] Patients (and their families) whose selfhood is constituted through the making of a diagnosis frequently challenge medical opinions. At times, people with disabilities are unwilling to succumb to a medical definition of disability that focuses unduly on their flaws even though their rejection may promote increased physical dependence.[30] Sometimes those with disabilities even reject the services available to them because of the implied subordination embedded in the conceptual designation of those services as "special," thereby signifying difference and inferiority.[31] In fact, there are multiple narratives of illness and disability that depart from strict medical perspectives, namely the political, religious, and environmental, and they do so because of the particular social circumstances and contingencies within which an individual is embedded.[32]

What all this suggests is that "health-talk" is capable of reproducing dominant narratives of health and well-being as well as generating contestation. As Fox insightfully posits, "[C]are is power, and the possibility for resisting that power entails a refusal of care *qua* care, and of the very meanings which are associated with professional carers."[33] A few social scientists have examined the micropolitics of resistance in the health care arena. Some have even suggested a more equitable sharing of power between physicians/therapists and patients/clients.[34] What is certain is that the "technologies of self" in the modern world as constituted through therapy and treatment are subject, at times, to intense ideological challenge. The resistance narratives of our respondents denouncing addiction treatment represents just such a challenge.

Avoiding Treatment

Our respondents offered three different but related sets of reasons for not seeking treatment. A large proportion of them, 34 percent, felt that treatment programs and self-help groups attributed negative qualities to people who were addicted. Most believed that these attributions would be detrimental to their ultimate recovery from addiction. Many of them also maintained that such programs assaulted their own sense of self by defining the individual as essentially an addict. Several others, 32 percent, felt that they simply did not need professional or self-help assistance, believing that they had the ability to transform their lives themselves. Finally, a smaller number of respondents, 19 percent, did not think that treatment programs or self-help groups were successful in arresting addictions.[35] Such reasons for avoiding treatment and self-help are not unlike those identified by Biernacki in his examination of heroin addicts who terminated their use without treatment.[36] However, his work provides little detailed analysis of why individuals avoid treatment. Because of this each of our respondents' accounts for avoiding treatment and self-help will be closely examined.

NEGATIVE IMAGES

Many of our respondents who had negative impressions of treatment programs and self-help groups raised concerns which were not unlike the many popular critiques of Alcoholics Anonymous.[37] Some of them felt that such programs were cultlike in their collective religious belief structure. The AA's perceived militant insistence that a "higher power" is responsible for one's recovery disturbed some respondents. Comments such as this one by a thirty-eight-year-old waitress were not uncommon: "The thing about AA that always bugged me was its higher power thing. It never interested me." Similarly, a forty-year-old substance-abuse worker said, "I find people who are in AA fanatics. They remind me of Southern Baptists." For this woman, the expression of collective religious beliefs, whether by Southern Baptists or members of AA, was inconsistent with her more restrained spiritual disposition. Another respondent commented, "I don't like everyone joining hands and saying prayers. That stuff pisses me off." Another characterized self-help groups as "mind control" and their members as "brainwashed."

However, most of those who rejected the ideology of treatment and self-help did so because of the way such therapeutic modalities construct the problem of dependency. The principles of most addiction treatment and self-help groups are premised on the notion of "powerlessness." Indeed, self-help groups such as Alcoholics Anonymous or Narcotics Anonymous, as well as the many formal treatment programs that incorporate a self-help ideology, encourage people to accept that they are "powerless" and have lost control of their lives. Most of our respondents vociferously rejected this "technology of the self" that attributes to people a sense of powerlessness over their lives. As one forty-one-year-old counselor who had had a twenty-one-year dependency on alcohol commented:

> I don't like the powerless message. You're not as powerless as these groups preach. I don't feel powerless anymore, I never did. I don't want to sit down at a table and say, hello, I'm Sharon and I'm an alcoholic. I have trouble with that word because it suggests that I'm powerless.

Other respondents expressed similar objections toward the constitution of the addict as powerless. For instance, a forty-four-year-old systems analyst who described herself as a lesbian and a feminist felt that treatment and self-help as typically practiced conflicted with her views on personal change. As she commented:

> Having read their credo, I thought it was bullshit. I believe that a person has the power within themselves to make happen whatever they want. I think they have a very negative

way of looking at things. I have done a lot of reading on feminism and participate in feminist groups. What I have come to understand is that it's your own sense of yourself and your own power over yourself and what you choose to do that matters. Dependency comes from a sense of powerlessness. It's understanding that the world doesn't happen to you, you happen to the world.

While alcohol and drugs had consumed their lives at an earlier point, these respondents believed that they retained power over drugs rather the reverse. This dialectical struggle between the power of individuals to make choices versus the power of drugs to enslave and limit their choices struck at the heart of their decisions to avoid therapy and self-help. By accepting treatment, they would have acquiesced to the premise that the drugs they consumed were more powerful than their ability to change their lives. For these respondents, such an admission was unacceptable. As one person summed it up, "You have to admit defeat to yourself and I didn't want to do that."

Respondents also objected to the hegemony of the disease model of addiction that focuses on drug use as being their primary problem. One woman who was alcohol dependent for ten years explained that she had experienced sexual abuse earlier in her life and that the treatment options available to her focused too heavily on alcohol alone. Another respondent, commenting on the professional staff at a treatment facility, explained: "I was absolutely furious that they never discussed with me any of the psychological problems that I had, like depression. It was just merely the drugs that was the primary problem [in their mind] and all my other problems would go away." These respondents found unacceptable the reductionist tendency of many treatment programs to overemphasize substance problems and inscribe use as their central problem.

Not only did these men and women see treatment and self-help as reductionistic, they also took exception to the programs' propensity to "essentialize" alcoholics and drug addicts. Our earlier discussion of Foucault is particularly relevant to this form of criticism. Foucault and other poststructuralist thinkers, including poststructural feminists and "queer theorists," have accused essentialist claims of human behavior of attempting to colonize the mind through arbitrary classifications like addiction.[38] Essentialist views locate the self as internal and existing independently of the context of an individual in society. The concept of addiction can be seen principally as an essentialist metanarrative having no universal basis in the world. In fact, as some have pointed out, the concept of addiction was "invented" by alcoholics, academics, and physicians who lobbied government agencies as well as society at large to support a disease orientation to alcohol and drug addiction.[39]

Although the disease concept of addiction advances a singular inexorable model that is considered universally applicable, there is substantial evidence that alternative models of addiction exist.[40] In reality, the concept of addiction lacks a coherent structure and is characterized by difference. This emphasis on difference offers addicts an avenue of resistance by providing them with recovery possibilities that depart from the hegemony of the disease concept. For our respondents, their perceived difference from the disease model of addiction was a potent source of resistance and became the path by which they overcame the illusion of its coherence.

In some respects, the critiques of treatment and self-help offered by our respondents were consistent with a poststructuralist analysis of addiction. They adamantly refused to be placed in the rigid category of addiction and dependency, preferring instead to see themselves in less definitive, more fluid ways. For instance, one respondent, a thirty-six-year-old graduate student, eloquently articulated her reason for avoiding treatment:

> I went to one session and I couldn't believe these people. . . . The therapist was trying to intimate that I had all these problems because I was an incest victim or something, which I wasn't. . . . We are all different, we all have different reasons for our drug abuse and why are they trying to say that this is the only way I can get well. . . . Another thing that bothered me about it was this concept that there's a monkey on your back. You're a drug addict or alcoholic and you're going to be this way the rest of your life and this is who you are. I said I'm far beyond this. I have some intrinsic purpose for being here and it's not to spend the rest of my life being a reformed addict.

Similarly, a forty-seven-year-old engineer was put off by what he perceived as the dogmatism of Alcoholics Anonymous and its unwillingness to consider and acknowledge other avenues of recovery. He decided to "go it alone" after attending a couple of AA meetings:

> I went to a couple AA meetings but I don't think of myself as very traditional and I just didn't feel it was the right place. I met a few people at this one meeting I went to and they tried to tell me I wasn't an alcoholic if I quit drinking six months earlier and this was my first AA meeting. I just resented that so I didn't go back. I had quit drinking in January and I probably didn't experience my first AA meeting until July, about six months later. So basically this guy was rejecting what I was saying.

These people found that their experiences of addiction and recovery, and ultimately their difference, were not validated by treatment programs or self-help groups. One respondent felt marginalized, or as poststructuralists would say, "territorialized," by the essentialist claims associated with addiction. As this thirty-three-year-old former cocaine addict who now on occasion drinks alcohol, commented:

> I went to a couple of meetings and found them extremely militant in their methods. . . . The people in AA kept giving me shit about being an alcoholic. My problem was with cocaine. I'm not an alcoholic. . . . I wish that some therapists and people in AA could have more insight into people. I wish they could tell that we're not all the same. Just because you have a big A [for addiction] on your face doesn't mean that you're the same as the addict next door. There are different reasons why you use. For me it was my family. It wasn't due to any inadequacies, but they made me feel extremely inadequate. . . . I have found that therapists need to be more open. I got into trouble because I was honest. This one guy couldn't believe that I used alcohol occasionally because he learned in some seminar that most people who have trouble with one drug can't control any drug. They tried really hard to pigeonhole me. I had to put my foot down. I'm not this kind of an addict.

Another described his objections to these programs as threatening his subjective "safety":

> I never felt safe in the couple of AA meetings I went to. They are just doom and gloom. It's like, you know, I'm an alcoholic so I'll never be anything else. It's like that's who they were first and I resent that. I think that we are human beings and we are entitled to mistakes and we're entitled to do things wrong but to be so set in their ways of thinking about who we are was not healthy for me to be around.

By circumventing treatment, these respondents were resisting the essentialist logic of these "technologies of the self" which inscribed one-dimensional "addicted" consciousness onto their bodies. In short, they were unwilling to accept a uniform, standardized, and undifferentiated view of addiction. By claiming that they were different, they were engaging in a form of cultural resistance against the dominant addiction-as-disease paradigm.

DOESN'T WORK

Not all our respondents were as critical of treatment or self-help groups as those described above. While the latter did constitute the largest subgroup in our sample, they did not represent the entire universe of reasons for avoiding treatment and self-help groups. For several respondents, the decision to circumvent treatment had more to do with their belief in the futility of such efforts. Although not as trenchant in their criticism, they believed that such approaches are often superficial at best, and potentially destructive at worst. However, most of them believed that treatment and self-help could be useful strategies when they worked for others, but maintained that they rarely did so.

Although there has been considerable evidence over the years documenting the moderate success of treatment and self-help groups, our respondents did not reach their conclusions about the ineffectiveness of treatment through critical engagement in the relevant research. Rather, their views were shaped by their association with a network of users and the stories they had learned about treatment through these networks. While it is widely known that drug-use careers are influenced by the networks of relations in which an individual participates, it might also be said that recovery careers are similarly affected by such associations. In some cases, failure stories are urban myths generated in an addict subculture, while in others such a perception is the direct result of the personal experiences of friends and acquaintances.[41] Whichever way they developed, such perceptions convinced a number of our respondents that treatment and self-help were largely ineffective.

Several respondents reported knowing people who had undergone treatment or had participated in self-help groups, but with few, if any, positive effects. One respondent explained, "I had so many of my friends that went to treatment and went back to doing the same shit they were doing before, so I figured what's the point of wasting all this money if it's not going to work." Two themes regarding the ineffectiveness of treatment and self-help emerged from respondents' accounts. The first of these was that treatment and self-help operated at fairly low emotional or intellectual levels. One respondent believed that he was simply too smart and critical to accept the group's beliefs about recovery, although he had no problems with those for whom it worked. Another commented that the programs were "so superficial" and that he knew they would not work for him. However, as with the previous respondent he had no hostility toward treatment and self-help, saying, "If it helps them, great."

However, not all respondents were so tolerant. For instance, some were suspicious of the proliferation of treatment programs and self-help groups, seeing them as mostly entrepreneurial schemes. Explaining her reasons for avoiding treatment, one respondent commented:

> If it works for them, if it's what they need, then that's fine. I don't condemn anyone for doing it. But, I'm real leery of the proliferation of all these hospitals and care centers because I wonder if their best interest is the patient or themselves. I feel like there is a fine line between self-interest and other interests.

Although not critical of those for whom treatment and self-help worked, respondents were nonetheless skeptical that such modalities would work for them.

Another variation on the ineffectiveness theme was the belief that treatment programs, and particularly self-help groups, bred a kind of dysfunctional dependency that inhibited real personal growth. This theme is reflected in popular critiques as well as among "12-steppers" themselves who acknowledge that people can get "stuck" in their progress through the program.[42] In AA parlance this phenomenon is sometimes referred to as the "dry drunk syndrome," suggesting that although an alcoholic may be sober, he or she nonetheless continues to exhibit the symptoms of an active alcoholic. Such people may rely on their 12-step group as a stopgap measure without trying to bring about a corresponding change in behavior. Frequently, they "fall off the wagon" and return to a life of active drinking.

This was the tendency our respondents appeared to be identifying when they rejected self-help groups. A forty-eight-year-old ski instructor who had been dependent on alcohol and cocaine voiced this concern as follows:

> They [people in AA] are just addicted to something else. I think they are really good for the people for whom they work, but not for me. I think I feel stronger and better for not having to go and use that.

Another respondent, commenting on his decision not to attend a 12-step program, said:

> I think they've helped a lot of people. I think I see certain personality types that use them. I really feel uncomfortable because a lot of the people I met [who were in 12-step groups] I didn't feel were sincere. They were needy people. That's just

how I felt. Mainly I just thought that they were so dependent on the program. I really respect it because it's helped a lot of people, but it's not for me.

Similarly, another believed that such programs impaired the necessary self-change work needed for growth:

I knew a few people who were in these programs. They never seemed to have gotten on with their lives. A lot of people just stay in the same place. I don't think I would have gotten sober if I went to AA.

One respondent even suggested that such programs might be detrimental since they bred a dependency on the recovery program itself that was not unlike dependency on a substance. For her, this approach to recovery went against the principle of taking personal responsibility for oneself:

There's something to be said for taking personal responsibility for your own destructiveness. There's a deeper question here than me just going to AA and promising that God's going to help me not to drink anymore. I think a lot of the people in those groups are dependent on AA and they're not really growing personally. The whole idea is to learn to walk, to learn something new, to learn a new strategy of life besides dependency. I wasn't going to spend 5 hours of my life a week sitting around a table with a lot of people who smoke and drink coffee and feel sorry for themselves and not doing anything but sitting there. For me, hanging around with people who are dependent would not be healthy. I said, there's got to be a better way and I found it.

Like other respondents who had either had direct but brief contact with treatment and self-help, or who simply knew people who had employed such "technologies of the self," this respondent characterized such interventions as substitute dependencies. Had she entered into such a program, it would ultimately have limited her own personal growth as well as her ability to overcome her dependency on drugs. Our interviews suggested that our respondents had thought deeply about their own "recovery" needs and had acted to realize those needs. Rather than assume a position they perceived as passive, they took responsibility for their lives, both during their dependency as well as their recovery.

DIDN'T NEED IT

Several of our respondents chose not to attend treatment or self-help programs because they felt they simply didn't need them. While ultimately all our respondents felt this way, some were more vocal about it. They did not hold treatment and self-help in contempt as did many of those in the previous section; rather they were able to end their addictions without professional or other organized assistance. In fact, many claimed that they would have used these programs had they not been successful through their own efforts.

However, by not choosing treatment or self-help programs as their preferred method, these respondents resisted the common American tendency to see dependency and addiction as a disease requiring medical or other therapeutic care. In a sense, by emphasizing their own ability to overcome their addiction, they were implicitly "demedicalizing" and normalizing their excessive alcohol and drug use. The health-talk contained in their words reflected elements of resistance in that they refused to see themselves as victims of a disease over which they had little control. In many ways, they were tapping into the classically American values of self-determination, diligence, and perseverance, which contrast with the victimization implicit in medicalized views of addiction.

Many of those we interviewed believed they possessed the resolve to change. For instance, a forty-six-year-old male nurse explained that he didn't need professional or self-help assistance because he was determined to change his life. He commented:

> Contrary to popular opinion, I guess I'm the exception. I think that determination and strong will are what did it for me. . . . The only way for me was to do it alone. For me, the people oriented track was superfluous and irrelevant and the only way that it could be done was through my own will and determination.

Several of our respondents articulated a similar belief that human beings possess the personal strength and resilience to change themselves. For instance, one thirty-six-year-old businessman said:

> I think basically I've been a pretty strong person and when I set my mind to something it's pretty hard to get me out of it. I believe that you can do it yourself. I think most of it comes from intestinal fortitude. I say that a lot because I believe deep down it has to come from within.

Another told us:

> It's just coming to realize your problems and then wanting to overcome them and find reasons for quitting. . . . I can and did just do it on my own. I have incredible will power. I guess some people need that, they need that support from the group to help them stay sober. I was able to support myself.

Still another respondent attributed his success in overcoming his dependency on cocaine and depressants to his unrelenting personal drive to succeed:

> I think 95 percent of those people [in treatment or self-help] are either going to fall off the wagon or go back to their

original problems. . . . They are focusing on support. I live a normal life and I don't have any time constraints on me except for normal time restraints. I don't have to go spend an hour a day to be able to handle this thing. It is my own attitude, my own drive and my own will to succeed that does it.

The fact that these respondents did not need treatment or self-help should not necessarily be interpreted as a denunciation of such conventional recovery approaches.[43] Nor does it suggest that our respondents were "in denial." Their experiences highlight the need to recognize that just as there are alternative experiences with alcohol and drugs, there are variant methods of pursuing and experiencing recovery. The narratives offered by our respondents are testimony to this assertion.

Identity Work among Untreated Addicts

The question of how our respondents constructed their identities in relation to their past addictions naturally follows from their decision to reject treatment. A fundamental insight in sociology is that identities are formed out of and in the institutions and roles in which individuals are embedded. We are not born with identities; rather, our identities are social in that they form and change over time through the course of our interaction with others. To say that one is a college professor, a musician, an athlete, a white or a black male, or a husband is to engage in a process of identification with roles. Roles generally "consist of the activities people of a given status are likely to pursue when following the normative expectations for their positions."[44] The identities that emerge from these roles relate to the self-conceptions of the individuals who occupy a particular role. Thus, from the perspective of "role theory," identities arise from the multiple roles that we either voluntarily occupy or are assigned to by others. However, not all these roles are accorded the same status. Sociologists have frequently examined how some roles achieve ascendance over others.[45]

These different levels of role salience lead to personal identities of different degrees of prominence, creating what Everett Hughes referred to as a "master status."[46] This master status locates an individual's position in society and influences how people define themselves and their relation to others during the process of interaction. Such a status locates individuals "within their social group, institution, and community, providing them with a structured set of ties, duties, and relationships."[47] In addition, identities and conceptions of self cohere to these more salient roles, thereby producing a "real self."[48]

However, one must be cautious not to "overdetermine" individual identities. People are not simply "cultural dopes" who unreflectively assume identities. Often, they resist and reject the identities implicit in the roles they occupy. In their ethnographic study of the homeless in Austin, Texas, David Snow and Leon Anderson found that street people carve out a sense of meaning in an attempt to "salvage the self."[49] Although relegated to the role of the homeless by other people and institutions, they constructed explanatory accounts of their situations to neutralize the spoiled identities implicit in the role they occupied. They preferred to think of themselves as being "down on their luck" rather than simply an object of common vilifying images cast on them by those with whom they came into contact. Thus, people aren't simply reflections of their roles but frequently challenge and construct identities contrary to those roles.

Resisting identities that flow from the roles people occupy or are assigned is a common practice in society. Baseball players in Mexico intentionally integrate vestiges of Latin culture into their games in order to preserve their cultural identity.[50] Rock stars challenge the rigid identities assumed to inhere in "maleness" by engaging in "gender-bending" performances that denote androgyny and sexual fluidity.[51] Law school graduates entering corporate law practices maintain images of themselves as being public interest oriented.[52] All these examples illustrate how people seek to resist the identity attendant on the roles they perform.

Whether or not a substance-dependent person assumes the identity of an "addict" or an "alcoholic" is relevant to these comments about identity and the self. From the remarks above, we might assume that an individual does not assume the identity of an addict solely through the heavy use of substances. However, while some roles are definitive, that of an addict is fairly amorphous. At what point does a person become an addict? The renowned sociologist Alfred Lindesmith once suggested that a person becomes an addict when he or she recognizes that narcotics will reduce the discomfort associated with withdrawal.[53] Another related view, however, might suggest that individuals become addicts, that is, assume the identity of an addict, only through their participation in recovery institutions that teach them that they are addicts.[54] From this perspective, the identity of addict is mediated by their participation in institutions which label them addicted.

Our untreated respondents raise interesting sociological questions about the nature of addiction and the identity of addict. Since they had not participated in treatment or self-help programs, one might guess that they did not view themselves as addicted. In other words, because our respondents had not participated in role-constituting activities associated with treatment, they distanced themselves from any accommodation with the identity of addict. However, because all our respondents experienced withdrawal and used substances to relieve their withdrawal, and experienced a host of drug-related problems as de-

Table 5

Perceived Identity among Alcoholics
and Drug Addicts

	Alcohol Users (N=25)	Drug Users (N=21)
Addict	12	1
Nonaddict	13	20

tailed in chapter 2, and because they were told they were drug dependent by friends and family, one might conversely speculate that they assumed the identity of an addicted person. We explore the issue of identity among self-remitters below.

In exploring this issue with our respondents, we found that only a minority subscribed to a disease-based view of their addiction. Interestingly, most of the respondents who identified with a disease model of addiction had previously been addicted to alcohol only. As indicated in Table 5, with the exception of one person, none of the previously drug-addicted individuals we interviewed perceived themselves as addicts. For most, the identity of addict was totally nonexistent. This was not the case among alcoholics, almost half of whom defined themselves in terms of their addiction.

Given the popularity of the disease concept of alcoholism in the popular culture and its widespread acceptance, it is not surprising that those who were alcohol-troubled would have gravitated toward such an identity, despite their avoidance of treatment. Also, a number of them reported having family members with alcohol problems who had participated in treatment or self-help. Undoubtedly they were influenced by their relatives' perspectives on alcoholism.

There were various elements of a disease concept in the "identity talk" of these respondents.[55] Consistent with the traditional disease narrative of addiction of "once an addict, always an addict," seven of our alcohol-using respondents and one drug user defined themselves as addicted despite the fact that they were no longer actively drinking or using drugs. Each of these people chose to remain totally abstinent from mind-altering substances. A forty-five-year-old house painter who had abstained from alcohol for thirteen years, explained: "I'm a recovering alcoholic. I'm going along with the ten [sic] steps I read about on AA and I recognize myself as a recovering alcoholic. I can't take another drink and that's it." Each of these respondents accepted the general view of addiction as a lifelong disease requiring abstinence and constant vigilance. Invoking the traditional disease metaphor, a woman who claimed to have read a copious amount of personal growth literature such as that popularized by John Bradshaw and Thomas Moore, commented:

> I used to use, I don't now, but I can't ever lose sight that it can hit me again. I have to think of where I was, where I want to go, and that I'll never be cured of it. It's always going to be there to haunt me. . . . It's a major disease. It can strike anyone and that's where I see it as a disease because a disease don't care who it hits. I'll never be cured of it. I'll always have to work at it. It's like a cancer, in a way.

Similarly, a thirty-four-year-old businessman continued to see himself as an alcoholic despite his lengthy period of sobriety: "When I think about an alcoholic, well, I am one. . . . I still think today, it's one day at a time. I think that it's a disease." Thus, despite their lack of involvement in treatment or 12-step groups, these respondents presented an identity of an addict that was congruent with those who identify with such programs. For them, their identity as addict ranked high among other identities.

However, those who perceived themselves as "sick" were by far the minority among our interviewees. The overwhelming majority of our respondents distanced themselves from the identity of an addicted person struggling to maintain control. For some, though only a very few, addiction was a thing of the past—a kind of bump in the road of life. These people identified themselves as having recovered completely from their dependent use. Having recovered, they no longer defined themselves in terms of addiction. A thirty-three-year-old woman, for instance, adamantly claimed: "I used to be an addict. I'm not anymore. I'm not even in recovery. I'm recovered. As far as I'm concerned, that's a past life." Those in this small group, although admittedly once addicted, no longer even thought about addiction as part of their current lives. Another person said:

> I regard myself now as fully recovered, past tense. I don't think that it's an active issue. I was hopelessly addicted and with all the symptoms. I had withdrawal, convulsions, insomnia, you name it. It was at a crisis point. Either I was going to die of it or I was going to quit. So I quit, that's it.

Most of our respondents were reticent about even applying the concept of addict or alcoholic to their lives. Most had normalized their abuse of these substances and integrated it into their biography. They simply referred to their dependency as a period during which they had had a series of problems. Others described their dependency as a "weakness" and themselves as "immature" or as "a person with life challenges" and even as a "phase."

These people preferred not to think of themselves as addicted or alcoholic, not because they weren't dependent on these substances but rather because of their unwillingness to adopt a discredible image of themselves as permanently sick.[56] They resisted either labeling themselves or being labeled, preferring instead to define their abuse as something in the past. For them, such a label would have been inconsistent with their view of themselves as effective people:

> I don't see myself as an addict. I never did. I know that I'm a strong, independent person. I don't know if I would be this strong and independent if it [drugs] hadn't been part of my life. But I choose to ignore and pretend it's not there because I think if I dwell on the fact that I was an addict at one time in my life, it might pull me down. I don't want to think of myself or identify myself as an addict. I see myself as someone totally opposite to that.

Rather than denying their problems or disavowing their deviance, as sociologists might say, these people readily avowed their dependency but resisted the tendency to make it a salient part of their lives.[57] Their "identity-talk" placed addiction significantly outside their current sense of selfhood. As a thirty-six-year-old graduate student who had been dependent on cocaine for five years, explained:

> I don't see myself as a recovering person. That's always bugged me about AA and things like that. They emphasize that you have this problem, this flaw, and will always have it. I look back and say, I wasn't very mature at that stage of my life and very responsible. But I learned something from it. I can't look at myself as being terribly flawed by this for the rest of my life. I'm a graduate student now. I'm a mother, a wife, a community member. . . I just can't label myself as an addict or ex-addict.

Interestingly, some respondents actually felt that they had benefited in some way from their past lives as drug addicts despite the significant disruptions these had caused. Attributing benefits to their use—a perspective antithetical to traditional disease-based models of addiction—is consistent with our respondents' desire to avoid labeling. A woman who now owns a home, runs a successful business, and is the president of the PTA at her child's school refuses to "walk around with the language of being an alcoholic and an addict today." She stated:

> I would be just labeling myself into the ground and I would be very depressed about that. So I don't say that [I'm an addict]. I will say that I have used drugs and alcohol in my life and that it was very nonproductive for me. . . . As for who I am today, I know that who I am today is certainly inclusive of what I was then. Those experiences certainly made me who I am. I don't deny them and I would never discount them. I can't say that I would be real excited to have to go through it again but I feel like I have some understanding for why that had to happen to me. And so, I accept it and I just let it go.

Another respondent, a thirty-three-year-old former heroin user, similarly considered himself better off in the present for having gone through a drug addiction in the past. Unlike those who defined addiction in negative terms, he placed his use within the Buddhist principle of "out of chaos comes growth." "I almost feel a kind of superiority towards people because I've gone through it and they hadn't and I had come out of it with both feet firmly planted. I think I'm actually better for having gone through it." He neither saw himself as an addict nor defined his previous use as essentially negative. It was just one of the many experiences that had brought him to his present state in life. Heroin use, for him, was now merely a distant memory.

The fact that these untreated individuals maintained an identity that distanced them from their previous excessive use raises some compelling questions about the possible deleterious effects of treatment and self-help on a person's self-concept. This question will be explored in a later chapter. Suffice it to say here that the majority of those we interviewed were presently composing their lives almost entirely independently of their previous use of intoxicants. They neither thought about it much, nor incorporated it into their identity "tool kit." In the main, they thought about themselves in a variety of different ways, but least of all as addicts.

Conclusion

Almost thirty years ago, David Robertson, a research sociologist at the Institute of Psychiatry at the University of London, wrote a provocative article in one of the premier addiction journals in America, the *Quarterly Journal of Studies on Alcohol*.[58] Most of those associated with the addiction treatment and self-help industries would consider the thesis of this article to be heretical. The article, sardonically entitled "The Alcohologist's Addiction," examined the implications of having lost control over the disease concept. By subjecting the disease concept of addiction to critical inspection as opposed to simply accepting its ideology at face value, Robertson advanced a litany of consequences associated with its blind acceptance. Among these consequences—including the conceptual ambiguity of addiction within medicine, the possibility of defining an ever-increasing range of conditions and behaviors as diseases, and the possibility that medicine would gain control over expanded areas of life—was his fear that disease conceptions of addiction would turn responsibility for rehabilitation over to experts and professionals. In his critique of the disease concept, Robertson suggested that by labeling addiction as a disease and placing individuals in what Talcott Parsons referred to as a "sick role," the addict came to believe that the disease could be arrested only by outside intervention.[59] No amount of self-restraint, willpower, or "natural" solutions would suffice to overcome addictive behaviors.

The consequences of being "addicted to addiction," as identified by Robertson and others, are directly applicable to the lives of those who recover without treatment.[60] As illustrated in this chapter, although the individuals we interviewed were seriously addicted to alcohol and drugs, they were not so severely addicted to addiction. In other words, they did not accept the addictionologist's essentialist claims about disease, powerlessness, and the inextricable nature of addiction. Our respondents actively resisted this dominant metaphor and its related "technology of the self" by circumventing treatment and self-help. They did so because they were contemptuous of the treatment and self-help ideology, didn't believe such programs worked, or simply felt they didn't need it. Ultimately, their belief that they were the navigators of their own lives and their unwillingness to be completely disillusioned through dependency allowed them to change their lives without recourse to treatment and self-help.

In addition to terminating their dependencies on drugs, an added benefit of recovery without treatment was that they were able to distance themselves from a self-identification as addict. Unlike many who adopt the identity of addict as their "master status," our respondents proceeded through life without much thought to their prior dependencies. They recognized that they had had problems, had been dependent, and needed to avoid substances and users, but, for the most part, they did not characterize themselves as addicts or alcoholics. That period in their lives had been one of much pain as well as much growth. Now that it was over, they simply moved on with their lives. In the next chapter we examine the broader social factors that assisted them in their natural recovery from addiction.

Chapter Five

THE SOCIAL CONTEXT OF RECOVERY WITHOUT TREATMENT

Peter's personal and professional life was in turmoil from his more than twenty-year dependency on alcohol. A partner in a large urban law firm, Peter began drinking excessively during law school to relieve the stress of being in such an intellectually challenging environment. Although he had become a successful attorney and had made it to the level of partner, by his early forties his professional life was beginning to crumble. His competency at handling complex legal matters deteriorated, as did his professional demeanor with clients and colleagues. Peter worked hard at keeping up appearances but in his private moments feared that he would be sacked by the law firm because of potential professional malpractice problems.

His fears hit close to home when a close and well-respected colleague was "kicked out of the office after twenty years" due to problems with the local bar association caused by his colleague's drinking. As Peter explained, "the fear of that kind of thing happening professionally was pretty important. I knew at that moment I had to do something." Although Peter had grown up the son of alcoholic parents and had been dependent on alcohol for over twenty years, this incident propelled him to walk away from his dependent use without treatment. When we interviewed Peter, he had been abstinent for nearly eight years and life had improved significantly. His professional career was back on track and his personal life with his second wife and two teenage children had become deeply satisfying.

Like the other respondents we interviewed for this book, Peter's dependency on alcohol and his eventual self-change occurred in a larger context of social relations within the family, peer group, and the workplace as well as in a broader social and cultural framework. As we have illustrated throughout this book, the meanings that our respondents attached to use, the personal transformations they experienced, and their constructed identities did not emerge independently of the contexts within which they were embedded. Use and abuse of intoxicants are intimately tied to local interactional settings as well as to the larger social structural dimensions of social life.

Drug use emerges out of peer and familial relations but also out of the circumstances of social class and cultural norms. Although use and abuse are not simply "determined" by these conditions, they are nonetheless mediated by them. As Anthony Giddens points out in his theory of structuration, social structure provides the rules and resources involved in human action, both enabling and constraining people to act in certain ways.[1] For structuration theory, social "action and interaction are constrained by, yet generative of, the structural dimension of social reality."[2]

Applied to our research, structuration theory suggests that the patterns of use, the social meanings of substances, the approaches to personal transformation, and the emergent identities associated with self-healing are mediated by the larger social context in which individuals are embedded. From this perspective, the structural location of our respondents is critically important to understanding their experiences with alcohol and drugs as well as their untreated recovery and associated identities. In previous chapters we examined how our respondents developed meanings about substances that contributed to their dependencies, how they transformed their identity, and how they constructed a normalized sense of self that abrogated an identity as addict. The present chapter shifts the level of analysis from the microprocesses of identity and personal change to an examination of how our respondents' experiences with drugs and self-healing were shaped by the macrostructural contexts they occupied. Specifically, it examines how our respondents' structural location in society enabled them to overcome their addictions without treatment. An understanding of this broader structural context not only has implications for treatment, as we discuss in the next chapter, but also has much to say about drug policy and efforts to prevent substance abuse, topics we will reserve for our concluding chapter.

Social Structure, Modernity, and Dependence

That dependency is related to the structural features of social life is a fundamental proposition advanced by social scientists who have studied addiction. The concept of structure is a complex and highly debated one in sociology. Many sociologists, particularly those associated with what has come to be known as the "astructural" version of symbolic interactionism, maintain that human action occurs in local social situations that are unencumbered or unconstrained by the structured patterns of life that operate around them.[3] However, others see human action as more directly tied to a broader social structure that shapes the internalized roles associated with race, class, and gender as well as other social statuses. For these sociologists, the concept of structure has multiple meanings and applications. Structure implies a system of patterned social relations within which an individual exists. Such patterned relations include those pertaining to social class, gender, and race as well as those more generally associated with roles, organizational hierarchies, institutionalized practices, and social formation. From this perspective, structure is part of social reality but is not immediately visible within ongoing relationships. A person's structural social position influences his or her consciousness, experience, social networks, opportunities, and dispositions. People may operate freely in these structured environments but not necessarily under freely chosen circumstances. However, structure is not simply recursive, that is, it does not merely impose a unidirectional effect on individuals. Rather, as Giddens asserts, structure possesses a duality that not only produces action but also allows individuals to act upon and shape society. Thus, human behavior shapes and is shaped by a context of structured social relations.[4]

This theory of the duality of structure, that is, structural conditions that are both enabling and constraining, has considerable utility in helping us understand the phenomenon of addiction and self-healing. In one of his more recent explorations of the relationship between social structure and identity, Giddens outlines the crisis condition of modern society and the implications this state of affairs has for the self. In his words, "personal meaninglessness—the feeling that life has nothing worthwhile to offer—becomes a fundamental psychic problem in circumstances of late modernity."[5]

Ironically, the expansion of opportunities and choices in contemporary society has made life existentially more troubling and has brought on an insecurity that "makes all of us increasingly vulnerable to a range of emotional disorders."[6] The sense of personal anxiety increases exponentially as people feel anchorless in the wake of what Giddens calls the "disembedding of social institutions," or the separation of social relations from their localized institutional foundations. Much of life has become decoupled from the reassuring institutional definitiveness that guides behavior. Community has become virtualized, public life has imploded, family life has become increasingly corporatized and is no longer a "haven in a heartless world."[7] The major modern institutions of science, law, and medicine fail to inspire awe, while politics have devolved into the lowest common denominator and the progressive social movements associated with labor, feminism, and race have factionalized into identity politics that inhibit commonality.[8] As a result, modern life has become increasingly crisis prone as its social institutions have lost their solidifying capacity. In such a society, Giddens claims, the self becomes a "reflexive project," that is, the self is no longer found in the constellation of social institutions, but rather must be actively explored, cultivated, and constructed as a narrative without the clarity of preexisting traditions.[9] Discovering "who I am" thus becomes a frustrating preoccupation in postindustrial society.

In such conditions personal problems like addiction become commonplace. As Giddens argues, addiction must be understood "in terms of a society in which tradition has more thoroughly been swept away than ever before" and in which the search for self correspondingly assumes critical importance.[10] Addiction and dependency become ways of coping with the personal fragmentation experienced in social life by providing a source of comfort, albeit more or less transient, through the palliation of anxiety. In a similar way, David Forbes describes addictions as "false fixes" that represent

> disturbed expressions within this culture through which we attempt to meet our needs for power, security, and self-expression. Addictive relations become a cultural problem as a result of our attempt to meet these social needs through drug use and other compulsive behaviors, since we are not meeting them otherwise as we mature.[11]

This inability to achieve basic social needs in contemporary society contributes to the development of addictions as a way of defending against an ontological insecurity and the associated limitations on self-actualization.[12]

In his thoughtful analysis of this crisis condition, Giddens proposes broad social solutions for the current maladies of the self in contemporary society. Drawing upon examples like self-therapy, he explores ways in which people can overcome their feelings of rootlessness and insecurity through the establishment of new and novel courses of action that depart from habit. Very often, such changes involve a "massive process of institutional reconstitution" in which people reorient their relationships with various institutions. Such reorientations can occur during personal crises and "fateful moments" such as those associated with dependency. These fateful moments possess transformative potential in that they represent

> phases when people might choose to have recourse to more traditional authorities. In this sense, they may seek refuge in pre-established beliefs and in familiar modes of activity. On the other hand, fateful moments also often mark periods of re-skilling and empowerment. They are points at which, no matter how reflexive an individual may be in the shaping of her self-identity, she has to sit up and take notice of new demands as well as new possibilities.[13]

While the condition of late modernity makes it likely that those experiencing various latent anxiety-based disorders will seek out professional therapy, Giddens maintains that it is "possible for an individual effectively to reorient his life without the direct consultation of an expert or professional."[14] In fact, the eradication of boundaries in modern society that contributes to the crisis of personal meaninglessness and the collapse of stabilizing institutions ironically may contain the seeds for personal salvation. Since contemporary society is no longer encumbered by the rigid traditions of past authority or what Roberto Unger refers to as "false necessities," new institutional arrangements and relationships can be visualized that remoralize and resolidify social life. Rather than locating the self in the liberating potential of individualistic pleasure, impulse, and ecstasy,[15] Giddens maintains that self-actualization is best pursued within social institutions, either those which are preexisting or new institutional arrangements and social relations that are emancipatory and empowering.

Unfortunately, the opportunities for emancipation from personal problems like addiction are not equally distributed in society. One's social structural position and associated social relations mediate the ability to experience self-change. In fact, Giddens recognizes the importance of one's structural location in affecting personal change by asserting that "access to means of self-actualization becomes itself one of the dominant focuses of class division and the distribution of inequalities more generally."[16] While dependency and recovery are not reducible to social class alone, these problems and possible solutions are not equality distributed in society. Rather, opportunities to develop alcohol and drug problems as well as opportunities to transform oneself are unevenly distributed. People who possess life options and resources because of their structural position in society tend to have a greater capacity for getting out of trouble with drugs.[17] According to social psychologist Jill Kiecolt, even the chances of developing self-efficacy are affected by such structural differences. As she writes, "[L]ocation in social structure sorts persons into 'contexts of action' which afford different amounts of resources and opportunities for engaging in efficacious action and building self-esteem."[18] Developing the self-efficacy to change oneself is significantly influenced by the social structural conditions present or absent in an individual's life. Thus, men may pursue self-change differently than women, whites may have different strategies than nonwhites, and the middle class may possess resources for change that are unavailable or in limited supply to those who are economically disadvantaged. As one moves up the social hierarchy, opportunities for developing efficacy leading to change increases, while those located near the bottom experience limited opportunities for self-change in the form of personal attributes and resources.[19] Consequently, the process of becoming dependent and the strategies for change are not merely contained in people's immediate settings, but are also greatly affected by their more general position in the larger social structure.

One way of operationalizing this unequal distribution of emancipatory opportunities is through the concept of "social capital." The concept of social capital is broadly defined by

> a variety of different entities having two characteristics in common: They all consist of some aspect of a social structure, and they facilitate certain action of individuals within the structure. Like other forms of capital, social capital is productive, making possible the achievement of certain ends that would not be attainable in its absence. . . . Social capital inheres in the structure of relations between persons and among persons."[20]

Social capital is, as Bourdieu postulates, "the sum of the resources, actual or virtual, that accrue to an individual or a group by virtue of possessing a durable network of more or less institutionalized relationships of mutual acquaintance and recognition."[21] These resources can operate at the broader levels of social organization as in the formation of civic groups and business norms pertaining to trust and cooperation or they can inhere more locally to individuals in particular social settings.[22] For instance, Granovetter and those sociologists who engage in "network analysis" have consistently demonstrated that occupational mobility and attainment are best predicted by observing how people use their available social relations and resources.[23] In most cases, the networks in which people are embedded greatly influence how they use and benefit from the resources available to them. As Granovetter summarizes it:

> people with certain characteristics get matched to positions with high or low potential for rewards. . . . But you don't have to think very long about matching processes before you see that they basically concern location in social networks and how these locations shape people's work lives and the kinds of positions that are available to them.[24]

Generally, however, social capital is unequally distributed in society. As Granovetter and Tilly conclude: "[S]ince personal relations are typically homogeneous by class, ethnicity, and region, this mode of allocation can effectively reproduce existing inequalities."[25]

While the concept of social capital has been applied to occupational mobility,[26] civic culture,[27] as well as to business transactions and economic behavior more generally,[28] it is also useful as a means of understanding personal problems such as addiction and efforts to overcome these problems. Like the above examples, personal problems and their solutions are embedded in a broader context of structured social relations and networks. Just as drug use is mediated by the structured relations in which one is embedded, so too are the opportunities for personal change and recovery. The opportunities for self-change among crack users in inner-city barrios are undoubtedly different from those in the middle class, who not only have better access to treatment but also have greater amounts of social capital that can facilitate change.[29] Ultimately, higher status confers more resources, access to social relations, and greater opportunities for self-change.[30] In the following section, we examine how the structural location of our respondents and their associated social capital were related to their ability to recover from their addictions without the benefit of treatment. This analysis suggests that recovery from addiction, particularly for those who do so without treatment, must be understood from a social perspective and not merely be seen as an individual act.

The Social Embeddedness of Natural Recovery

As illustrated in the previous chapters, people who overcome their alcohol and drug dependencies do so within a context of institutional life and social relations. Each of our respondents reengaged in conventional life pursuits and developed or reestablished meaningful social relationships, often in the institutions with which they had become disconnected. However, these emerging conventional commitments and social relations occurred within the structured set of relations in which our respondents were embedded. Their ability to immerse themselves in institutional life and develop meaningful social relations was thus influenced by the preexisting social capital they brought with them into their intoxicant dependency as well as the amount of social capital they were able to retain through their dependency. For the most part, because they had led relatively stable middle-class lives prior to and during their dependencies, the quality and quantity of social capital they possessed facilitated their recovery. As we illustrate below, although our respondents believed they had overcome their dependencies on their own, their recovery actually occurred within a structured context of social relations. The social capital that adhered to these relations offered them access to information, normative expectations, relationships, institutions, and other opportunities that were useful to them in accomplishing their personal transformations, and that might have been unavailable in different social contexts. We discuss three types of social capital below.

STABILITY

There were a variety of factors in our respondents' lives that assisted in their creation and maintenance of social capital. One such factor was the degree of stability they brought with them into their dependent use and the amount of stability they maintained during their dependencies. As discussed in the previous chapter, none of our respondents assumed the role of "street addict" or "skid row" alcoholic, nor were they incarcerated for a significant length of time. None had engaged in the sort of street crime, prostitution, or violence that is commonly portrayed in the media. This fact alone assisted them in their ability to maintain a degree of stability. However, their stability went beyond these factors. Contrary to the popular image of alcoholics and drug addicts, most of our respondents had had steady jobs prior to their dependent use and many remained employed during their dependency, even though they experienced significant disruption and a host of problems. In the words of an accountant with a ten-year addiction to cocaine:

> I really started using heavily and having problems. But through it all, I worked. I was an office manager for H & R

Block for about 5 years. . . . Then in 1985 I decided to commit myself to something, although I was still using heavily. I second mortgaged my house and pulled out $30,000 and bought a tax practice that had two thousand customers.

Having a stable employment history also provided our respondents with the opportunity to witness the consequences of their excessive use. Like Peter, whom we profiled at the beginning of this chapter, many of those we interviewed worked in jobs where they feared exposure. A forty-eight-year-old architectural engineer was worried about what his colleagues would think of his crack use:

I was pretty much in control of my life, in my profession. I moved here for job advancement, though I was having problems with alcohol and crack. Professionally I was doing good. I was pushing the edge. Then the crashing down became tremendously worrisome. I was using a lot of crack and became concerned that I would lose my job and the respect of my associates.

Another respondent, a case manager at a social service center, also became concerned about potentially losing his job. He explained:

Here I was all the way through college. I had a pretty good job and a family and a real bad addiction. . . . If they [his colleagues] found out that I was doing this [using cocaine and heroin] I would get fired. And now with drug testing, I would never get another job if I'm not able to pass a drug test.

Even when respondents experienced problems on the job, most were nonetheless able to keep them. In part, this was because they were employed in primary labor market jobs that featured "well-defined paths for advancement and the protection of rules of due process."[31] Unlike low-skilled secondary labor market jobs, employment in the primary labor market typically includes higher salaries, job security, and generous health benefits.[32] Where a person falls in this segmented labor market has significant implications for his or her level of stability.[33]

Our respondents were often protected by the normative prescriptions and legal rights associated with primary labor market employment. For instance, Dennis, the college professor's son introduced in chapter 2, was having problems at the tractor company where he worked. As a result of his "excessive tardiness and absenteeism," he was eventually fired. However, with the help of his college-professor father who retained legal assistance, Dennis "fought it [the decision] in court and eventually won and got reinstated." In his words, "I knew how to use the system to my advantage. I just used it the way it was written. The union backed me all the way and the arbitration rules were in my favor." Although Dennis continued his use of substances, the employment stability he experienced no doubt prevented him from sliding further into addiction.

Stable employment not only afforded these respondents access to nonabusing colleagues whose opinions they respected, but also provided them with an institutional investment that made it easy for them to eventually "just say no." In addition, even while they were actively using alcohol or drugs, this stability gave them financial security that mitigated the need to engage in criminal activities to secure drugs. Whether Dennis and others like him would have pursued criminal activities without such stability is not known. However, the demographics of our respondents suggests that they were unlikely candidates for such activities given their previous levels of stability and socialization. Most of all, their economic stability before, during, and after their periods of dependency had a profound impact on their ability to overcome addiction without treatment.

IDEOLOGY

Another type of social capital that mediated our respondents' untreated recovery was their possession of an ideology. As James Coleman points out, "An ideology can create social capital by imposing on an individual who holds it the demand that he act in the interests of something or someone other than himself."[34] The development of such ideologies depends in large part on the structural connections between an individual and others. The ideologies of our respondents, formed through their relations with others, helped facilitate their eventual recovery. While most respondents attributed their self-healing abilities to their own personal resilience and motivation, it is clear that these attributes emerged through their association with others.

For instance, many developed a strong desire to terminate their dependency because of their obligation to others. As Coleman points out, this sense of obligation to others is a type of social capital: "Individuals in social structure with high levels of obligations outstanding at any time, whatever the source of those obligations, have greater social capital on which they can draw."[35] This suggests that people with obligations to others are more motivated to act in particular ways. Those who do not possess or fail to recognize their obligations to others are free to violate personal trust, while those who have an ideology of obligation are somewhat more constrained in their actions.[36]

Many of our respondents possessed and acted on such obligations to others. This ideology, forged out of their own biographical experiences, provided them with powerful incentives to change. For instance, a retired military officer with an extensive history of alcohol dependency, described how his obligation to himself and others served as a catalyst to change:

> What it finally came down to, I just stopped. I gotta take a look at my life and what the fuck was going on. I'd seen other guys die. That didn't scare me because I've never been afraid of death. But what did scare the shit out of me was that I wasn't doing a damn thing with my life. I was brought up to be more than an alcoholic.

Another respondent, a forty-two-year-old business owner, had a strong sense of purpose that grew out of his early experiences growing up on the East Coast. As he explained: "I've always believed that I had a sense of purpose in my life and a certain amount of strength to accomplish things. I had seen my father accomplish a lot and he taught me that there's nothing I can't do if I try." Another respondent who was a manager in a local business, while attributing his self-healing to his own "intestinal fortitude," nonetheless spoke of his obligation to others. As he commented: "A lot of people have stuck by me during all my problems and I'll be damned if I'm going to let them down."

This obligation ideology also manifested itself in the desire to avoid being exposed to nonusing friends. Fear of exposure is a type of social capital in that it represents a preexisting social relation that influences behavior. In some cases, this fear prevented the escalation of use. One respondent who was dependent on heroin and cocaine said:

> I stopped shooting up, but I continued using for a long time. I had no marks and I wanted to stop before I had any marks. That was my biggest fear was that I would be discovered and the shame that would be surrounding it. It's OK, it's socially acceptable to snort, but not to inject.

Although, like the earlier respondent, he attributed his eventual self-healing to "sheer willpower," his eventual "will" to stop, like his determination to avoid needle tracks, was related to his involvement in social relations. Similarly, another respondent, who lived with a nonusing friend in Texas when she was trying to stop, indicated how her connection to this friend influenced her use:

> One of the things that happened [when she was trying to stop] was that I went down to Texas to stay with a friend. However, I took some stuff with me in case I got the urge. And I remember thinking that I was staying with this girlfriend of mine and her two kids and I remember thinking that she would kill me if she knew that I brought drugs into her house. And she had been my best friend and used drugs together years before, but she would kill to protect her kids.

This relationship ultimately helped her to discontinue her drug use: "I knew I couldn't tell Lisa. I came to realize that my life had nothing to do with the people that I really cared about. They never would expect that I would get so wrapped up with drugs." Rather than being merely an individual choice to stop using, our respondents' access to social relations and the social capital associated with these relations thus provided them with much of the incentive to change.

MAINTAINING RELATIONSHIPS

Another source of social capital that facilitated our respondents' recovery was that they had not "burned their bridges" with nonusing family members and friends. Although they frequently discussed relational turmoil, for many this stress had not led to the termination of their relationships. Respondents repeatedly spoke of the importance of family and friends in their natural recovery. This sympathetic investment on the part of others was critical to their personal transformations.

Respondents often claimed that without the help and support of family and friends, they might still have been using.

As David Karp points out in his work on depression, managing relationships with troubled people can be daunting.[37] As with depression, alcohol- and drug-dependent people test the limits of friends' and family members' patience. Many people who are dependent on these substances breach what Candace Clark refers to as the "emotional economy."[38] According to Clark, there are sympathy boundaries in all relationships that are constantly being managed. The margin of sympathy is determined by how much each has given and received in the past. Drawing upon this general concept, Karp likens this emotional economy to a bank. He writes:

> [E]ach of us expects to get approximately what we give and an individual who makes great sympathy demands without repayment may run out of credit altogether. Should a person become "bankrupt" in a particular relationship, he or she will have to draw on sympathy accounts that remain "open" in other relationships.[39]

Karp found that while the "emotional economy" of the family and friends of the depressed people he studied were often tested, intimates sought to honor their perceived commitments to loved ones suffering from depression. He concluded that such commitments by family members and friends were essential to relieving the profound emotional pain associated with depression.

Other people's commitments toward one are a type of social capital that often helps those suffering from depression or dependency. As suggested by the term "emotional economy," troubled individuals may draw upon this commitment as long as they have not exceeded their sympathy credit. For many of our respondents, the sympathy boundaries associated with the implied emotional economy, while strained, had not yet become insolvent. Because of this they were able to benefit from the relational investments of others. In other words, our respondents could use the resources of family members and friends to aid in their self-healing.

Friends and family often provided the emotional support respondents needed to overcome their dependencies. Respondents often talked about how they had gained emotional strength from the support of others. Jane, a twenty-six-year-old assistant manager with a longtime dependency on cocaine, discussed the importance of her friends as follows:

> My [nonusing] friends were very important to me. I had some dear friends that were supportive and it helped me to take a look internally as far as pulling up my own willpower and making the decision to quit.

Another respondent, a case manager in an alcohol and drug clinic, expressed similar sentiments about the importance of having good friends. Asked what strategies she had used to discontinue her drug use, she responded:

> I think through support of my friends and talking about the frustration and what I was going through. . . . I was living with one friend and another lived in the same apartment complex. There were many times I knocked on his door and cried, bawled my head off and he would sit there and listen. I would cry about the fear because I would get the urge to use and it would be overwhelming. That was the only place I could turn. . . . I have known this guy since third grade. We are great friends. I always tell him that he saved my life. I really respect his opinion. If it had not been for him, I probably wouldn't have been able to do it.

In such cases friends played the role of counselor in helping respondents struggle with the emotional demands associated with overcoming their dependencies. However, these intimates frequently provided something much more important than a sympathetic ear and good advice. They offered a sense of belonging. In the words of one respondent, a thirty-six-year-old former heroin addict: "They [her friends] were just there and they made me feel like there was a place for me. I think a lot of drug addicts feel like you don't matter, no one cares what happens to you." Knowing that her friends still cared provided her the reassurance and strength she needed to overcome her addiction to heroin.

In addition to the emotional investments of others, respondents were also able to directly benefit from the more tangible resources and connections of family and friends. These resources were often made available to them at a critical juncture in their dependent careers. Such resources often corresponded to the turning points our respondents experienced. Sometimes, the resources possessed by friends facilitated employment. Friends provided them with the "ties" and connections necessary to acquire good jobs.[40] Sally, who during her dependency on cocaine and crank worked full-time as an environmental activist and attended school, discussed the importance of having stable friends in the labor market. She eventually left her job and the drug scene by going to stay with an old friend. Upon returning to Colorado and in need of employment, she easily acquired another environmental job: "I came back and I made a phone call to a friend and I had a job." She continued, "It was a good feeling, being able to do that kind of thing after all I had been through, knowing that I can still get a good job."

Similarly, another respondent reflected on how a friend had led to her developing a new life that began with acquiring a job:

I had a very strong connection to this friend and she opened the right doors at a time that I needed it. She got me involved with [a civic organization]. They were embarking on their . . . program that was a three-year alcohol awareness type program that was implemented nationally. I signed up to be on a committee and I ended up chairing it. I went to Washington for some large conference. It was really neat for me to do. I was only a short way into my sobriety when all this happened. The doors just opened for me. I have really good friends.

Being embedded in structures of social relationships that were capable of providing resources such as access to meaningful employment was critical to our respondents' eventual recoveries. Not only were they relieved of any financial burdens that might have promoted the desire to use, but their networks also facilitated their recommitment to the conventional world of work. Each of them renewed their "stake in conventional life" through the social capital they possessed.

This recommitment to institutions also occurred in arenas other than work. For instance, in a previous chapter we explored the religious conversions of some of our respondents. These conversions did not occur independently of the context of social relations. Rather, our respondents used the social capital of their friends to connect them to religious institutions. One respondent, for instance, while believing that change must "come from within," nonetheless experienced his spiritual awakening by utilizing the resources of a friend. He explained: "I got involved in a Buddhist religion through a friend. I knew that she practiced. She got me involved in it and I felt that some type of spiritual faith might help me. I think it has because I continue to practice." Another explained how his "Buddha buddies" got him involved in Buddhism. For him, this became his main support group.

The resources of parents also proved beneficial to many of our younger respondents. For instance, Andy, another heroin addict who at the time of the interview worked in the film industry, discussed how he was able to use the resources made available by his parents. Andy dropped out of high school in 1980 after completing his sophomore year. Life grew increasingly ugly for him as he became involved in stealing cars to support his habit. As things began to deteriorate around him, he made the decision to "get out of that environment." With some financial assistance from his parents, Andy moved to Hawaii to stay with some relatives in order to "clean up his act." Although he completed his high school education while in Hawaii, he nonetheless returned to the intravenous use of heroin. After three years living in Hawaii, he decided to move back to Arizona where his parents lived. At this point Andy's parents provided him with the finances to attend college where he finally was able to stop using heroin. As he explained:

> My family helped out with my schooling and then once I was in this academic environment, I really took advantage of it. I made dean's list each semester. I graduated with a 3.7 GPA. . . . Once I graduated I started applying my degree in broadcast journalism. I decided to start a business and wanted to go to a big city to do it, like Denver. I wanted to go out West but a journalist friend of mine was moving to Denver. So, I acquired a loan, with the help of my parents, bought a bunch of video equipment and moved here.

Andy owed a great deal to his parents who continued their emotional investment in him, even through the hard times. This allowed him to utilize the resources they and other relatives were able to make available. Had he breached the sympathy boundaries of his parents by "burning his bridges," he might never had been able to build the kind of institutional recommitments and social relations necessary to break his heroin addiction without treatment. Through his parents' resources, he was able to receive a good education, grow a successful video production business, and become actively involved in community life through dance and theater. Ironically, even his involvement in dance stemmed in part from social capital established while living in Hawaii. Andy had met and studied with his present dance teacher while she was visiting Hawaii several years earlier.

Daria, a twenty-five-year-old college student with a five-year dependency on heroin, provided a similar account of supportive parents. Daria contacted us after hearing about our study from another student who had attended a lecture given by one of the authors. Like many of our respondents, she was anxious to tell her story. Daria began injecting heroin at age seventeen while working as a teenage fashion model. Her use escalated rapidly, so that by age nineteen she was, in her words, "really addicted." "We just did it and did it and did it," she recalled. "Eventually I was at the point of waking up and thinking about it because the first thing I did before going to pee was shoot up." After experiencing several overdoses, she made the decision to stop. Rather than going to a detox clinic, however, she was offered the comfort of a mountain "getaway" to quit cold turkey. As she explained:

> My husband and I set up a plan. I was going to go up to a secluded house in the mountains owned by my dad. When I went up there I was really sick from detoxing. We did it but I was really miserable but I wasn't using. I think we were there about forty-five days.

After finally getting off heroin, Daria sought to reestablish her relationship with her parents. Although relations had been strained over the years of her heroin addiction, they nonetheless were able to reconcile their differences. In fact, Daria's parents provided additional support for her determination to remain drug-free. When asked about her relationship with her parents, Daria commented:

My mom is trying to make a relationship now when I'm 25. . . . I don't want to put her through more than she needs. I'm working on building trust with my parents now. She still doesn't completely trust me when she gives me money for school to pay my tuition [at an expensive private school] but I know they're really proud of me now that I'm clean.

As with Andy, Daria's termination of heroin use after several years of addiction was facilitated in large part by the unyielding support of her parents who provided her with valuable resources. Not only did she have the opportunity to remain isolated from a subculture of drug addicts by withdrawing to the comfort of a peaceful Rocky Mountain environment, but her parents also subsidized her education at an expensive private college.

Being a member of the upper-middle class and having access to financial and other resources meant that Daria's recovery from heroin addiction was extremely different from that of a street "junkie." Unlike street junkies who often have little to look forward to after they stop using, Daria had access to resources that encouraged her to develop a renewed stake in conventional life. She was surrounded by a supportive safety net that eased her transition into a drug-free lifestyle. Like Andy, she was finally able to walk away and stay away from heroin because she did not have to work hard to reintegrate into the conventional world. Because Daria's physical, emotional, and financial needs were taken care of, when she finally made the decision to change her life, she was able to move forward toward her own self-actualization without treatment. Today, Daria spends little time dwelling on her heroin-addicted past. Instead, she occupies herself with her horses and her academic studies, and with ambitions of working with animals and fighting for the rights of endangered species.

Conclusion

Few social scientists would deny the impact that social structure has on alcohol and drug dependency. Structuralist arguments are useful in challenging the pharmacological determinist dictum that places the power of drugs above the ability of individuals to control them. Neither addiction nor violence are properties that adhere to the pharmacological characteristics of drugs.[41] Rather, such properties are mediated by the social circumstances that surround their use. Whether it is poverty that precipitates alcohol and drug dependency as suggested by some[42] or whether addiction is caused by the deterioration of community under conditions of late capitalism,[43] one thing remains clear. The structural location of a person in society mediates the use and abuse of substances.

As with abuse, so with recovery. Opportunities for personal transformation are unevenly distributed in society. How a person experiences what Mills calls "private troubles" and the options he or she possesses to overcome these problems are restricted by his or her social circumstances. As Giddens points out, structure both promotes and restricts behavior.[44] The opportunities for self-actualization are affected by the structural conditions associated with class, gender, and race, and one's financial status, ideology, and connections. People's private troubles are, in part, reproduced by the social conditions which surround them."[45] Working-class boys do not see school as a valuable asset for the future,[46] girls sacrifice academic success for relationships,[47] and young African-American males have few networks to help them get into good jobs.[48] Thus, to paraphrase Marx, people do choose their options, but not under their preferred circumstances.[49]

As we have demonstrated in this chapter, recovery from drug and alcohol dependency is affected by the social capital that one possesses. The social capital that had been established and maintained prior to as well as during their dependencies played a significant role in helping our respondents overcome their problems. The fact that they had a fair amount of social capital in no way diminished the seriousness of their substance problems. However, they were able to maintain these important relationships despite their excessive substance abuse.

Social capital possesses a malleable quality in that it can be created and maintained, as well as destroyed. The destruction of social capital can have serious consequences. In fact, it is quite common for those experiencing drug and alcohol addictions to have "burned their bridges" to the point where few will support and assist them. Proponents of concepts such as "tough love" might see the kind of support and assistance given to our respondents as having contributed to their continued addictions. Testimonials from "tough love" advocates attest to the burned bridges syndrome. One distraught woman, obviously at the limit of her emotional boundaries, wrote to a newspaper with the following advice:

> If you want to help addicts, don't lend them money, wash their clothes, dry their tears, write them letters or invite them into your home. Don't let them use your phone, your car, your shower or your bed. Don't listen to or advise them or give them articles to read. Don't think you can be their best friend. Only a professional can help them. What you think is "help" may only make them worse. Addicts are master manipulators, more seductive than the drugs they're hooked on, and their word (with a hand on the Bible) doesn't mean a thing. They have no conscience. If their lips are moving, they are lying. I have learned a lot from attending more than 40 Al-Anon and Nar-Anon meetings in five cities. The faces are different, but the stories are the same. The more you involve yourself with addicts, the more misery and devastation you will suffer, and

you won't help the addicts one damn bit. You need Al-Anon or Nar-Anon. I know because I have BEEN THERE AND DONE THAT. (Emphasis in original)

Perhaps it is understandable that parents and friends, because of several failed attempts or simply because it is a convenient excuse for the lack of real intimacy, wish to terminate all interaction with substance abusers. However, those we interviewed suggested that having caring and nurturing friends and family members who did not condone their behavior but were there to provide support, was critical to their natural recovery.

If our respondents offer any guide, the maintenance of intimacy is essential to the ability to overcome dependencies. True intimacy does not mean condoning all behavior, including behavior associated with alcohol and drug abuse. Nor does it mean, however, that one should make love and nurturance contingent on authoritarian demands. As Giddens writes, "intimacy is not being absorbed by the other, but knowing his or her characteristics and making available one's own."[50] While establishing personal boundaries is a part of any healthy relationship based on intimacy, it does not necessarily imply the retraction of affective ties. Rather, and in the case of troubled individuals, it may involve "loving detachment," or "the emerging capacity to sustain care for the other without shouldering the burden of his or her addiction."[51] Unfortunately, concepts such as tough love end up holding the dependent individual hostage to the insecurity or inability of family members and friends. Sometimes tough love becomes an excuse for parents to minimize or obscure the toxic effect poor parenting skills have had on the personal well-being of their children. For such individuals, tough love becomes a therapeutic justification for continued emotional brutality.

As our respondents demonstrate, intimacy not only provides the emotional benefits associated with being accepted by others, but perhaps more important, it gives continued access to the social capital of others who can offer resources and networks. The destruction of social capital through the burned bridges syndrome, a syndrome that may give rise to tough love practices, prevents a person in need from having access to the capital of others. This impediment can often exacerbate personal problems. Though we live in a society that glorifies a meritocratic ideology of "pulling oneself up by the bootstraps," this is largely a cultural myth. Few people accomplish much in this world, whether in their chosen occupations or in overcoming life's many challenges, without the assistance of others. Whether through the direct action of "networking" or through an accident of circumstance, we are both aided and restricted by the structure of social relations within which we are embedded.

It is in this sense, then, that "natural recovery" is indeed natural. The experiences of our respondents, who subscribed to an individualistic ideology of recovery, actually attest to the importance of the social relations that surround and envelop them. The "natural" communities of friends, family members, and relatives, and the social capital available through these connections, contributed significantly to the personal transformations of our respondents.

PART TWO

IMPLICATIONS OF NATURAL RECOVERY

Chapter Six

LESSONS FOR PRACTITIONERS
FROM SELF-REMITTERS

Thus far our analysis has focused on the processes through which our respondents successfully overcame their addictions without treatment. As we have demonstrated, self-remitters develop a stake in conventional life that provides them with satisfying relationships and new involvements in social life that are incompatible with their addictions. This emerging stake in conventional life was mediated by the larger social context in which our respondents were embedded. In forgoing treatment for their addictions, our respondents were engaging in a type of paradigm subversion, that is, they not only rejected the "false necessity"[1] of treatment but also resisted the identity characteristics that typically adhere to the role of addict.

We now turn our attention to the implications our respondents and their stories have for practitioners working in the field of dependency treatment. Although the body of research on re-covery without treatment is diminutive when compared with literature on addiction treatment, it is nonetheless substantial in its conclusions. In his comprehensive review article of recovery without treatment, Glenn Walters, a clinical psychologist at the Federal Correctional Institution in Minnersville, Pennsylvania, reviewed several studies conducted between 1971 and 1996.[2] He convincingly points out that these studies undeniably document the existence of natural recovery and notes the processes of self-change illustrated in each study.[3] While these studies have made the processes of self-change comprehensible, there has been only scant discussion of what recovery without treatment can offer to practitioners working with drug-dependent clients.[4] And while several of these studies have included brief discussions of the implications for practice, a fuller elaboration of these impli-cations has not yet been articulated.[5]

Using the narratives from our interviews along with the find-ings of other studies as a guide, this chapter explores the impli-cations of recovery without treatment for practitioners working with alcohol- and drug-dependent clients. In this chapter, we specifically examine: (1) the prevalence of recovery without treatment, (2) the comparative advantages that adhere to recov-ery without treatment, (3) implications for treatment strategies, (4) implications for brief interventions, (5) the role of recovery capital in overcoming alcohol and drug dependency, and (6) threats to recovery capital that undermine efforts to terminate a dependency on intoxicating substances.

Prevalence of Untreated Recovery

Perhaps the most striking observation made by those who have studied natural recovery, and one that runs counter to stereotypic views about addiction and treatment, is that recovery without treatment is pervasive.[6] Overcoming alcohol and drug problems unassisted by treatment is widespread and perhaps more common than recovery with treatment. As we discussed in the introduction of this book, the results of two population surveys in Canada conducted by noted researchers Linda and Mark Sobell, report that 77.5 and 77.7 percent of those who overcame alcohol problems did so without treatment.[7] In an earlier study, Goodwin, Crane, and Guze discovered during an eight-year follow-up of felons that, among those that had been alcohol dependent, 40 percent had remitted without treatment.[8] Some have estimated that the rate of untreated to treated recovery ranges from a low of 3 to 1 to as much as 13 to 1.[9] While methodological constraints prevent researchers from making conclusive estimations, recovery from addiction to alcohol,[10] cocaine,[11] and heroin[12] unassisted by treatment has been estimated to be widespread.

For instance, Walters, reviewing results from nine studies that estimated rates of recovery among nontreated individuals, presents an impressive conclusion concerning the rate of natural recovery.[13] Extrapolating from the available research on natural recovery, he posits that if you were to follow a group of 100 substance-dependent people for ten years, 55 of them would self-remit during that period. However, after factoring in return to problematic use (by his estimate, 20), he asserts that the net result of self-remitters would be 35 of the 100, with the remaining 65 either continuing to use or entering treatment. Although the extrapolations from Walters's study are speculative, his estimates coincide with the work done by the Sobells and others on recovery from alcohol problems without treatment.[14] While there are few controlled studies comparing treated with untreated remitters, we may conclude from the above discussion that recovery without treatment occurs at least as often, and possibly quite a bit more often, than treated recovery.

As we have argued in this book, recovery without treatment is anything but unusual or rare. For those who have been exposed to the unsubstantiated belief that such occurrences are nonexistent, the mere recognition of this fact can be liberating in overcoming dependency. Simply knowing that many people overcome severe drug problems without entering treatment may remove much of the mystical power and horror associated with the concept of addiction. As we have illustrated in this book and as others have suggested, many people with alcohol and drug problems find the prospect of entering drug treatment plainly unappealing. For such people, recovery without treatment might not only be a viable option but their only option.

Self-Recovery and Its Advantages

While the literature on recovery without treatment has alluded to the potential advantages of untreated recovery, for the most part this literature has not included a detailed discussion of those benefits.[15] Our respondents' experiences are pertinent to such a discussion. This discussion is offered not as a rejection of various treatment modalities, since treatment does benefit significant numbers of people.[16] In fact, as we have pointed out earlier, there is a functional equivalency between natural recovery and effective treatment approaches.

Before identifying the advantages of natural recovery, however, it is necessary to point out that it may not be a feasible option for everyone suffering from addiction. The experiences of our respondents suggest that having structural and individual resources, what we describe later in this chapter as "recovery capital," can be a critical element in a person's ability to overcome dependency problems without treatment. As suggested by our respondents and supported by the extant literature, those who possess an assortment of resources are better able to overcome dependency without treatment than are those with limited resources. Resources such as education, occupational skills, financial stability, and supportive families and friends, that is, the wide spectrum of human and social capital, all mediate success in overcoming these problems without treatment. Conversely, people from impoverished backgrounds who are financially, educationally, and socially disadvantaged may not be the best candidates for natural recovery. They possess fewer resources that they can draw upon to facilitate self-change.[17] Similarly, people whose identities and values are overly intertwined with a "street subculture" may experience a multitude of serious cultural, economic, and social challenges when they seek to transform their lives.[18]

Indeed, as suggested by our respondents, having resources may significantly increase the likelihood of successful outcomes, with or without treatment. The distinction between these two groups may be that self-remitters are able to actually draw on their personal, familial, and community resources in ways that facilitate a successful recovery effort without needing to resort to formal assistance.[19] It is also important to note that such individuals are likely to have a greater stake in conventional life than the street addict or alcoholic with limited resources who has abandoned conventional roles and relationships.[20] While vocational skills and financial stability are easily seen as resources that can be useful in a recovery effort,[21] possessing a stake in conventional life is an important resource to be considered. The purpose of discussing these issues is to point out that recovery without treatment is contingent on a variety of personal and social factors that require important consideration.

This said, we would like to address the range of potential advantages of natural recovery. These include less cost, less life disruption, less addict identity and stigma, an increased sense of self-efficacy, and an increased sense of individual empowerment.

LESS COST

The diminished financial burden of treatment to individuals and society is a tangible advantage of natural recovery that can be easily appreciated. While the financial burdens associated with self-help groups are negligible, by contrast formal treatment for dependency can be extremely costly, and for many, prohibitive. Whether the treatment facility is a private agency, a public agency, or some combination of both treatment is expensive. According to the Health Care Financing Administration that identifies national health care expenditures, in 1996 $5 billion were spent on the treatment of alcohol misuse and an additional $7.6 billion were allocated to drug abuse treatment. The cost of treatment in the twenty-eight-day inpatient program at the famous Betty Ford Clinic in California is more than $12,000, about $15,000 at the popular Hazelden Foundation in Minnesota, and $17,500 at the nationally advertised Cottonwood De Tucson in Tucson, Arizona.[22] Local programs in the Denver area on average cost approximately $1,000 per day for inpatient drug treatment.[23] Interestingly, a twenty-eight-day stay would result in a cost of about $28,000, considerably more than the cost of some of the nationally known treatment programs (and perhaps more than what some drug-dependent people spend on substances during their dependencies). It is not unusual for some to incur excessive out-of-pocket expenses for inpatient alcohol- and drug-dependency treatment. Conversely, there are few costs for people who recover without undergoing formal treatment. Given the financial restraints imposed on managed care facilities that now provide addiction services, as well as the overall cost of treatment to society, the reduced costs associated with natural recovery are particularly attractive.

LESS DISRUPTION

While the disruption of intoxicant use and the activities that support it are clearly the goals of both recovery with and without treatment, the disruptions of other conventional life activities by long-term treatment can be problematic for people. Undergoing treatment, including attending group meetings, can be extremely disruptive. These disruptions assume different levels of importance depending on the unique situation of the individual seeking help and the course of treatment pursued. For example, women who are the primary caregivers of their young children might find these disruptions overwhelming if, as is often the case, treatment isolates them from their children and prevents them from meeting their parental responsibilities.[24] For single mothers who may risk losing their children temporarily or, in extreme cases, permanently if they enroll in formal treatment, the implications can be monumental.[25] For the primary income earner in a family, particularly a person employed in the secondary labor market that offers little job flexibility or leave opportunities, attending treatment, even if briefly, can lead to loss of income and potential loss of job.

If you view the various modes of intervening in dependency problems along a continuum from the most disruptive to the least, long-term residential treatment is the most disruptive of all. Long-term treatment programs such as therapeutic communities often require a commitment to treatment of one to three years.[26] Conversely, while most would agree that participation in self-help groups is generally less disruptive than most formal treatment, Stanton Peele and others maintain that involvement in 12-step groups can be quite disruptive.[27] Peele observes that participation in such groups can actually result in more rather than less disruption since new members are encouraged to attend daily meetings, particularly during the first ninety days of participation. Peele also points to the potential for significant disruption stemming from the principle of lifelong participation espoused and practiced by some groups.[28]

Clearly, natural recovery is at the opposite end of this spectrum. Unequivocally, recovery without treatment is less disruptive than any other means of recovery from alcohol and drug problems. People are not required to become residents of hospitals, treatment centers, or other institutions for extended periods of time and are not encouraged to attend an inordinate number—much less a lifetime—of meetings discussing their addictions. This is not to say that self-recovery is completely free of disruptions and personal challenges. Several of our respondents reported making fundamental and difficult changes in their lives in order to overcome their addictions. However, the disruptions associated with recovery without treatment are more natural than artificial, and are consistent with other growth-promoting change strategies that people who are not drug dependent employ throughout their lives. These inherently self-imposed strategies are flexible enough to allow people to maintain and expand upon their conventional roles and responsibilities. The logistics of rearranging one's life to enter an inpatient or residential treatment facility, particularly for extended periods, can be overwhelming and therefore should not be taken lightly.

LESS ADDICT IDENTITY AND STIGMA

Enrolling in treatment or joining a traditional self-help group is a serious decision that has a variety of profound lifelong implications for one's identity.[29] Treatment symbolically confirms to the user and to others that the treated individual is an addict. In a sense it assents to the view of that person as "essentially" flawed. For many, entering treatment can be significantly disruptive of normal identity processes.[30] As Burke writes, this in turn often leads to "a lessening of a person's feelings of efficacy or mastery."[31] Additionally, entering treatment causes others to react to one as essentially an addict, and as a result causes the person to see him or herself in those terms.[32] In contrast, as discussed in chapter 4, our respondents avoided many of these negative identity-conditioning situations. The adoption of the identity of an addict is the reified product of social reaction, particularly, of the addiction-treatment industry and self-help groups that hold rather narrow views about the complex phenomenon of addiction.[33] Entering treatment frequently results in being labeled and adopting the identity of an alcoholic or drug addict who has a progressive and lifelong disease. More important, as Peele suggests, the internalization of a "spoiled" identity has potentially dire consequences that can undermine the recovery process itself.[34] While modern society has become more tolerant of people who have experienced dependency and has accepted the medicalized relabeling of excessive use,[35] it would be naïve to think that being a drug addict or alcoholic carries no stigma. Such a stigma can carry considerable social costs and, under certain circumstances, lead to outright persecution.[36]

Not at the same level of concern, but not to be ignored either is the fact that treatment requires the maintenance of a formal record of a person's participation in treatment. While there are laws in place to protect the privacy of such records, institutionalizing one's alcohol or drug problem by documenting it can be potentially detrimental, and may actually compound an already difficult situation. For example, employment applications often include questions about prospective employees' participation in alcohol and drug treatment. It is naïve to think that answering in the affirmative poses few potential consequences other than in the rare cases where one is applying for drug treatment-related jobs. Additionally, with computer technology so pervasive, people have increasing access to individuals' private lives. That some professionals share information with their families and friends about their clients and patients should also to be noted.

Participating in self-help groups represents a different kind of challenge to one's anonymity. As a rite of passage, addicted people are often required to proclaim that they are drug addicts, in the presence of a roomful of total strangers. While members espouse the principle of anonymity, new recruits are encouraged to admit their alcohol- and drug-related wrongdoing to others. Although these practices might occasionally, be therapeutically beneficial, they can simultaneously subvert one's anonymity by calling attention to a person's circumstances. The response of Allen, a twenty-nine-year-old former alcoholic, illustrates some of the potential labeling problems associated with participating in traditional self-help groups. When asked how he saw himself in relation to his previous dependency on alcohol, he responded:

> I don't like the term recovering addict or "once an alcoholic always an alcoholic." I don't feel that it's going to haunt me for the rest of my life. I feel like it's part of my life that's behind me. That's the reason why I don't like AA meetings, because they like wail on it so much. They have a hard time getting rid of it. It's OVER! It's time to move forward. I'm not proud of it or glad that it happened. I'm more of a seasoned individual now. I learned a lot from it.

Although there is generally no formal record of one's participation in self-help groups and anonymity is an intrinsic principle, one's identity in relation to past problems is indeed compromised. Additionally, the lifelong label of addict inherent in traditional self-help programs can be of even greater detriment to group participants than loss of anonymity or other concerns about privacy. Ultimately, the medicalization of behaviors like excessive intoxicant use can mitigate against attempts to take personal responsibility for one's actions and for the development of social policies that seek to create a world that responds to the genuine human needs of community, health, efficacy, and security.[37]

INCREASED SENSE OF SELF-EFFICACY

Another advantage of recovery without treatment is the increased sense of self-efficacy that is associated with solving problems with intoxicant use unaided by conventional interventions. According to the social psychologist Albert Bandura belief in one's self-efficacy is critical to a person as he or she goes about his or her daily activities.[38] As Bandura writes:

> [People] who have a high sense of efficacy visualize success scenarios that provide positive guides for performance. Those who judge themselves as inefficacious are more inclined to visualize failure scenarios that undermine performance by dwelling on how things will go wrong.[39]

For Bandura, a self-efficacious person has a sense of self-determination, motivation, goal-attainment, and confidence. As Bandura remarks, the irrepressible self-efficacy of Gertrude Stein allowed her to continue submitting poems to editors for twenty years before one was finally accepted.[40] Bloom has described self-efficacious people as those for whom "the muses frequently work overtime."[41] The point is that self-efficacy is the cumulative expression of a variety of traits that increase an individual's resiliency and capacity to function in effective ways. It generally results from the acquisition of knowledge and skills, powerful vicarious experiences, verbal persuasion by others, and physiological arousal, each of which prepares a person to perform competently and achieve his or her desired goals.

The experiences of our respondents lead us to believe that when people overcome severe and longstanding drug problems on their own, self-efficacy is enhanced. Given the profile of the respondents in our study, we can assume that they were discernibly self-efficacious prior to ending their dependency. Recall that the primary reason that many of them avoided treatment was that they felt sufficiently confident about their ability to overcome their substance-use problems on their own. Thus, it is unlikely that self-efficacy was created by their ability to overcome alcohol and drug dependency without treatment; rather, it was bolstered as a result of their actions. As our respondents indicated, their enhancement of self-efficacy went beyond their sense of personal mastery over drug dependency and related problems. It generally carried over into other areas of their lives as well. For many, self-recovery gave them an increased sense of personal power over future events, foreseen and unforeseen. The poignant response of Audrey, a thirty-seven-year-old formerly alcohol-dependent woman, illustrates this point. When asked about the benefits of having terminated her dependency on alcohol, she stated:

> It gave me mastery. If I can do this, I can do anything in the whole world. I didn't even think I could sing three years ago and now I sing in two choruses. I guess I feel like I can do anything now.

Similarly, the response of Barb, a thirty-year-old woman formerly addicted to alcohol and cocaine, testified to her ability to draw upon a sense of self-efficacy, a trait apparently instilled in her by her mother. Explaining her ability to quit on her own, she stated:

I was thinking about that today, about maybe something was instilled when I was a child. I remember my mom always saying you can do anything you want; you can be anything you want. If you want it bad enough, you can do it. That always stuck. No one can save you but yourself. You have to do what you can. But the meat and potatoes is [*sic*] that it's your job and you can't blame anybody else. And this crap when people say my parents weren't affectionate or I had this problem as a child. It's like ok, you're an adult now, you know it and you better fix it.

INDIVIDUAL EMPOWERMENT

The concept of empowerment has gained considerable acceptance among clinical practitioners over the last two decades and is used in an increasing number of professional circles, including social work, nursing, education, management, and psychology.[42] Two practitioners of "empowerment" describe it as a "construct that links individual strengths and competencies, natural helping systems, and proactive behaviors to social policy and social change."[43] As practiced in the helping professions, empowerment denotes making choices and executing strategies that result in one's increased capacity to solve immediate as well as future problems. According to Zimmerman, empowerment integrates perceptions of personal control and a proactive approach to life with a critical understanding of the sociopolitical environment.[44] The term compels us to think of wellness versus illness, competence versus deficits, and strengths versus weaknesses.[45] When people cultivate their potential strengths, draw upon existing natural networks, and cultivate community resources to solve pressing personal problems they are personifying the concept of empowerment. As practitioners of empowerment therapy note, the processes of empowerment, that is, the methods used to solve one's problems, can be as important in creating a sense of power as solving the problems themselves.[46]

The strategies used by our respondents and the results of their efforts to arrest their addictions without entering treatment personify many of the elements of empowerment. By drawing on their inner strengths, finding support in the naturally existing relationships of family and friends, and avoiding toxic relationships and repressive institutions they achieved the kind of empowerment referred to by scholars. Similarly, their sense of empowerment was evident in their increased sense of self-efficacy and control and their development of "spontaneous sociability," as exhibited through their enhanced participation in social life.[47]

While it is relatively easy to appreciate the empowerment qualities of self-recovery as reflected in the narratives of our respondents, the sociopolitical dimension of empowerment inherent in self-recovery is not as immediately apparent. Typically, the concept of empowerment invokes the ideals of participatory democracy and mutual aid, as well as activist-oriented efforts to transform the sociopolitical landscape.[48] It is this dimension of empowerment that differentiates it from more general concepts of self-efficacy. Practitioners of empowerment are "transformative intellectuals"[49] who seek on the one hand to politicize the personal problems of their clients by helping them to locate themselves in a broader social, economic, political, and historical context, and on the other to transform repressive institutions and social practices by encouraging individual and collective struggle.[50]

Unlike other troubled individuals who achieve empowerment, such as those experiencing poverty, our respondents did not unite with other alcohol- or drug-dependent people around activities that promoted their interests in natural recovery, nor did they necessarily place their dependencies within a broader political context. In fact, unlike treatment participants, they were rather secretive about their former problems during the course of their recovery. However, we believe that their deliberate avoidance of treatment in the face of the widespread treatment imperative promulgated by the drug-treatment industry and their ability to maintain a normalized identity in a society intent on demonizing use, let alone abuse, represent political acts of empowerment. Their natural recoveries were individual acts of defiance against the status quo. Though the collective sociopolitical element of empowerment might be less salient in natural recovery, it is not altogether absent. Thus, from this perspective self-recovery can foster individual empowerment, leading to increased involvement in and engagement with one's own natural communities.[51]

Implications for Treatment Strategies

As pointed out earlier in this chapter, not every dependent person is a good candidate for natural recovery. However, those who decide to enter treatment for alcohol and drug dependencies can benefit from this examination of the phenomenon. For counselors, therapists, or others working directly with individuals in treatment settings, there are a number of important implications suggested by self-recovery. First, practitioners must understand that people have been overcoming substance-use problems without treatment long before formal treatment and self-help groups ever existed. And as demonstrated in the discussion of the prevalence of untreated recovery, self-recovery continues to be widespread despite the availability of treatment. The fact that we are promoting the recognition of this phenomenon does not imply that we feel treatment is unnecessary. On the contrary, we agree that our drug-war resources should be redirected to increased funding for effective treatment and prevention.

An understanding of natural recovery can help practitioners in their practices by allowing them to compare the strategies for change that they employ with their clients with the processes of change described by self-remitters. This might be especially useful since our respondents' narratives suggest that many of their recovery strategies correspond with what actually occurs in effective treatment. Practitioners might consider incorporating the strategies of self-remitters into their practice with alcohol- and drug-dependent clients. As discussed in chapter 3, the variety of cessation strategies our respondents used to overcome their dependencies clustered around three general areas. These were: alternative activities, relationships, and avoidance techniques. Specifically, they included becoming deeply immersed in gratifying alternative activities, renewing or cultivating meaningful relationships with nonusing friends and family members, and avoiding or severing relationships with users and related networks. Our respondents' success in applying these general strategies suggests that practitioners would be well-advised to consider them when they develop treatment plans with their clients. Since these change strategies have been discussed elsewhere, many practitioners are already aware of their significance.[52] Nonetheless, the prominence of these strategies in our research and the research of others leads us to advocate their inclusion in practice.

A distinct strategy identified in chapter 3 that warrants special attention in this section is the conversion experience. The concept of conversion captures the experience of many of our respondents as they transformed their lives, and holds enormous promise for those who undergo treatment. To reiterate, a conversion experience refers to a powerful personal experience wherein a person undergoes a radical transformation in identity by becoming deeply immersed in activities that create new meaning in life and a reorientation toward it. Becoming deeply involved in spiritual beliefs and activities or, as in the case of numerous formerly drug-dependent African-Americans, joining the Nation of Islam would represent conversion experiences. Interestingly, the religious conversions experienced by our self-remitters were similar to those who become devout members of 12-step groups. A number of respondents from our study offer compelling examples of such conversion experiences.

However, as our respondents demonstrate, conversions do not have to be religious in nature. Becoming deeply involved in physical fitness or immersed in a new social role as a college student can produce a similar type of conversion experience. This suggests two important considerations to practitioners: first, that the conversion experience can be a key intervention strategy when working with drug-dependent clients and second, that a wide range of situations can serve as conversion experiences (not merely religious ones as suggested in self-help ideology) and should be explored with the client. Of course, to be effective treatment must be tailored to the individual circumstances of the client and thus the appropriateness of the conversion experience would vary from client to client.

Implications for Brief Intervention

Perhaps one of the most important treatment implications to emerge from our study lies in the potential utility of a practice approach that has come to be known as brief intervention. Nick Heather of the Centre for Alcohol and Drug Studies in England writes that over the past few years, "the topic of brief interventions has attracted a great deal of attention."[53] Known also as minimal intervention, the general concept can be summarized as follows: feedback of risk, personal responsibility, clear advice, a menu of change options, empathy, and enhancement of self-efficacy.[54] The principles of brief intervention in the context of dependency treatment suggest that employing the least intrusive treatment techniques possible in the least restrictive settings can render effective client outcomes.[55] While some alcohol- and drug-dependent people may benefit from long-term treatment regimes such as therapeutic communities, extensive outpatient services, or numerous years of participation in AA, advocates of brief intervention maintain that significant numbers of people overcome addictions with short-term, minimal interventions.[56] Indeed, long-term treatment of addiction is not a prerequisite for successful recovery. Realizing this, some supporters of brief intervention have suggested implementing such initiatives on a widespread basis. As Bien and his colleagues write, "[T]hough our knowledge is far from complete, there is sufficient evidence to warrant the implementation of brief interventions in a variety of settings."[57] A close examination of the profiles of those who have solved alcohol and drug problems on their own can aid the process of identifying likely candidates for brief intervention. Conversely, such an examination could also produce an insight into those who, because of the absence of certain qualities, might be poor candidates for brief treatment intervention.

Generally, brief intervention is a term used to describe treatment techniques that are of short duration and intensity.[58] Its form can range from providing reading materials about the potential problems of intoxicant use[59] to actual face-to-face contact between a dependent person and a professional who specializes in brief intervention treatment. Because of its shortened time frame compared with other forms of treatment, it is not surprising that brief interventions are gaining recognition, given the increasing concerns in insurance companies and managed care settings over the apparent runaway costs of treatment. Indeed, as the cost of treatment has escalated sharply over the years, such cost-effective options have become increasingly attractive. Brief intervention has attracted international attention and has gained strong support for its efficacy in moderating alcohol intake among problem drinkers and mitigating related problems.[60]

Thus far, most of the research on brief intervention has focused predominantly on problem drinkers with a lower severity of intoxicant use.[61] While some have serious concerns about the utility of brief intervention approaches for severely dependent people,[62] the experiences of the self-remitters in our study suggest that this type of intervention could be promising for a wide variety of users. However, the success of such minimal interventions may depend on identifying those who, because of their personal and social characteristics, are most likely to respond to brief intervention. In this regard, our respondents may provide useful instruction. For example, all our respondents possessed a fair degree of social stability despite their excessive and dependent use. All but two of our respondents had graduated from high school or held GEDs, and many had college and graduate degrees. Most were employed or owned their own businesses for significant periods during their dependencies and also held fairly conventional values about work, family life, relationships, and personal fulfillment. Understanding the role such resources play in recovery efforts is instructive in discerning who may best respond to brief interventions. Indeed, it is likely that people possessing the characteristics of the self-remitters whose experiences we have documented in this book would be good candidates for brief interventions.

Such interventions might take the form of several educational counseling sessions or short consciousness-raising sessions that focus on the effective strategies used by other self-healers. In the appendix of this book, we present a thorough discussion of the self-recovery strategies that can be introduced and explored in a brief intervention context. While there are numerous brief intervention options, one of the most critical phases in any brief intervention process is the assessment period. If it is determined during an assessment that a person is not motivated to change, it is important to realize that possessing social stability, resources, and conventional values may do little to bring about change. However, having these attributes can increase one's motivation to change. Conversely, if the desire to change is not accompanied by social stability, the appropriate resources, and a stake in conventional life the positive outcome is likely to be limited. All this suggests that treatment professionals working with alcohol- and drug-dependent clients must identify the resources, namely, the social, human, and physical capital that their clients can draw upon to support their recovery. Given the importance of these factors in the lives of self-remitters, it is critical that practitioners focus on the broader "recovery capital" of their clients.

Recovery Capital and Treatment

While much has been written about the advantages of brief or minimal intervention, there has been little discussion among practitioners of the contextual factors that seem to influence successful treatment outcomes. As we have demonstrated throughout this book, a person's structural location in society and the relationships, networks, and other assets that adhere to one's social position greatly affect one's chances for recovery. In some ways, the intensity of intoxicant use may be less important in overcoming dependency than the contextual factors that surround addiction in a person's life. In fact, all the people described in this book were severely dependent on the substances they consumed. Unfortunately, in many disease-based treatment circles the contextuality of use and recovery is overlooked in favor of the use itself, isolated from its social embeddedness.

Attention to the social context of use and recovery naturally draws our attention to the various assets that individuals possess that can be drawn upon to facilitate recovery. As we have seen in this study and in others, such assets are critically important in understanding use, dependency, and recovery. These assets—or what some social scientists refer to as forms of social, physical, and human capital—can be drawn upon to support recovery. This capital, which we collectively refer to as recovery capital, represents critical elements that an individual possesses or that exist within his or her immediate surroundings and that function to promote and sustain a recovery experience.

The term recovery capital is consistent with the work of social scientists who have examined the function of certain resources and relationships in specific social structures.[63] Recovery capital is used here to refer to the sum total of one's resources that can be brought to bear in an effort to overcome alcohol and drug dependency. It is embodied in a number of tangible and intangible resources and relationships, including those that existed prior to a person's drug involvement, during the period of drug use, and conditions likely to prevail in the future. It encompasses attitudes and beliefs that one has toward the past, present, and the future. It also includes one's mental status and other personal characteristics that can be drawn upon to resolve a dependency problem.

As employed here, the term recovery capital refers to the convergence of resources subsumed under three major classes of capital: social, physical, and human. James Coleman distinguishes between these three classes in the following way:

> Social capital . . . is created when relations among persons change in ways that facilitate action. Physical capital is wholly tangible, being embodied in observable material form; human capital is less tangible, being embodied in the skills and knowledge acquired by an individual; social capital is even less tangible, for it is embodied in the *relations* among persons. (Emphasis in original)[64]

Recall that in the previous chapter we offered an extensive discussion of the importance of social capital to the recovery of our respondents. To reiterate, their social capital consisted of the resources developed and available to them through the structure and reciprocal functions of social relationships within which they were embedded, that assisted them in their recovery. As we illustrated, our respondents' social capital facilitated a fairly intangible but nonetheless effective bond to family, community, and social institutions. Because social capital is a resource, like other resources it can be used to facilitate actions taken in one's own interests.[65] For example, it can take the form of favors owed to you, access to particular information and situations, emotional support, expectations others have of you that foster attainment of goals, preferential treatment by others, and trust by others, to name a few. As we demonstrated in the previous chapter, a person attempting to overcome an addiction would be drawing on his or her social capital when responding to the confidence reposed in him or her and the expectations of others. Similarly, if the person's drug use or recovery effort had caused him or her to lose employment, his or her social capital might be used to expedite access to other employment options.

Of the three concepts—social capital, physical capital, and human capital—social capital is the most elusive. Physical and human capital are somewhat easier to grasp. As Coleman states, physical capital is tangible.[66] It is reflected in the material resources available to someone and can be experienced by the senses. Money, property, automobiles, and the like are straight-forward examples of physical capital. This form of capital plays "a central role in establishing and maintaining economic relations."[67] Whether people overcoming addictions remit on their own or undergo formal treatment they are at a distinct advantage if they have access to physical capital. In fact, physical capital can facilitate access to drug treatment programs. For those pursuing a path of recovery without treatment, access to physical capital makes a variety of recovery strategies possible, including those identified by our respondents and discussed in the previous chapter. For example, if a person feels the need to extricate him or herself from drug-using family members, friends, or networks, access to physical capital will increase the opportunity to do so. For those who feel they need to enroll in formal treatment, access to physical capital such as insurance and/or adequate sums of money can give them treatment options that the lack of physical capital would preclude. Unfortunately, in some communities where there are long waiting lists at public treatment programs, the absence of physical capital results in no treatment at all, other than participation in traditional self-help groups.

Human capital generally refers to the knowledge, skills, and other personal attributes that can be used to achieve one's desired goals.[68] Possessing a college degree, having vocational skills, or possessing knowledge and understanding that can be drawn upon to negotiate personal difficulties are all examples of human capital. In the context of our discussion of natural recovery, human capital can be viewed as all the personal characteristics an individual possesses that can be used to combat a problem with addiction. Having ample human capital can prevent people from becoming overly immersed in a drug subculture with its attendant aberrant values and related criminal activity.[69] It provides people with the resources needed to successfully negotiate conventional life. As Faupel found among the heroin users he studied, those who possessed adequate human capital, namely, had stable occupational lives and skills that they could capitalize on, were less likely to become ensconced in the underworld of a drug subculture.[70] Whether one is attempting to arrest a dependency problem with or without treatment, the presence or absence of marketable employment skills, interpersonal skills, emotional stability, and other human capital resources can be instrumental to successful recovery. In fact, among the host of obstacles to recovery faced by urban minorities, the lack of employment skills, that is, human capital, represents one of the major barriers to achieving stability.[71] Thus, human capital in its various forms plays an important role in achieving the kinds of metamorphoses needed to carve out new lives without drugs.

A form of human capital that warrants special attention when examining addiction is mental health. There are a number of apparent and not so apparent reasons for the nexus between mental status and drug dependency. Diminished or impaired cognitive capacities, emotional instability, depression, persistent impulsiveness, and a vast array of other compromised mental health states can thwart the best recovery efforts.[72] It is estimated that mental health problems are at the core of a number of alcohol- and drug-dependency problems.[73] Mental health problems can be the cause or the result of dependency. Intoxicant-induced conditions can range from the mild and temporary, such as the irritability associated with withdrawal conditions, to the acute and inveterate, characterized by chronic organic brain syndrome. On the other hand, reasonably good mental health with its attendant characteristics such as self-awareness, self-esteem, internal locus of control, and a positive outlook on life, for example, represent critical forms of capital that should be considered when planning a recovery effort.

The major point of this discussion as it relates to treatment services is that people can draw on a variety of different types of resources to facilitate overcoming addiction. As suggested by this study and others, recovery capital is differentially distributed among alcohol- and drug-dependent people. Those who overcome their drug dependencies without treatment, or with only brief interventions, may possess more of this capital than those who are involved in treatment.[74]

The crucial point for practitioners working with substance-dependent clients to remember is that those who possess large amounts of recovery capital—perhaps even independent of the intensity of use—will be likely candidates for less intrusive forms of treatment such as those associated with brief intervention and natural recovery. Conversely, the lower the individual's recovery capital the greater may be the need for more intrusive forms of treatment. Longer periods of treatment may be required to build up the kind of recovery capital needed to overcome dependency. In fact, effective treatment should be directed at enhancing clients' available recovery capital or helping them establish it. This relationship between recovery capital and the treatment needed is the principal rationale for suggesting to practitioners who are not already doing so that they view treatment on a continuum from least intrusive to most intrusive.[75] While recovery without treatment is clearly the least intrusive of all possible options and has numerous advantages, particularly for those who have a good supply of recovery capital, brief intervention comports well with the concept of natural recovery and should be considered by treatment professionals as a viable option for many who are struggling with addiction.

Recent work on recovery without treatment as well as our own research suggests that intensive treatment might be better directed toward people with the least amount of recovery capital. Similarly, people with high levels of recovery capital might not need as many resources expended on their treatments. The potential merits of this position are obvious when one realizes that the principal function of most treatment is to actually provide or help people create their own recovery capital. Whether treatment includes educational classes, group meetings that create new networks and relationships, job training, or temporary housing services in public treatment facilities away from the drug scene, effective treatment produces and expands recovery capital.

There are currently no assessment instruments to identify resources conceptualized as recovery capital. Nonetheless, practitioners can determine the level of recovery capital available to their clients by using current assessment skills. In our view, an assessment for recovery capital should be part of routine assessment procedures, in conjunction with an assessment for those conditions that encroach upon one's recovery capital or otherwise undermine one's ability to draw upon it. We will refer to the conditions that impinge on one's recovery capital or ability to use it as threats to recovery capital. In the next section we explore these threats and further examine the role of recovery capital in facilitating effective self-change.

Threats to Recovery Capital

While the results of this and other studies suggest that people who overcome addiction without treatment tend to possess fair amounts of recovery capital, unquestionably many people who have such resources continue to be plagued with problems. Their persisting addictions in spite of the advantages that their recovery capital creates for them suggests that there are other compelling factors at play that continue to make people vulnerable to drug dependence. While most of our respondents were able to quit on their first try, some were only able to quit after a few attempts. Thus, self-remitters as well as those in treatment frequently remain vulnerable during their attempts to terminate use.

Among the many possible reasons why people remain vulnerable is the lack of motivation to quit, which might be interpreted as a critical gap in recovery capital. The important point for practitioners to understand is that recovery capital is not a fixed set of traits that individuals possess. Rather, it is a continuous operating loop of resources available to people, but in different configurations and different amounts.[76] Practitioners have no one formula of recovery capital to rely upon to assist them in their clients' recovery process. One person's recovery capital may facilitate recovery, while the same amount of capital may be insufficient to produce a change in another person. The point is that recovery capital, while composed of human, social, and physical capital, is itself deeply contextual and therefore individual-specific. For example, a substance-dependent person could have substantial recovery capital, but may find it difficult to succeed because he or she maintains primary relationships with people who are drug dependent and continues to be exposed to using opportunities. Similarly, a drug-dependent person who has an equivalent amount of recovery capital might find it nearly impossible to stay clean because he or she continues to self-medicate an unrecognized underlying psychological condition.

The concept of threats to recovery capital resembles the notion of risk factors associated with relapse. Over the years, there has been a considerable amount of work on relapse and the precipitating conditions associated with it.[77] Before initiating this discussion of relapse, however, we want the reader to know that, given the kinds of concerns we have regarding the reifying properties of the language used in the addiction field, the term relapse gives us pause. The conventional use of the term generally ignores the various means by which people reduce their intoxicant-use problems and subverts growing recognition of the psychosocial explanation of drug dependence.[78] Webster's *New Collegiate Dictionary* associates relapse with recurrence of a disease after a period of improvement. For many treatment professionals, the term relapse generally conveys similar disease-based imagery. A more contextualized understanding of relapse, one that is consistent with the concept of recovery capital, would be more useful in understanding why some have difficulty in overcoming dependency. For example, Alan Marlatt and his colleagues as well as Helen Annis and her colleagues take a social cognitive approach to relapse which does not necessarily invoke disease imagery.[79]

What are some of the conditions that might threaten the recovery effort of an alcohol- or drug-dependent person? Cummings, Gordon, and Marlatt, and Marlatt and Gordon focus on high-risk situations that interfere with the creation, maintenance, or implementation of recovery.[80] They assert that most relapses are associated with one of three types of situations: negative emotions, interpersonal conflict, or social pressure. Following on Marlatt and his colleagues' early groundbreaking work on relapse, Daley states that high-risk factors fall into two categories. There are internal factors such as negative thoughts, feelings, desires, or urges and cravings, and external factors such as relationships, events, activities, places, and material possessions.[81]

Gorski's approach to identifying high-risk situations is individualized, being contingent upon the individual histories of dependent people.[82] His technique for identifying those conditions is to take a personal intoxicant-use history and a recovery and relapse history to identify high-risk situations that can lead to relapse. Annis, like many others, draws heavily on the work of

Marlatt and his associates.[83] Interestingly, much of her work examines the relationship between self-efficacy and relapse prevention. Recall that one of the advantages of people resolving their alcohol and drug problems on their own appears to be the building of self-efficacy. In some cases, the work on relapse prevention has led to the development of assessment instruments to help identify relapse potential. One such instrument is Annis's *Inventory of Drinking Situations* that assesses a variety of attributes such as unpleasant emotions, physical discomfort, positive emotions, testing personal control, urge/temptation to drink, conflict with others, social pressure to drink, and personal relationships.[84]

While the concept of relapse prevention is a valuable one, it does not adequately capture threats to recovery capital as we conceptualize them. Although the relapse literature acknowledges the importance of social context, it places most of its emphasis on psychological factors affecting people independently of their social structural foundations. In our view, however, social context is always an important consideration. For instance, in their recent study of youth crime, sociologists John Hagan and Bill McCarthy highlight the critical importance of social capital in the lives of young people.[85] They found that homeless and criminal youth came from families with diminished social capital. Additionally, since communities have social capital as well as individuals, Hagan and McCarthy found that youth crime was differentiated across distinct community settings. Communities that provided few resources or support services for youth tended to experience higher rates of youth crime. These youth were more likely to be in possession of criminal capital stemming from their embeddedness in street life.[86]

The point is that emotional states that are conducive to wellness and conformity are never independent of the contextual settings in which people live. While emotional states have generally been relegated to the realm of psychology, it is critical to point out that emotion is fundamentally a social process that must be considered alongside the social contexts in which people find themselves.[87] Emotion is the individual response to a host of social and cultural conditions which an individual experiences as part of his or her daily life. Consequently, the psychological disposition associated with relapse cannot be thought of in isolation from the social context surrounding an individual in the stages of recovery.

Because we recognize the importance of social context we prefer the concept of recovery capital to that of relapse prevention. As suggested by our respondents, lack of access to recovery capital, whether physical, human, or social, poses significant barriers to one's eventual recovery. As numerous sociologists have demonstrated over the years, recovery is often "raced," "gendered," and "classed." That is, the intersection of these variables often mediates one's ability to avoid and overcome alcohol and drug problems.[88] The social context of dependency and recovery must be taken into account when determining the ongoing treatment needs of those combating addiction. Just as Hagan and McCarthy found that the emotional well-being of youth was influenced by their access to social capital,[89] so too should treatment professionals learn to appreciate the relationship between recovery capital and the emotional well-being of addicts. Developing a contextual understanding of recovery could go a long way toward better differentiating between those needing minimal services and those requiring more intensive services. In the long run, a contextual focus on recovery and efforts by treatment professionals to either utilize the already existing recovery capital of an individual or to build new recovery capital could lead to improvements in treatment services.

Conclusion

Recovery from severe alcohol and drug dependencies without undergoing treatment is a widespread phenomenon that has for the most part been overlooked by treatment practitioners. For years, the treatment industry has promulgated the belief that overcoming an alcohol and drug problem requires extensive treatment. The experiences of the people interviewed for this study, as well as those of self-remitters in other studies, challenge these claims regarding the necessity of treatment. As the narratives of our respondents demonstrate, the decision to resolve their alcohol and drug problems on their own has been to our respondents' advantage in profound ways, ways that many of them may never fully realize. Because of their success in terminating their dependencies, they offer valuable insights for professionals working in the field of dependency treatment.

The processes of natural recovery as identified here and elsewhere are not, as some might believe, antithetical to treatment.[90] As this chapter has shown, there are a number of advantages associated with self-recovery; we have also sought to examine the implications these advantages have for practitioners. We examined the ways in which practitioners might benefit from a better understanding of those who have recovered from dependencies without treatment. Among the current treatment options, brief intervention comes the closest to employing the lessons of natural recovery. Such approaches may be particularly appropriate for those who possess a high degree of recovery capital. Access to and availability of recovery capital could be a critical consideration for practitioners' ability to determine who would likely be good candidates for brief treatment interventions.

Treatment programs of all kinds may be more successful if they incorporate the experiences of self-remitters into their practice.[91] The concept of recovery capital offers treatment providers a broader conceptualization of dependent people. All too often treatment professionals see alcohol- or drug-dependent people in stereotypic ways. The concept of recovery capital significantly challenges the overly medicalized views of addiction and recovery and offers a corrective to the essentialist claims offered by the treatment industry. Social structures and cultural values have a significant influence over the recovery experiences of individuals. As Biernacki points out, "a white, middle-class, high-school educated, male addict will have more personal and social resources to draw from when he decides to give up drugs than will a Chicano addict living in a barrio."[92] In the first scenario, recovery capital is high, while in the second it would undoubtedly be low. Treatment professionals, although cognizant of the contextual nature of recovery, often fall prey to overtly disease-based explanations that often disregard structural explanations. By building upon the factors that create recovery capital, factors that were present in the lives of the self-remitters we studied, treatment professionals may increase their levels of success. Furthermore, such a focus might also lead to the creation of a range of differentiated services while simultaneously reducing the costs associated with treatment.

This chapter has focused primarily on the treatment implications associated with natural recovery. The final chapter of this book broadens the scope of our analysis by exploring the implications natural recovery has for prevention and drug policy. In it, we also examine more general questions regarding the current state of social life in postindustrial America and the implications and challenges this life poses for natural recovery from addiction.

Chapter Seven

CONCLUSION

Addiction, Society, and Social Policy

In this book, we have sought to accomplish several objectives. By exploring the social lives of individuals who have recovered from alcohol and drug addictions without treatment, we have tried to highlight the role social context plays in facilitating recovery without treatment. Our central aim has been to examine the personal, interactional, and structural dimensions of our respondents' natural recovery experiences as well as to illuminate some of the treatment implications that follow from them. More specifically, we have crafted a sociological analysis of the natural recovery process that focuses on the social and interactional nature of self-remission from addiction. In doing so, we have added to the understanding of natural recovery in the following ways: (1) by paying close attention to the social context of recovery without treatment, we have demonstrated how the reactions of others and the social networks in which individuals find themselves facilitate the natural recovery process; (2) by examining both alcohol- and drug-dependent people together, we have been able to identify some of the similarities and differences in the natural recovery process across different substances; (3) we have highlighted some of the parallels between natural recovery and conventional approaches to addiction treatment; and (4) we have suggested some of the benefits of natural recovery, identified those for whom it might be particularly appropriate, and explored the implications natural recovery has for the treatment world.

In this concluding chapter, we turn our attention to the broader theoretical and policy-based contributions suggested by this study. We begin by examining general theories of the self, particularly as they relate to addiction and self-change. We then move to a discussion of the implications natural recovery has for prevention, drug control strategies, and for the broader dimensions of social and cultural life. It should be pointed out that since our sample of self-remitters probably does not represent the larger natural recovery population, our conclusions are speculative. However, while this data lacks the breadth of larger statistically based investigations, like other qualitative studies its strength lies in its ability to capture the deeper meaning and context of human experience. Because of the depth associated with qualitative studies like this one, consideration of broader implications is a legitimate and valuable exercise.

Recovery, Identity, and Society

Throughout the preceding chapters we have illustrated the social and psychological processes that contribute to the addictive use of intoxicants as well as those associated with natural recovery from addiction. In our interviews we found that addiction emerges out of a search for everyday meaning and social connectedness. Our respondents did not commence their substance-using careers as full-blown addicts. Rather, their addictions occurred over a lengthy period of time during which they sought to find meaning, pleasure, and satisfaction from the substances they used. Whether it was to seek hedonistic pleasure or to escape personal discomfort, the excessive use of substances served a positive function for all our respondents, if only temporarily.

Interestingly, this search for meaning ultimately assisted our respondents in overcoming their addictions without treatment. After experiencing a series of stressful, crisis-provoking events, our respondents successfully overcame their addictive patterns of alcohol and drug use. Their ability to terminate these powerful addictions was intimately related to their capacity to develop deep personal commitments to conventional roles. These roles and their attendant social identities facilitated a profound change in our respondents' belief structures and behaviors that were fundamentally incompatible with the frequent and heavy use of substances. At critical junctures in their addictive careers, they were able to immerse themselves thoroughly in satisfying social roles associated with work, family, and community.

While there were many similarities between the alcohol-dependent individuals and the drug-dependent ones we interviewed with regard to the natural recovery process, there were some important distinctions as well. Among the formerly drug addicted, there was a much greater tendency to physically leave the geographical areas in which they resided as a way of breaking their drug habits than among those experiencing alcohol problems. Many former drug addicts spoke of an urgency to break away from their drug-using networks. This urge to put some distance between themselves and their drug-using networks—a finding supported by other research—may suggest that the social networks surrounding the subculture of drug use provides a greater compulsion to use than the networks associated with excessive alcohol use.[1] Because alcohol use is a legal activity and therefore not as forbidden, the need for physical distancing may not be as great for the cessation of alcohol addiction.

As we have demonstrated, the discontinuation of addiction among those we interviewed did not occur, as some of them seemed to believe, solely as a result of their own psychological will to change. Rather, much of the impetus and motivation to change was associated with "conditioning factors" in their social environments that supported their desired change.[2] The process of change, as demonstrated by our respondents, rarely occurs in isolation. Instead, personal transformation is a social product that is greatly influenced by the situational social contexts in which an individual is located. The social relations that surrounded and enveloped our respondents facilitated their natural recovery from addiction. Their motivations, cessation strategies, opportunities to change, and their ultimate success at accomplishing a natural recovery were largely a product of their social interactions with others. This axiomatic sociological principle has important implications for the way we think about addiction and recovery.

One of the most significant findings presented in this book, and one supported by previous work by Biernacki, concerns the nature of our respondents' identities as they relate to their addiction.[3] For the most part, they—and particularly those who were former drug addicts—refused to identify themselves as addicts despite their obvious addictions and related problems. Although those experiencing alcohol problems tended to identify themselves as addicted more often than did respondents with drug problems, the overwhelming majority refrained from identifying themselves through a disease narrative. At no time during their period of addiction did they become deeply immersed in an addict lifestyle or develop a commitment to the role of an addict. As we have pointed out throughout this book, while our respondents experienced considerable personal and interpersonal turmoil, they rarely "hit bottom" in the classic sense or came to define themselves "essentially" as alcoholics or "dopefiends."

The data we report regarding our respondents' tendency to eschew an addict identity and gravitate toward conventional social roles whose competent discharge was incompatible with the excessive use of intoxicants can be further illuminated by what sociologists describe as role identity theory. For many years, sociologists, particularly symbolic interactionists influenced by the early writings of Cooley and Mead, have sought to elucidate the distinctive components of the self.[4] Interactionists, for whom the self is an important concept, conceive of the self principally as a social object formed in the field of actual experience.[5]

At its core, role identity theory views the self as both a social product and a social process.[6] As both product and process, the self carries with it shared social meanings and "reflected appraisals"[7] or the judgment of others. It also possesses the ability to actively and creatively make adjustments in and otherwise manage the "presentation of self" to others.[8] Social psychologists such as Sheldon Stryker view the self as being composed of distinct identities that are associated with the many roles people occupy in society.[9] Accordingly, a person's self is made up of a multiple set of hierarchically assembled role identities, some of which the individual considers more important or salient than the others.[10] From this perspective, differences in behavior stem from variations in the salience ordering that people assign to their identity.[11] For instance, some may place the identity associated with being a parent above that of being a worker[12] while others, by contrast, may do the reverse.[13] Thus, a person's self is always contingent on the patterned constellation of role identities assembled by him or her.

The ordering of identity salience, however, is not simply a psychological artifact unrelated to an individual's social setting and network of social relationships. Any particular ordering of role identities ultimately has much to do with social context. The level of a person's commitment to any role is greatly affected by the perceptions and evaluation of others.[14] Commitment to a particular identity is high to the degree that an individual perceives that many of his or her important social relationships are predicated on the occupancy of a given role.[15] As role theorists have asserted, the ability to commit to a stable identity or set of identities is mediated by the sum total of social forces, pressures, and drives that influence people to maintain a congruence between their identities and the judgments or "reflected appraisals" of others.[16] Connection and ties to others as well as the support provided by role partners give people the incentive to commit to particular role identities. Thus, the more strongly people are associated with particular roles, the more likely they will experience a high level of commitment to that role. The analysis of commitment levels is certainly relevant to this discussion of addiction and recovery, for as Richard Stephens asserts, "the greater the degree of commitment to the street addict role, the greater will be the extent of heroin use."[17]

The experiences of our respondents, who have terminated their excessive use of substances, are illuminated by the sociological tenets of role theory. As we have seen, our respondents discontinued their addicted use of substances in large part because they were able to commit to more conventional identities. This supports Stephens's assertion that the more role strain and conflict addicts experience, the more likely they are to attempt to come clean.[18] Our respondents' ability to do so provided them with a source of motivation to change their patterns of substance use. Motivation for change, as previous research has consistently demonstrated, is a critical dimension to any recovery effort.[19] In fact, one treatment approach known as "motivational enhancement therapy" seeks first and foremost to increase an addicted person's desire to change. This technique generally encourages alcohol and drug users to compare the consequences of their excessive use with their core personal values. When the mismatch between use and values is great, users often develop their own impetus to change.[20]

Consistent with the sociological insights of role theory, however, motivation to change, like all emotional responses, must be understood within its broader social and cultural context. It is not merely a psychological quality of mind. Rather, it is a social product rooted in the communities in which people find themselves.[21] The motivation to change, as in the efforts of our respondents to discontinue their excessive use of substances, occurs in response to the social forces and pressures to establish and maintain a balance between their identities and the evaluations of their identities by others. Our respondents were able to recover despite their circumvention of treatment largely because they were motivated to commit to a role identity that they deemed incompatible with the excessive use of substances. Additionally, they were able to achieve a degree of congruence between this conventional identity and the reflected appraisals of others. Thus, the social capital to which they had access and the networks in which they were embedded facilitated their commitment to conventional role identities, thereby making their natural recovery possible.

While the recovery experiences of our respondents may be understood in relation to the social psychological principles of role theory, it is important to point out that they all had opportunities to commit to meaningful roles that distanced them from the excessive use of intoxicants. As we discussed earlier, all our respondents reported having stable working-class or middle-class backgrounds prior to their addictive use. For the most part, all were able to maintain a fairly stable lifestyle during their addictive years in spite of the numerous social, physical, and financial problems they encountered. They also had the opportunity to enhance their social and human capital that gave them increased access to meaningful roles. Thus, their capacity to recover without treatment was enhanced by the personal and social assets they brought with them into their addictions. These assets and attributes provided them with fairly stable and supportive relationships, employment and job skills, relatively high levels of education, and conventional values, all of which made them perfect candidates for successful recovery even without treatment. As research has consistently pointed out, "people who are married, hold down jobs, and have stable lives have by far the best chance for overcoming alcohol [and drug] problems."[22]

The experiences of our respondents and our analytic conclusions based on these experiences illustrate the value of a sociological perspective on natural recovery. Our analysis of the natural recovery experience highlights the connections between the substance used, the person, and the environment. Addiction and recovery are much more than a biological or a psychological phenomenon. They are also inherently social. All too often this social dimension of the addiction and recovery experience receives too little attention. However, as Zinberg has shown, it is the interaction between the substance, the person, *and* the social setting that contributes to addiction, and as we have argued, to recovery as well.[23]

Because our respondents recovered from their addictions without treatment, they illustrate the importance of understanding this relationship. What mattered for these respondents was their embeddedness within social life, their ability to maintain some level of stability, their values and expectations, their access to social resources and social capital, their relationships, and, of course, their opportunities to forge conventional role identities that were productive, rewarding, and satisfying.[24] The experiences of our respondents and the analysis we have woven together in this book underscore the critical sociological insight into the relationship between the individual and society. In addition, they have also illuminated the processes of natural recovery. These processes have important implications for prevention, drug policy, and the organization of social life more generally. It is to this discussion that we now turn.

Does Prevention Work?

The current mantra of substance-abuse prevention professionals is that "prevention works." Unfortunately, some of the most popular prevention programs have been unable to live up to this lofty standard. Over the years, substance-abuse prevention has been profoundly ideological.[25] The history of alcohol- and drug-prevention efforts has been marred by a prohibitionist ideology that typically has demonized the use of mind-altering substances. Prevention efforts have usually been more preoccupied with the substances people consume than with the actual circumstances of their use. From the inception of Scientific Temperance in 1902 (an alcohol-education program developed by the Women's Christian Temperance Union) to the contemporary drug war-inspired "Just Say No" campaigns of the 1980s and 1990s, a good deal of prevention rhetoric has propagated a shallow moralism about the "evils" of substance use. Frequently, this moralistic rhetoric has fallaciously equated use with abuse, a position that has had more to do with political and ideological expediency than with scientific fact. Not only are such programs often ineffective, but they may even be dangerous in that they impede deeper exploration of and investment in effective prevention, and lead to counterproductive results. At best, traditional prevention strategies "convert the converted" and at worst, actually encourage use.[26]

One of the most pervasive and popular prevention programs in the country is the Drug Abuse Resistance Education program, better known as Project DARE. Created in 1983 by the Los Angeles Police Department, DARE uses uniformed law enforcement officers to teach an antidrug curriculum that "seeks to shape students' attitudes and social skills so that they will be able to resist peer and media pressures to try drugs."[27] Since its inception, DARE has been adopted by nearly 70 percent of public schools nationwide.[28] Notwithstanding its immense popularity, scientific evaluations of DARE programs generally have not been favorable. While DARE may increase adolescents' knowledge about drugs and favorable attitudes toward police, research studies have found little reliable scientific evidence to indicate that these popular programs have been successful at preventing substance use or abuse.[29]

The impact of DARE is not unlike other discredited "scare tactic" or moralistic approaches that have traditionally produced increases in knowledge without corresponding changes in attitudes or behavior.[30] In fact such approaches may be counterproductive in terms of the stated goals of prevention. Some recent evaluations of DARE programs have reported that participants experience an *increase* in their use of various substances. In a six-year study of a DARE program in Illinois, Dennis Rosenbaum, head of the criminal justice department at the University of Illinois, found that not only did DARE fail to significantly reduce drug use among participants, but it actually led to higher levels of drug use than among nonparticipants. Concern about the ineffectiveness of such programs as well as their excessive cost has led many cities, including Houston, Oakland, Omaha, and Spokane to discontinue DARE. Recently, several cities in Colorado, including Boulder, have "given DARE the boot."[31]

However, DARE remains popular despite the lack of significant outcomes related to substance use or related targets such as social skills or self-esteem, and despite the exorbitant costs of such efforts, which in 1993 were estimated to be $700 million annually. In fact, one of the most prominent achievements of DARE programs has been in public relations. In addition to its abstinence-based curriculum, DARE sponsors high-profile "drug-free" events in cities across the country, encourages children to report friends or parents who are using drugs, and has a growing presence on the Internet. Overall, the symbolic capital of DARE programs as a "drug war" initiative has substantially outpaced any demonstrable positive effects in reducing substance use or related risk factors.

One of the greatest limitations of DARE and educational programs like it is the failure to see that the use of substances is a meaningful social activity for users that can never be understood solely in individual terms. Traditional prevention programs have turned a blind eye to the purposeful aspects of substance use. Such programs typically portrayed drug users as diseased, irrational, and degenerate souls who are to be feared and rejected. DARE and programs like it simply deny the fact that experimentation with substances and other types of risk-taking behaviors is normative for adolescents. The denial of this fact, as well as of the fact that most users derive social benefits from the substances they use, has no doubt led many young people to reject the moralistic exhortations of these programs that masquerade as fact. Such "prophylactic lies," as in the infamous television spot "This is your brain on drugs" in which an egg sizzling in a pan is used as a metaphor for the effect of drugs on the human brain, may actually do more harm than good.[32] Indeed, the militancy of such antidrug messages can foster resistance to such evidently false and distorted messages among young people "who often know better" and help tear down restraints against use.

Although these largely symbolic prevention activities are extraordinarily popular among politicians, moral entrepreneurs, and a large contingent of the general public, they fortunately do not constitute the universe of prevention. Some of the very best prevention initiatives adopt a risk and resilience model that sees substance abuse in relation to the broader social contexts in which it occurs. Such approaches to prevention see individuals as embedded in a broad sociocultural context that influences values and practices with regard to the consumption of substances, as well as within the interpersonal and institutional environments of families, peer groups, and schools.[33] Adopting the principles of social learning[34] and social control[35] theories, these and other "scientifically based" prevention experts recognize that the use and abuse of substances occurs within a context of risk factors that are primarily associated with the extent of an individual's bonding to conventional "prosocial" groups. From this perspective, the more an individual is bonded to prosocial life within the family, peer groups, and the school, the less likely will he or she be to develop patterns of substance abuse.

Other "structural" dimensions of social life, however, mediate the building of social bonds. For instance, it is well known that conditions such as poverty, overcrowding, and social disorganization are associated with an increased risk of substance abuse. People living under such economically disadvantaged conditions tend to be characterized by "low achievement motivation and the absence of other prosocial values and involvements; social, academic, and family alienation."[36] These structural factors can often reduce an individual's commitment to conventional life, which in turn leads to an increased risk for developing drug problems.

Thus, from a risk-based perspective, efforts to increase adolescents' attachment and commitment to conventional groups, as well as their involvement and belief in related norms, expectations, and values offer the greatest potential for promoting healthy lifestyles. Efforts that seek to reduce the antecedent risks to abuse, including economic deprivation, neighborhood disorganization, norms favorable to abuse, family conflict, low bonding to family, academic failure, lack of commitment to school, social influences favorable to drug and alcohol abuse, and alienation are especially promising. Although prevention efforts that seek to minimize the effects of known risk factors may not ultimately be as flashy as high-profile programs like DARE, they nonetheless have a much greater potential for success. Indeed, prevention of alcohol and drug problems works best when it is directed at helping young people develop more substantial and enduring sources of satisfaction that can replace their search for a sense of personal value and accomplishment through self-defeating means.[37] Better scientific evaluation of such prevention efforts and harm reduction initiatives will help determine which approaches are most effective in minimizing alcohol and drug problems.

One type of activity that is concordant with the experiences of the individuals we interviewed is community-based prevention. Interestingly, some community-based youth programs that do not strictly target substance misuse, could in the long run be more effective in impeding drug and alcohol addictions, as well as a whole range of other destructive behaviors, than programs specifically designed for that purpose. One such program is the University of Denver's Bridge Project, operated by the Graduate School of Social Work. The program specifically targets youth that reside in Denver's most socially disorganized public housing projects. While the focus of the program is stated to be education, including tutoring for school-age children and full four-year scholarships to the university for deserving high school seniors, exposure to appealing prosocial influences has created core changes in many of these youths' values and expectations. In so doing, the seeds for building their stakes in conventional life are being planted and nourished through the activities in which they are involved. There is considerable mentoring and modeling of positive behaviors at various levels of the program. For example, each scholarship student is connected with a mentor who not only provides guidance to that student but also introduces him or her to activities that most of us take for granted. Such activities as going hiking in the surrounding mountains or attending a Broadway play, for example, can open a whole new world of possibilities to a poor inner-city adolescent. An added benefit of this program is that scholarship students return to the housing projects to tutor other school-aged children, thereby increasing the community's own indigenous resources.

The strength of the Bridge Project lies in its ability to improve community capacity, and in the sense of "pushing the residents and organizations of a community toward their full potential."[38] Community-based programs like this one have attempted to increase the level of social capital within a community in order to organize and mobilize the natural healing components of that community. The importance of community for promoting health and well-being, as suggested by our respondents as well as other scholars, cannot be overlooked. The political scientist Robert Putnam has postulated the empowering impact that organized communities have on citizens as follows:

> Researchers in such fields as education, urban poverty, unemployment, the control of crime and drug abuse, and even

health have discovered that successful outcomes are more likely in civically engaged communities.[39]

Such community capacity building, however, cannot occur solely through the interventions of the government or a few committed professionals. In fact, the presence of these entities may even undermine the development of community by suggesting that prevailing social problems are being attended to by professionals, without any citizen involvement.[40] As John McKnight's provocative thesis suggests, the professionalization of community care may actually and ironically "destroy the sense of community competence."[41] In short, the professionalization of care and health promotion may censor a community's own natural capacity to care for itself. Building resources within communities, increasing the amount of social capital in a community, and expanding opportunities and incentives for people to develop conventional stakes in social life may ultimately be more effective in preventing alcohol and drug problems than providing young people with information on "how to say no" to alcohol and drugs. Unlike these relatively simplistic efforts, community-based measures focus on constructive ways to give kids something to say "yes" to.

The Misguidedness of America's Drug War

In addition to the implications for substance abuse prevention strategies, particularly those designed to foster increased commitment to conventional roles, the experiences of our respondents and the related research on natural recovery also speak volumes on America's misguided drug war. The financial and human costs of the war on drugs over these many years have been exorbitant. Although America has witnessed substantial reductions in drug use since the late 1970s, such reductions have occurred in large measure despite, rather than because of, the drug war. After spending an estimated $65 billion in domestic and foreign drug enforcement from 1981 through 1994 to finance the war on drugs, America now leads the industrialized world with the highest rate of incarceration. The obsessive reliance on a punitive approach to drug control has led to numerous human rights violations in the domestic and international spheres, significant corruption and abuse of power among government officials, increased crime and health problems, and intensified racial conflict. It has also produced a general climate of intolerance that threatens to undermine long-standing democratic and constitutional principles. Given the extensive collateral damage associated with fighting the drug war it is not surprising that vocal and bipartisan opposition to its directives has emerged from various quarters. Prominent figures as different as William F. Buckley, Baltimore Mayor Kurt Schmoke, economist Milton Friedman, psychologist Thomas Szasz, biologist Stephen Jay Gould, former Surgeon General Jocelyn Elders, Hoover Institute fellow and former police chief Joseph McNamara, presidents of the American Bar Association and the American Judges Association, as well as the millions of ordinary citizens who have participated in ballot initiatives nationwide, have all called for alternatives to our current drug war mania.

While there have been many criticisms of the drug war, none have been more trenchant than those that focus on incarceration. Since 1980, the incarceration rate for drug offenders has increased eightfold, reaching an all-time high in 1997 of 400,000 people. Because of mandatory minimum sentencing laws that were implemented as part of the Anti-Drug Abuse Act of 1986, nearly 60 percent of all federal prisoners are presently incarcerated for drug law violations. Over the past decade and a half, arrests and sentencing for drug offenses have grown at an alarming rate. According to Bureau of Justice Statistics, in June 1997 the nation's prisons and jails held 1,725,842 men and women—an increase of more than 96,100 over the prior year. The increase in drug offenders has accounted for nearly three-quarters of the growth in the federal prison population between 1985 and 1995, while the number of inmates in state prisons for drug law violations has increased by 478 percent over the same period. Drug offenses represent the fastest-growing single offense during this time period, far exceeding other nonviolent and violent offenses. In addition to rising rates of incarceration of drug offenders, the length of sentences, particularly for nonviolent drug offenses, has similarly increased. For the most part, those most burdened by the punitive policies of the drug war have been society's least powerful: women, minorities, and the poor.

The present drug war expenditures show no sign of abatement, given the policy of what Reinarman and Levine aptly call "punitive prohibition," the doctrine supporting the "heavy reliance on criminal law and imprisonment for use and personal possession of illicit drugs."[42] The 1998 National Drug Control Strategy developed by the Office of National Drug Control Policy (ONDCP) allocates $17.1 billion in federal spending alone for antidrug efforts, representing an increase of $1.1 billion (6.8 percent) over the previous year. The author of the strategy, National Drug Control Policy director and former military commander General Barry McCaffrey, explains that the strategy begins a ten-year plan aimed at reducing "the availability and demand for illicit drugs" by 50 percent and cutting the number of "chronic drug users" in half.

While increased spending has gone to treatment and prevention, most of this budget is directed at continuing and expanding punitive strategies. Over 60 percent of this massive budget has been awarded to law enforcement agencies, both domestic and foreign, to continue their worldwide, state-sponsored assault on drugs. Fifty percent of the current budget, or 8.54 billion of tax-payer dollars, will enrich the coffers of the criminal justice in-dustrial complex, while an additional 11 percent, or $1.81 billion is earmarked for interdiction initiatives. Regarding the latter, the strategy calls for such expenditures as $75.4 million to support Department of Defense counterdrug activities in the Andes, the Caribbean, and Mexico, and for the National Guard, $45 million for crop eradication and alternative development campaigns in the Andes, and $35.7 million to enhance Coast Guard interdic-tion capabilities, particularly in the Caribbean. Much of this state-sponsored war chest, supported by the hard-earned tax dollars of American citizens, will undoubtedly be used to pur-chase military hardware, including sophisticated equipment such as infrared radar and other high-tech surveillance devices, Heuy and Blackhawk helicopters, weapons, and to support a net-work of troops and drug-dealing CIA informants, and perhaps even provide the needed resources to finance military incursions into foreign countries to protect democracy from the evils of drugs. Indeed, the combined criminal justice and military-indus-trial complex continues to prosper through America's perma-nent drug war economy.

The consequences of this lopsided spending have been de-tailed elsewhere and do not need to be elaborated here.[43] How-ever, there is one grave consequence of the current punitive poli-cies that has particular bearing on the untreated remitters ex-amined in this book. None of the former drug addicts we interviewed were victims of the drug war. Although all of them were actively using drugs during the drug war buildup of the 1980s and 1990s, none spent time in any of our nation's prisons. Given that all but one were white and all were either middle class or stable working class, perhaps this is not surprising. Whatever the reason, none of them became an imprisoned casu-alty of the drug war. None of them was forced to face the ravages of prison life with its brutal and spirit-killing effects, none was degraded by over zealous DEA officials or treated like criminals, and none of our "crack"-addicted women had their children forcibly taken from them by the courts. Fortunately, all our respondents survived their addictions, but perhaps equally important, they survived the drug war which would probably have seriously impeded their efforts to recover from their addictions on their own.

As demonstrated by our interviewees the social processes that allowed them to develop commitments to conventional roles and identities facilitated their natural recovery from addiction. Making this commitment was contingent on their possession of resources and positive relationships, referred to in the previous chapter as recovery capital. While some might suggest that the threat of prison can deter drug use, prison life typically destroys much of the opportunity to utilize or develop the necessary recovery capital to terminate an addiction. It promotes relationships with hard-core criminals identities and breaks down networks of stable relationships. Prison life subjects people to degradations and indignities that are hard to overcome upon release. Although treatment programs are available in many prisons, life inside prison walls often thwarts the kinds of transformations experienced by our respondents.

Despite the overutilization of incarceration for drug offenders during the past two decades, the evidence suggests that "get tough" policies offer few positive deterrents for future drug use. The little empirical work on the topic suggests that tough sanctions do little to deter drug offenders from offending again.[44] One reason why tough sanctions may be associated with low levels of specific deterrence is that despite a high lifetime likelihood of arrest, the probability that a person will be caught committing a particular offense is incredibly low. Inciardi and Pottieger's work provides an especially striking example of this phenomenon. In their sample of 254 crack dealers from Miami, approximately 87 percent had been arrested at some point within the year of the survey. However, out of over 220,000 offenses the likelihood of arrest for each particular incident was less than 1 percent.[45]

Writing in the *Maryland Law Review*, William McColl argues that "the appalling fact is that because the system fails through a lack of resources or resolve to effectively treat the problem of drug abuse when the offender first encounters the system, the same individuals return over and over again."[46] Renowned criminologist Elliott Currie generally concurs with this assessment. In his opinion, "[W]e have no evidence that the long-term problems of drug abusers can be addressed any more effectively inside the prisons than outside them."[47] Instead of relying on incarceration, Currie believes that efforts should be made to "firmly separate the addict from the in-prison drug culture" by linking offenders to a broad range of community services.[48]

The increasing rates of drug arrests combined with the overcrowding of prisons, high recidivism rates among drug offenders, and the growing recognition of the shortcomings of incarceration have led many jurisdictions to develop specialized drug treatment courts. Begun in Miami in 1989, drug treatment courts are "sweeping the nation" and numbered well over a hundred nationwide in the early 1990s.[49] The rise of these courts may suggest that the punitive response to drug offenders is under attack. Rather than demonizing and punishing drug users, treatment-oriented drug courts view drug users as redeemable and explore rehabilitative alternatives that assist and empower them.[50] These treatment-oriented drug courts, like the Denver Drug Court, seem to offer a compromise between an ineffective hawkish paradigm of drug control and a policy that would separate users from the criminal justice system entirely.[51]

The overall goal of drug courts like the Denver Drug Court is to reduce substance abuse and related criminal activity among offenders through the provision of early intervention, community treatment, and/or sanctions. The court adopts a therapeutic ideal that is associated with a number of judicial innovations such as indeterminate sentences and nonadversarial courtroom procedures. In such courts as this, "the role of the trial judge is changed dramatically. . . . Instead of being a neutral arbiter, the judge becomes the center of courtroom attention."[52] With the assistance of a drug court staff including designated probation officers and case managers, the judge closely monitors offenders' participation in treatment programs. The judge assumes various roles such as "confessor, task master, cheerleader and mentor, in turn exhorting, threatening, encouraging and congratulating the participant for his or her progress or lack thereof."[53] A carrot and stick approach is utilized, whereby the court applies graduated sanctions in response to violations and rewards program compliance.[54]

Research on treatment-oriented drug courts has been mixed. While most drug courts manage drug cases more efficiently, not all courts have demonstrated significant outcomes with regard to recidivism or reduction in drug use. Because of this, drug courts have been subjected to vociferous criticism. This is due largely to the fact that the drug war has emphasized punishment and its assumed benefits. Proponents of punitive antidrug policies have often condemned drug courts for "coddling" drug users. For instance, commenting on his opposition to drug courts, former New York State Senate majority leader Ralph Marino has argued, "These are not the innocent drug addicts they are made to seem. . . . If you're going to sink new spending into this area, we ought to deal with additional bed space."[55] Critics of drug courts question whether these special courts are actual "courts" because they depart from standard adversarial practices and seek to avoid incarceration. The critics denounce the drug courts for being too lenient on drug offenders.

The "harm reduction" principle of such courts is that the drug user must be separated from criminals for treatment to be effective and that drug users should be given several chances to rehabilitate themselves. Given this separation from criminality and the "second-chance" nature of these courts, it is not surprising that the drug courts are currently at odds with the "war on drugs" rhetoric. However, a criminal justice approach based on a principle of adversarialism and punishment is too limited to effectively deal with drug use and addiction. The drug courts can offer an alternative approach in which the perspectives of multiple parties—the judge, the offender, the family, the prosecutor, the therapist, and the public defender—all collaborate to reach a working solution. Instead of seeking the "truth" as mediated through legal arguments, such courts are in a position to become problem solvers by involving the parties in multiple perspectives. As one legal scholar has suggested, an emphasis on nonadversarial procedures permits "more voices, more stories, more complex versions of reality to inform us" and allows "all people to have views that are not fully determined by their 'given' identities in our culture."[56] By transforming drug users from a legalistic category to a therapeutic one the drug courts have the potential to direct the future of drug policy. In fact, as Eva Bertram and her colleagues suggest, they may actually organize a community in ways that could help build resources for recovery capital:

> Drug courts guided by the principles that are advocated in Miami and Oakland could help legitimize the importance of comprehensive treatment programs that address the environmental factors emphasized by a public-health approach. More-over, through the coordinating mechanisms of a drug court, prosecutors, judges, probation officers,

prison officials, treatment agencies, and community groups that may formerly have been uncooperative or even mutually hostile agencies might come to forge local programs that focus on treating drug abuse and addiction not mainly through the threat of punishment but by creating a continuum of care and decent educational, housing, and economic opportunities.[57]

The drug court movement is by no means a panacea. Since it is part of the criminal justice complex, it can still be and often is excessively punitive. Some people on the left of the political spectrum have been critical of drug court developments for helping "sustain a drug war that criminalizes those with substance abuse problems."[58] For harm reduction proponents, it is the criminalization of drug use that poses the greatest danger to individuals and society, not the use itself. Additionally, drug courts can and often do impose mandatory treatment protocols on users that have a traditional disease focus. Resistance to such treatment approaches, like resistance to treatment or AA in prison, is often not only futile but is also seen as being symptomatic of addiction. We believe that all these criticisms are valid. Nevertheless, drug courts do offer an alternative to the rising tide of incarcerated drug offenders. Many drug courts seek to enhance and build the recovery capital of those experiencing drug problems by not only connecting users to treatment, but also, and perhaps more importantly, by helping to mobilize the personal and social resources that are consistent with an individual's own capacity for natural recovery. Ultimately, we agree with harm reduction advocate Ethan Nadelmann, who writes that it is more effective to concentrate on "integrating and reintegrating [addicts] into their communities" than to adopt ill-fated punitive practices that sever them from the very communities that can provide assistance.[59] Unfortunately, in all too many cases "current federal drug law enforcement policy and local policies that mimic it are more likely to rip apart community fabric than to strengthen it."[60]

Culture, Community, and Social Life

Although it is unpopular to say so, licit and illicit intoxicant use as well as addiction will never be completely eliminated. While politicians and moral entrepreneurs espouse "zero-tolerance" platitudes, we are unlikely as a society to ever arrive at this final destination. This admission, one that many drug warriors would consider treasonous, is not made out of a sense of defeatism. Rather, it reflects a realism that is consistent with most intelligent investigations into the use of intoxicants. History has taught us many things, including the fact that intoxicant use has existed from time immemorial. As Reinarman and Levine write, "persons of all ages, genders, races, and classes have ingested chemicals to alter their consciousness in virtually every culture and every epoch."[61] The use of intoxicating substances has not ceased after more than a century of prohibitionist drug wars and almost a century of mostly proscriptive prevention efforts. It has not gone away despite the fact that America now incarcerates more of its drug-using citizens than any other country in the world, or the fact that America has undertaken numerous military efforts to eliminate drugs from their source. Intoxicant use has not gone away despite all these repressive measures, nor is it likely to do so anytime in the future.

Like it or not, intoxicant use is part of our cultural fabric. The use of substances of all kinds has been a normative and largely accepted activity for more years than not. For centuries, individuals have found intoxicant use of all kinds alluring, and alcohol and drugs have often provided them with a source of solace, creativity, or simply a release from life's challenges. History also teaches us that in the overwhelming majority of cases people control the substances they use. For instance, although colonial Americans drank excessively by today's standards, intoxication was a relatively rare occurrence. Similarly, a country like Italy that has been characterized by high levels of alcohol consumption has historically also had low incidences of intoxication and "loss of control." By contrast, other cultures such as the Irish have tended to exhibit high levels of intoxication and alcoholism.[62]

These differences in consumption practices point to the importance of culture and social life. In his book *Drug, Set, and Setting*, Norman Zinberg, the late clinical professor of psychiatry at Harvard Medical School, argued that controlled drinking practices began to subside in America around the time of the Revolutionary War and the Industrial Revolution.[63] During these historical epochs the natural regulatory norms and rituals of social life that fostered controlled use deteriorated under the impact of rapid social change. The Revolutionary War and the Industrial Revolution created conditions that were ripe for alcohol abuse. In each case, men were brought together in large numbers, away from the regulatory function of family life, and under oppressive and fearful circumstances. Not surprisingly, in these timorous and turbulent settings the excessive consumption of alcohol was used to ease the psychological tension associated with wartime and to provide a means of escape from the proletarian drudgery and alienation that characterize factory life.[64]

The path-breaking work of Lee Robins and her colleagues on the use of heroin among Vietnam veterans supports the claims concerning the influence that social and cultural settings have upon use.[65] She and her associates found that while heroin addiction among soldiers fighting in Vietnam was substantial, few remained addicted or sought out heroin after leaving this highly volatile setting. Like the previous examples, for those who were in the midst of battle, the Vietnam War contributed to a severe breakdown in rudimentary rituals of control. It had dramatic consequences for those who were unable to extricate themselves from this emotionally potent setting. However, most returnees from Vietnam were able to reintegrate into community life and reestablish rituals of control once the conditions favorable to their use disappeared.

Controlled use after periods of excess may also be explained by the development of rituals. During the early 1960s there was great anxiety about the adverse psychological effects of new psychedelic drugs like LSD that were becoming popular among young people. Ironically, as the use of psychedelic drugs increased, the number of "bad trips" associated with use began to decline.[66] The standard sociological explanation for this counterintuitive pattern points to the importance of rules and rituals. Control over these substances was not established until sanctions and rituals emerged among the community of users. Once sanctions developed, such as "use only at a good time, in a good place, with good people" and once users began to interpret the effects of the substances, the proclivity toward negative psychotic experiences abated.[67] The same may be said for the decline in problems associated with cocaine use in the 1980s. It took several years of relatively unrestrained and problematic use before cocaine users themselves developed rules and rituals that resulted in new levels of control.

This core sociological insight regarding the impact that "users' norms, values, practices, and circumstances" have on the use and abuse of intoxicants, has great significance for recovery, particularly for those like our respondents who do so without treatment.[68] Practices surrounding the use or nonuse of intoxicants do not simply happen. Rather, they evolve out of participation in groups and in a cultural and social context more generally. This is especially the case in contemporary American culture that places a premium on pleasurable and ecstatic experiences. Capitalism in America gave birth to a rapacious individualism and consumerism that knows few boundaries. As a result, hedonistic commodity consumption has become normative. Americans identify themselves increasingly on the basis of their material possessions and the images they are able to create through the products they consume. In such a cultural condition, the use and abuse of intoxicants in the pursuit of pleasure and meaning becomes inevitable. Indeed, the recent fashion of socializing in trendy cigar bars that serve high-priced cigars and expensive liquors is consistent with this consumer-oriented culture in which intoxicants provide avenues for personal meaning, status, and identity.

The hyperconsumption that so characterizes the American landscape has significant consequences. Over the years, many social critics have described a kind of cultural revolution that has been taking place in advanced capitalist societies like the United States. This "cultural logic of late capitalism" is said to be characterized by the collapse of established patterns of social and community life.[69] As a result, America has seemingly lost its core as more and more people feel that their world is spinning out of control.[70] Instead of feeling "trapped" by restrictive social institutions, as C. Wright Mills once proclaimed, nowadays people feel that their private lives are a series of meaningless activities.[71] As David Harvey has suggested, the contemporary condition of cultural life has produced a "profound shift in the structure of feeling," in which people increasingly experience their lives as fragmented, ephemeral, disconnected, and chaotic.[72] In such a cultural condition, the self becomes increasingly "saturated" and temporary. As the psychologist Kenneth Gerson has written, "the fully saturated self becomes no self at all."[73] This saturated self is incapable of developing an authenticity or of arranging a consistent hierarchy of identities because people are consumed with the continuous construction and reconstruction of selves in a world where anything goes. Each new self becomes as real and as ephemeral as the preceding one as people engage in an unending but ultimately frustrated search for meaning and social connectivity.

A sense of social isolation and loss of community characterizes this pervasive crisis of meaning. For many, the social institutions of family, work, religion, and education no longer provide the comfort, support, and continuity necessary to foster meaning and satisfaction. The dramatic population shifts in America, along with its raging "culture wars,"[74] unpredictable upward and downward mobility, major technological change, and the globalization of markets have produced increased levels of fear and vulnerability in society, leaving people feeling increasingly dislocated and disconnected. This sense of dislocation is further exacerbated by the continuing capitalist revolution that "undermines local communities as jobs are moved overseas or to wherever else capital can earn its highest return; families are uprooted; and loyal workers are laid off in the name of downsizing."[75] As a result of these dramatic changes, America has been described as being in the "twilight" of collective social life.[76] No longer do Americans feel a sense of community and commonality with others that naturally produces conditions of mutual trust and commitment. For the most part, there has been a collective turning inward, a kind of mass privatization of social space that inhibits the expression and experience of community.

The people whose voices we have heard throughout this book are part of this cultural landscape. They used and ultimately abused a variety of substances in an effort to find meaning and relationships. Some simply sought hedonistic pleasure, while others sought relief from painful emotional experiences. For all of them, the excessive use of alcohol and drugs provided a sense of meaning and purpose that they found temporarily satisfying.

Not unlike the alcoholics studied by Denzin, our respondents might be characterized as social critics in that they reveal a kind of "felt truth of the culture and the times."[77] In a sense, addictions of all sorts provide people with comfort and security in a world that is increasingly experienced as being out of control.

Our respondents have much to say about this current condition of social life. They all attempted to find personal meaning in the substances they used. The more they sought this through intoxicants, the more ensnared they became in their addictions. However, through it all they were able to overcome their addictions, not through treatment but by becoming involved in social institutions that provided them with the personal significance they desired. Their success was related in part to the social institutions and relations that were available to them in contemporary society. Because of this, our respondents offer some emancipatory potential for what "postmodern" critics see as a socially morbid situation. Critics of the contemporary "postmodern" condition have asserted that the truth claims of traditional institutional narratives such as community, work, family, religion, law, politics, and education have eroded to the point where they no longer produce the necessary "collective efficacy" for building cohesion, trust, and meaning.[78] Postindustrial society has lost its core and its inhabitants are said to be adrift in an ocean of collective disenchantment.

The people we interviewed for this book, however, would suggest that the dire conclusions of these critics are only partially correct. Our society has become increasingly fragmented and disconnected, patterns of social and community life have deteriorated, and our major social institutions have undergone dramatic change to the point where they no longer appear as paramount as they once did. Living in such a world does produce the feeling, as Anthony Giddens has commented, of "riding a juggernaut."[79] However, our respondents discovered meaning in these traditional institutions or were able to create new institutional relations that promoted self-renewal. They were able to "remoralize" old institutions and visualize new possibilities. Some of them found solace in the conventional roles associated with work and family life, while others redefined and reconstituted work and family life, chose alternative lifestyles, or developed new identities made possible through "postmodern" institutional arrangements. Ultimately, each of our respondents found the answer to their troubled lives in the recesses of the social lives they had once found dissatisfying.

Lest the reader gets lulled into a false sense of optimism about the ability to "rediscover community," we offer the following qualification. Our respondents did become part of a "responsive community" whereby they became involved in and committed to the roles associated with these communities.[80] While a revival of community life has many positive benefits, the opportunities to experience meaningful community may be restricted by economic circumstances. The fact that all our respondents were from middle-class or stable working-class backgrounds should not be overlooked. Each of them possessed the social and human capital, which we collectively referred to in the previous chapter as "recovery capital," needed to promote the transformations they experienced. For the most part, they all had educational credentials, skills, social networks, and other resources. Their access to these resources significantly facilitated their natural recovery. Such is often not the case, however, for those whose social and economic circumstances are impoverished. There are significant limits on the extent to which our nation's poorest individuals can experience satisfying community life. The severe social disorganization that has been cultivated in these poor neighborhoods during the past twenty years, the breakdown of traditional informal means of social control,[81] the decreasing potential for good, stable employment,[82] and the expanding opportunities for criminal activities such as drug dealing all create impediments to forging new identities and commitments to social institutions.[83] Indeed, the "demoralization effects" of poverty may not provide the opportunity, much less the incentive, to develop conventional stakes in social life.[84]

Fortunately, social class does not completely determine destiny. Many people have overcome the challenges associated with being economically disadvantaged. Despite their hardships, in large measure they accomplish this much the same way as those interviewed for this book changed their lives. They had access to social and human capital as well as to others who provided love, support, and encouragement, and they acted on their limited opportunities to find conventional sources of meaning.

In our attempts to build community and create opportunities for personal resilience, we must never lose sight of the fact that economic differences have important consequences. As a society we must be attentive to the multiple ways of developing and reinvigorating community life. Indeed, the manner in which we create sustainable community and provide opportunities for people to overcome life's many challenges and vicissitudes is the true measure of our national character.

IMPLEMENTING NATURAL RECOVERY

Suggestions for Personal Change

Given the promise that natural recovery holds for people with drug and alcohol problems, this book would not be complete without providing some practical suggestions for overcoming addiction without treatment. Drawing on our research, and based as well on our experiences as practitioners and teachers in the area of drug and alcohol dependence, this appendix identifies key strategies that have been successfully used by people who have overcome addiction to drugs and alcohol unaided by treatment or 12-step groups. Because we want to provide useful information to those wishing to attempt a natural recovery from addiction, we deliberately avoid the kind of academic writing style used throughout this book. The material in this chapter is presented in the spirit of practical suggestions to people struggling with substance-dependency problems. Although it is not characteristic of researchers to do so, we felt a strong obligation to share our insights with those presently in the throes of addiction who may not find the academic style of this book accessible or engaging.

The strategies that follow do not represent an exhaustive list of the techniques employed to overcome addiction without treatment. We have included only those strategies that, from our perspective, seem to have been particularly salient in the lives of the self-remitters we interviewed.

Starting Out on Natural Recovery

Before embarking upon a "natural" road to recovery, it is important to first address several key issues that you will need to consider as you contemplate recovery without treatment. While each addiction situation is unique, there are four questions that everyone needs to ask him or herself before undertaking natural recovery. These questions are: Do you have the desire to change? What is your personal plan for change? Should you share your plans with others? and Do you need to adopt a regime of complete abstinence?

DO YOU HAVE THE DESIRE TO CHANGE?

One of the most basic therapeutic tenets observed by many in the helping professions is that resistance to change or uncertainty about the need to change is a major obstacle to recovery. In fact, among professionals who treat drug- and alcohol-dependent persons like yourself, motivation to modify the intake of these substances is seen as a necessary condition for change. In many treatment programs, providing opportunities for their clients to develop a strong desire to change is an integral part of program planning and structure.

This same principle applies to recovery without treatment; that is, the most elegant plans for recovery are likely to fall short without a sincere desire on the part of the troubled person to change. Like the self-remitters we interviewed for this book, you must find a reason to initiate a change in your life. Finding a reason to change will require that you examine and develop your own positive capacities, strengths, and relationships. You will need these to facilitate change.

A critical component of the desire to change is to ask yourself "why?" Alcoholics and drug addicts have a hard time changing their lives when they perceive that they are benefiting from the intoxicants they are using. Even in the midst of assorted personal and interpersonal problems, people can derive pleasure and profound meaning from the use of mind-altering substances, as did the people we interviewed. While the significance of such benefits is often not readily apparent or understandable to those unfamiliar with the addiction, such benefits are no less real. For example, people from poor backgrounds with limited education or job potential, few employment opportunities, diminished faith in conventional values, and a sense of hopelessness in their lives might feel that they have little reason to change. Often their feelings of alienation, coupled with opportunities to use substances and their status in the drug subculture, have strong appeal. One of the authors is reminded of an encounter during his years in social work practice with a very bright but poorly educated young African-American male heroin addict who was living on the streets. When asked about his continuing drug use, he exclaimed, "Why should I quit? It's my reason to wake up everyday. Besides, what else could I do?"

While heavy alcohol and drug use might not be as meaningful in the lives of others as it was for this man, chronic substance use does more than merely ward off withdrawal symptoms or other physical discomfort. The essential point is that in order to overcome alcohol or drug dependency, you must first develop a strong desire to change your life. Starting out on natural recovery from this position will substantially increase your chances of success.

WHAT IS YOUR PERSONAL PLAN FOR CHANGE?

As in the case of other major life changes, ending an addiction to alcohol and drugs is an undertaking that is best approached thoughtfully and strategically. You should adopt a proactive rather than a reactive posture that anticipates obstacles and challenges along the way. Developing a plan for change will go far in assuring the success of your effort. Such a plan will help ease the difficulties you might experience through your efforts to change. As with the individuals we interviewed, change is often difficult and it is normal to experience discomfort while it occurs. No change can occur without some amount of uneasiness.

As you move into your attempt to recover without treatment, you should avoid "just letting things happen" or being passive. This can result in a return to old ways and habits. There are a variety of questions you should ask yourself: When should I begin the process of natural recovery? Do I need to take time away from work? Will it be necessary to actually extract myself from the surrounding environment by temporarily, or even permanently, relocating? What personal strengths and resilience can I most rely on for change? Where are my primary social support groups that can help me reach my goals? These and other questions will need to be considered prior to any attempt to resolve addictions without treatment. Thoughtful planning can help you think about these questions as well as help you identify appropriate action. Later, when we discuss actual recovery strategies, the relevance of planning to successful recovery will become even more apparent.

Though planning can be a crucial component in the process of natural recovery, it is also important that you guard against overplanning. Too many plans, particularly initially, can put inordinate amounts of pressure on you, perhaps even setting yourself up to fail. This problem can be compounded when these expectations are not met, resulting in frustration, doubts about your ability to succeed, and lowered confidence levels. Additionally, you should be somewhat flexible in your planning since you can never fully anticipate the array of life circumstances likely to be encountered in the self-recovery process.

SHOULD YOU SHARE YOUR PLANS WITH OTHERS?

Because of the profound negative effects that drug and alcohol dependency can have on family members and others who are close to the user, sharing specific plans to change with them is akin to making a commitment to them. Sharing your plans to change with others may help you locate a network of family members, friends, coworkers, and other associates who can be used as a support system. However, while such natural support systems are extremely valuable, our work in the area of natural recovery suggests that the person attempting to make the change should give some thought to whom they are sharing their plans with. Other people's expectations can have both positive and negative effects on your effort to recover.

On the one hand, sharing your intentions can produce a sense of accountability to others, create support networks, and generate a strong motivation to succeed. On the other hand, however, these same expectations, particularly in the early stages of a recovery effort, might lead others to make unreasonable demands on you that could actually put you at risk for using again. Unfortunately, because the belief in the disease concept and the necessity of treatment is so pervasive in our society, some people might not accept your claims about natural recovery as sincere. Instead they may prescribe an abrupt, "straight and narrow" course of recovery that precludes the kind of gradual and often wavering process that many people experience before they finally overcome drug and alcohol problems.

Sharing one's plans with others can also compound feelings of failure and inadequacy when success is not immediately achieved. These feelings could reinforce beliefs that support reified myths about addiction and suggest the folly of natural recovery. Popular beliefs held by others, such as "once an addict always an addict," or other disease-based tenets can create major obstacles to natural recovery and have important implications for your attempts to change. Conversely, by undertaking natural recovery independently of the traditional expectations and beliefs of others, you might be able to minimize these shortcomings by reframing your experience not as a failure but as a necessary learning experience. Change takes time and you may not be successful the first time around.

While we do not want to discourage you from taking full advantage of existing relationships that can aid you in natural recovery, given the prevailing myths about addiction we simply wish to alert you to the pros and cons of sharing your plans with others. In most cases, it will mean sharing plans and gaining support from those who accept and validate your desire to change in your own way. These are the people who will help bolster your confidence, not those who constantly remind you of your "disease." Such people can have toxic and corrosive effects on any sincere natural recovery plan.

DO YOU NEED TO BECOME ABSTINENT?

The decision to pursue a course of abstinence versus the reduction of substance use is an important consideration and one that many who contemplate this kind of change struggle with. It is erroneous to assume that the only path to success is abstinence. Many, even after many years of chronic alcohol or drug dependence, are able to reduce the harmful intake of these substances without completely terminating use. Conversely, though reduction of use might be appropriate for some, others might find it nearly impossible to cut back, even after many attempts to do so. Most of the self-remitters we interviewed made the decision to abstain from any future use. However, those who do reduce their intake of intoxicants generally develop and implement strong personal rules limiting use. In a sense, they teach themselves to use in a controlled fashion. For those interested in decreasing the use of alcohol, instructional books by Mark and Linda Sobell and Audrey Kishline could be very useful. The title of the Sobells' book is *Problem Drinking: Guided Self-Change Treatment*. The title of Kishline's book is *Moderate Drinking: The Option for Problem Drinkers*. You might also wish to browse the various Internet web sites, such as "The Stanton Peele Addiction Web Site" at www.peele.net/.

Strategies for Natural Recovery: Early Phase

Overcoming addiction is a gradual process. A person gains momentum, strength, and resilience as the time between addiction and recovery passes. It can be understood as a developmental process distinguished by early and later stages. Each of these stages is characterized by common yet unique challenges. We begin this discussion of strategies by identifying some that appear to be particularly germane to the early phase of the self-recovery process. We then explore strategies associated with the latter or maintenance phase of natural recovery.

DETOXIFICATION

At the outset of your natural recovery, you need to make a decision about whether or not medically supervised detoxification is necessary. Many alcoholics and drug addicts with long-standing habits gradually get clean by weaning themselves off of these substances, while others, including most in our study, quit abruptly. While you may find that natural recovery is a viable option in your own case, a desire to pursue this course should not blind you to the potential dangers of acute withdrawal syndromes associated with certain substances, including alcohol and other central nervous system depressants such as barbiturates and benzodiazepines. Although withdrawal from dependence on stimulants like cocaine and opiates such as heroin can be extremely uncomfortable, this process is generally not dangerous or life-threatening. On the other hand, heavy cocaine and opiate users might be oblivious to their coexisting addictions to alcohol and other depressants that can produce dangerous withdrawal effects.

Where there might be such dual addictions, formal detoxification should also be considered. Although such a process is clearly a form of treatment, medically supervised detoxification is of relatively short duration. It generally takes from seven to fourteen days to complete fully. Many complete detoxification and go on to productive lives free of drug and alcohol addictions without any further contact with treatment or without attending support groups. We do caution, however, that some detoxification programs subscribe to traditional disease-based notions of addiction and some of their daily activities promote such views to the exclusion of other more "natural" explanations.

In addition to the discomfort of physical withdrawal, the early phase of recovery is often a fragile period. The range of emotional and physical sensations can include, for example, ambivalence, loneliness, sadness, irritability, lethargy, and insomnia. An effective response to these uncomfortable feelings requires you to take a proactive posture. It is important to realize that such feelings are temporary and will pass. Unless there are chronic underlying physical or mental health problems these feelings are normal and will generally abate.

Self-remitters use a number of strategies to reduce the frequency, intensity, and duration of these uncomfortable feelings. Our respondents reported being active, engaging in physical exercise, partaking in soothing and invigorating nonexercise activities, modifying diets, and reducing or eliminating the intake of common stimulants such as nicotine, caffeine, and sugar.

BEING ACTIVE

During the early period of natural recovery you should strive to become active. Being active fills much of the void felt in the early stages of recovery. When drinking and drug taking are eliminated from the user's life and social connections with users are terminated there is generally a profound sense of emptiness, further compounded by increased boredom and idle time. Being active discourages one from having pronounced thoughts about using during these idle periods and can mitigate some of the boredom and stress that often lead to resumed use. By being active we do not mean you should engage in frenetic and purposeless activity, but rather that you engage in activities that offer comfort and personal satisfaction. Examples include taking a walk, gardening, bowling, hiking, house cleaning, and various forms of moderate physical exercise. It is critical to understand the importance of "being active" as you start your journey of self-recovery so as to guard against the tendency to simply withdraw from the world through inactivity and reclusion. Such an approach would probably be counterproductive for most.

PHYSICAL EXERCISE

Physical exercise is, without a doubt, one of the best ways of being active. Because of the many benefits associated with physical exercise in both the early and later phase of the recovery process, this activity warrants separate attention. During the early period of natural recovery the level of intensity and duration of your exercise should be relatively moderate. The reason is that during this time, particularly in the first few days and perhaps weeks, people with long-standing histories of addiction may not have the physical stamina to undertake more rigorous exercise. People who are not in the habit of exercising on a regular basis can easily become disenchanted with it if they push themselves too hard too early. Also, they may be susceptible to painful injuries if they are overly aggressive.

During this early stage of natural recovery consider short or relatively easy daily aerobic workouts that gradually increase in intensity and duration, for instance, from ten minutes to twenty, and then to thirty minutes per session. Examples include walks, walk jogs, treadmill walking, moderate stairmaster walking, moderate bike riding, water aerobics, and a wide range of other low to moderate level aerobic activities available at public recreation centers and gyms, YMCAs, health clubs, and fitness facilities accessible in most U.S. towns and cities. Such regular workouts are enormously beneficial at the outset of recovery. Many people trying to recover from addiction have reported that they reduce boredom and tension, improve sleep, and lead to an overall increase in health and sense of well-being. Regular moderate physical exercise can aid in your body's return to normal health and accelerate the recovery process.

As you begin to regain your health and increase your stamina you will be able to increase the intensity and duration of workouts. This gradual increase further hastens the restoration of good health and makes it easier to move to more rigorous workouts. However, before beginning a regular routine of any type of physical exercise, even the moderate workouts identified above, you should consult with a physician or health expert. Years of heavy drug and alcohol use with attendant behaviors hazardous to health might put you at risk for an assortment of mild to severe ailments. Consequently certain forms of exercise could actually be harmful.

SOOTHING AND INVIGORATING ACTIVITIES

Interviews with the alcoholics and drug addicts in our study and discussions with others who have defeated long-standing addiction without treatment report on the value of activities that are soothing and invigorating. They point out how activities such as getting a massage, taking warm and hot baths, steam baths, whirlpool baths, and sitting in a sauna can ease some of the physical and mental discomfort common in the early stages of natural recovery. While this kind of relief can benefit most who are struggling with the discomfort of the early phase of the recovery process, formerly heroin-addicted individuals find this to be particularly helpful. Cessation of habitual use of heroin and other opiates often results in mild to extreme body aches, frequently characterized as flulike symptoms. These soothing and invigorating activities, while giving temporary relief from some of the discomfort, also allows the person to experience firsthand the transitory nature of his or her unpleasant state. In many cases, such firsthand experience can make the difference between optimism about the possibility of truly feeling better and gloom about the expectancy of continued discomfort.

IMPROVING YOUR NUTRITION

During the early phase of natural recovery, you may need to come to terms with the consequences of numerous years of potential dietary neglect. Many alcoholics and addicts have had very poor and often debilitating nutritional practices. The results of this nutritional negligence can exacerbate the already difficult task of recovery through poor health, increased discomfort, and decline in the body's ability to quickly return to a physical and mental state of normalcy. It is therefore crucially important that you begin to pay attention to your food intake as soon as possible in order to circumvent the deleterious effects of poor diet and to begin the process of rebuilding your health. The principal reason we emphasize this point is that the consequences of poor diet not only impair the ability of the body to return to health, but consuming certain types of foods and beverages can actually aggravate the negative emotional and physical states common during this phase of the recovery process. These heightened adverse states, of course, can place one at risk for using again.

Foods high in sugar and fats are good examples of what one might want to avoid during this period. If you wish to maximize the benefits of sound nutritional practices and minimize the negative effects of poor food choices you should consult with a nutritionist, other food experts, or with some of the literature on nutrition currently available at health food stores, book stores, libraries, and on the Internet. We suggest reading Andrew Weil's best-selling book, *Spontaneous Healing*, and, if possible, visiting his advice internet web page at www.drweil.com.

BEWARE OF COMMON STIMULANTS

We particularly caution against the heavy use of beverages that contain large amounts of caffeine during this period. Drinking excessive quantities of caffeine throughout the day can create a sense of mental and physical uneasiness that might put you at risk for resumed use. While coffee is an obvious concern, caffeinated soft drinks that have high levels of sugar can also be

quite troublesome. Smoking cigarettes or otherwise using tobacco products can also threaten one's success during this early
period. However, we do not suggest that those who are nicotine
dependent simultaneously quit their use of tobacco, at least during this initial period; that might prove to be too difficult. Because of the high potential for boredom and stress, we do caution
against increasing the use of tobacco products and would suggest
that users stabilize their nicotine dependence at a reduced level.

Both caffeine and nicotine use present unique challenges for
drug- and alcohol-dependent people beginning a course of recovery. While the up-and-down mood swings associated with
the use of these substances can compromise attempts to arrest
dependency on other drugs, an abrupt break with caffeine and
nicotine which have their own corresponding withdrawal syndromes may profoundly worsen the negative experiences of the
initial phase of recovery. It is important to note, however, that
some people who have overcome addictions on their own report
cessation of cigarette smoking, and to a lesser degree coffee
drinking, concurrently with the cessation of heroin, cocaine, and
alcohol use.

Strategies for Sustaining Recovery from Addiction
without Treatment: Maintenance Phase

The strategies that we have explored thus far are particularly
relevant to the early phase of a recovery effort. We now turn
our attention to more complex strategies that can help sustain
a recovery without treatment. As with the discussion above,
the strategies that we identify here do not represent an exhaustive list, but rather are tactics employed by many of the self-
remitters we interviewed. These strategies include changing
environments, gaining social support, finding alternative forms

of leisure and recreation, feeling good, engaging in meaningful work, assuming meaningful responsibility, experiencing conversions, and nurturing new identities.

CHANGING ENVIRONMENTS

Changing environments is a key tactic for many undertaking natural recoveries, particularly those who are addicted to substances like cocaine and heroin. Even with the strong desire to change, continuous exposure to the cues and conditions under which use occurred could undermine natural recovery. Visiting your old "hangouts," interacting with the friends with whom you used these substances, and continuing the old patterns of activity all represent the kinds of pressures that can inhibit recovery. Some former alcoholics and drug addicts who have employed natural recovery have talked about their need to permanently sever or at least temporarily cut off relationships with close friends and family members who contributed to their dependent use of drugs and alcohol. Others left spouses who refused to quit or reduce their substance use. In some instances people changed jobs or changed career paths altogether when their work environments exerted a negative influence over their attempts to quit. While it is widely known that bartenders and musicians who perform in nightclubs are overly exposed to alcohol and drug use, various kinds of service work such as those in Colorado's ski industry are also often associated with heavy alcohol and drug use.

Moving or relocating to another city is a strategy that many self-remitters have employed. This "geographic cure," as it is commonly called in the addiction field, responds to some addicted individuals' need to extricate themselves from the myriad of coexisting and often intertwined circumstances that keep them entangled in destructive substance use.

Whether or not you choose to physically relocate is a decision that only you can make. However, even if you do not take such a drastic step, you should try to at least detach yourself from the drug scene.

RELATIONSHIPS

As most researchers and users know, addiction to drugs and alcohol emerges in a context of social relationships with others and, in most cases, is sustained by those relationships. While these relationships often play a major role in maintaining addictions, they also serve some of the same needs that ordinary social relationships provide. The need for friendship, support, intimacy, acceptance, and the like are realized through substance-using relationships. As these social networks are abandoned it becomes necessary to cultivate meaningful relationships to replace them with those that do not reinforce heavy alcohol or drug use, but instead provide you with acceptance and support to help you through your personal transformation.

You can cultivate such supportive networks in various ways. Many of the self-remitters we interviewed established new relationships with individuals and groups where alcohol or drug use were not central activities. Others reestablished relationships with family members and friends who were not heavy substance users. Such relationships can be created or recreated in a wide variety of ways and settings. Many of the self-remitters we interviewed spoke of joining health clubs, choirs, church groups, and recreational sport teams as ways of meeting people. Some even contacted old friends or family members as a way of helping them stay clean. Reconnecting with family members and old friends can be rewarding for both parties.

The workplace also offers opportunities for establishing supportive relationships. Many workplace relationships can evolve into loving and nurturing ones that go beyond the walls of work. School is another setting where such relationships can evolve. Several of the people we interviewed developed new relationships with people they met when they returned to college or enrolled in adult education courses. Others found supportive relationships in a wide variety of civic activities undertaken through choir groups, political groups, community groups, and religious groups. These are only a few examples of the wide range of opportunities to replace abandoned substance-using friends and groups. Whatever specific strategies you employ, it is important to remember that relying on the assistance and support of friends, family members, and acquaintances will not only facilitate your natural recovery from addiction but will also contribute to major improvements in your life more generally.

LEISURE AND RECREATION

Heavy intoxicant use not only consumes a great deal of one's time and energy, but it can become an integral part of an addict's pursuit of leisure and recreation as well. As demonstrated by the addicts we interviewed, a life of dependency can be all-consuming. For many, when the addicted life is deserted so too are the primary means for thrill, excitement, and pleasure. Those addicted to substances for long periods of time have to find other channels of enjoyment, and some actually have to learn how to have fun without drugs or alcohol. For those who are completely immersed in the street subculture of illicit drug use, learning to enjoy life through conventional means can be particularly challenging. One heroin addict living in Italy told one of the authors that he didn't know if he could stay clean because "straight people were boring." While the suggestions that we offer here may appear fairly simple and straightforward, the former addicts that we interviewed said they had found them to be meaningful recreational outlets.

Joining community clubs and groups can create opportunities to participate in numerous forms of pleasurable activity. Choirs, book groups, outdoor groups, hand drumming groups, and other community-based informal organizations can provide such opportunities. Team and league sports such as volleyball, softball, basketball, and team tennis provide similar opportunities. However, keep in mind that among certain team sports drinking can be a central associated activity.

Those attempting to overcome addiction can also find pleasure in individual sport activities that are simultaneously health promoting. Such activities as jogging, swimming, racquetball, tennis, and the like have been found to be extremely beneficial. Similarly, health clubs and other kinds of fitness organizations offer a wide variety of enjoyable, health-promoting activities available in group as well as in individual formats. Some of the group activities include, for example, aerobic classes, step-aerobic classes, jazzercise classes, or martial arts classes. At the individual level, a wide variety of workout equipment is available where people can simulate jogging, rowing, cycling, cross-country skiing, and a host of enjoyable and invigorating activities.

HEALTH AND FITNESS

Much of what has been discussed so far has implications for improved health. Clearly, improving your state of health will greatly increase your chances for success in accomplishing a natural recovery from an addiction to mind-altering substances. Improved health reduces the deleterious effects of years of physical neglect and leads to an increased sense of physical and mental well-being, which in turn negates much of the potential discomfort that often results in resumed use. One of the principal reasons why persons addicted to alcohol and drugs for long periods of time find it difficult to stay off these substances is that they often feel uncomfortable and, as reported by many during the early phases of a recovery effort, outright miserable. Depending on the circumstances of your own use, this discomfort can range from mild to extreme. It can diminish appreciably over the course of a few days or it can linger for several months with almost unnoticeable improvements. For example, people who have been on high doses of methadone for extended periods and whose health has been significantly compromised through poor diet, inactivity, and other conditions report experiencing various levels of insomnia, body aches, restlessness, sadness, and an inability to focus for weeks and months after their last dose of the drug. They also complain about the "psychological discomfort" that seems to linger long after the physical discomfort subsides. Their experiences suggest that the feelings of emptiness, gloom, detachment, and similar conditions that characterize this state persist much longer than the physical uneasiness. Given these circumstances, it is not surprising that many people return to using these substances within weeks and, in some cases, within days of completing treatment or other attempts to stop.

Of course, the key to limiting the extent and duration of "feeling bad" is to increase your ability to "feel good" without necessarily using substances. A person's motivation to maintain a changed lifestyle will undoubtedly be compromised if he or she continues to feel poorly after weeks or months of abstinence or significant reduction. After all, as a former client of one of the authors stated, "Who wants to get clean to feel bad all the time?"

Again, attention to health is an effective means by which you can reduce these negative sensations. For many, the level of health that we recommend exceeds their presubstance-use levels of health; for others, getting healthy merely means a return to the state of health that they had enjoyed prior to their destructive use of substances. Although several of the self-remitters that we interviewed became involved in fitness activities, we are not suggesting that all addicted individuals need to become preoccupied with health and fitness to feel better. There are multiple avenues to "feeling good" without using substances. Your task is to find what it is that gives you pleasure and provides you with rewards that come from no longer being addicted to substances.

As stated earlier, regular physical activity and attention to nutrition can aid one's natural recovery effort in numerous and important ways. While the early phase of natural recovery should entail moderate workout regimes, in the latter phase of the recovery process you might consider moving to a more rigorous workout. Examples include jogging, lap swimming, cycling, rowing, stair climbing, cross-country skiing, and group workouts such as aerobic, step aerobic, boxing aerobic, and spin cycling classes. These kinds of workouts often result in heavy sweating and have been reported by some to have almost immediate effects on increased relaxation and sense of well-being. Again, you should consult with a physician before beginning a more rigorous and strenuous regime of physical exercise.

Nor can people overcoming long-standing drug and alcohol problems ignore well-documented research as well as volumes of other information on the benefits of good nutrition. You cannot expect to experience noticeable improvements in health and the attendant benefits of improved physical and mental well-being on a poor diet of foods high in fats and sugars. One cannot consume large amounts of caffeine and smoke heavily and still expect to enjoy an optimal level of health. While you do not need to become a "health zealot" to overcome drug and alcohol problems, you do need to be aware of the kinds of foods you consume and recognize that good nutrition can lead to noticeable states of improved physical and mental well-being.

You might also consider augmenting your diets with vitamins, minerals, herbs, and other nutritional supplements. For example, silymarin, the active ingredient in the milk thistle plant, has been shown to be effective in reducing some of the harm caused to the liver by years of heavy use of alcohol and other drugs. Since the liver plays such a vital role in the body's processing of nutrients and in the elimination of toxins from the body, restoration of proper liver function alone can benefit one's health in an appreciable way. Consulting with a nutritionist, herbalist, practitioners of Chinese medicine, or reading up on the subject of good nutrition can provide you with invaluable nutritional advice.

People who were formerly substance dependent but now enjoy markedly improved levels of health and well-being are often amazed that they can experience this state without using mind-altering substances. In fact, one of the reasons given by some for not returning to alcohol and drugs is that they do not want to jeopardize the physical and mental well-being that they enjoy and have become accustomed to. This of course does not suggest that good health is the panacea for relapse prevention. However, those contemplating natural recovery need to be keenly aware of the fact that they can realize substantially improved health and fitness with only moderate effort.

WORK

While involvement in work in the early stages of the recovery process can help fill some of the void that is often so pronounced during that time, continued employment in settings that are uninspiring can actually threaten natural recovery.

There is a large body of literature that underscores the importance of doing interesting, challenging, and gratifying work. This is particularly relevant to those who have long-standing histories of substance dependence and who are attempting to overcome such problems. Many of the self-remitters we interviewed talked about the value of changing jobs and careers as they began their recovery journeys. Several reported returning to college to prepare for new careers. Others started their own businesses as they proceeded with their change processes. Most of these self-remitters threw themselves into their new pursuits with a passion. While the people we interviewed were perhaps not representative of the total population of self-remitters, we feel strongly about the significance of meaningful work in sustaining a natural recovery. Mundane, repetitive work routines with little or no intrinsic personal reward can produce severe alienation, leading to a felt need to escape through the use of intoxicating substances. Also, such jobs typically do not provide the kinds of benefits such as health care, relative job security, and at least some limited flexibility, that people need when recovering.

One of the appeals of working as a service provider in a drug- and alcohol-treatment program, for those who have had substance use problems, pertains to this principle. Despite the often low wages, frustrating mounds of paperwork, and disappointing progress of many clients, this type of work can be very rewarding. The intense human contact, the excitement, and the sense of "making a difference" in this as well as other types of human service settings are very appealing for numerous people. We are not suggesting that you necessarily seek employment in alcohol- and drug-treatment settings or in similar human service organizations. In fact, there can be some drawbacks to becoming alcohol- and drug-treatment counselors for those whose lives have been so intimately anchored to addiction and who have recovered without treatment. Many self-remitters would find it difficult to enter into drug treatment work given its emphasis on traditional disease notions of addiction. However, this kind of human contact, along with the overall exciting climate inherent in a range of human service organizations, make such work conditions particularly appealing for many former users.

Of course, there are a host of professional careers that offer similar opportunities, such as medicine, law, psychotherapy, and teaching, for example. These professions may be beyond the reach of many because of professional-school entrance requirements for training as well as the length of training required to practice. Nevertheless, there are many occupations that do not require such extensive training while providing the kinds of personal satisfaction that we identify. The key is to find employment that is nonalienating, intrinsically meaningful, and personally rewarding.

Finally, we realize that meaningful work can mean different things to different people and that many people find work involving intense human contact totally unappealing. Obviously they would need to explore other types of occupations. We also realize that like some of those we interviewed, many people in professional jobs in medicine and law find their work rewarding, yet they get into trouble with alcohol and drugs, or worse, because of the stress of their work.

Ultimately, you need to carefully examine the work you do. Perhaps you are unhappy with the kind of professional practice you are doing. For high prestige professionals making large sums of money, this can often be the case. Making money does not necessarily bring about happiness, and may require you to make compromises that you find personally disconcerting. The kind of inner satisfaction you seek may be derived from jobs with lower stress and greater intrinsic meaning. Since you may spend more than half of your waking hours at work during the week, you must take into account how your work conditions might affect your efforts to recover naturally.

RESPONSIBILITY

Many people who have overcome substance addictions on their own have found that having family and work responsibilities as well as other obligations that they take very seriously have tempered their urge to return to using intoxicants. They have discovered that they value their new lives immensely and do not wish to threaten them by resuming old habits. Assuming responsibility in your life can bring about healthy and rewarding changes. For instance, some addicted women decide to get clean because of pregnancy or the birth of a child. Clearly, the responsibilities associated with being a parent can be uniquely rewarding. While unwelcome responsibilities can create unhealthy pressures to escape, obligations to others can actually serve as a buffer against the return to use or at least to use that is destructive.

Careers, professional positions, and jobs that are highly valued can serve a similar purpose. Commitments to organizations and institutions beyond the workplace can also result in a decrease of chronic substance use. Membership in churches, other religious organizations, community groups, civic groups, as well as participation in social and political movements can create forms of responsibility that many find gratifying. This is not to suggest that you should try to shoulder inordinate amounts of responsibility as part of your natural recovery strategy. Excessive responsibility, particularly early on, could actually undermine your recovery. We are suggesting, however, that for people who are attempting to terminate their destructive patterns of substance use, taking responsibility for your own actions as well as for meaningful activities that you truly cherish can help you reach your goal.

BELIEF

In chapter 3 of this book we explored the concept of conversion and its apparent role in the recovery process for many untreated as well as treated remitters. Recall that the conversion experience can be characterized as a fundamental departure from one's addicted life and its accompanying roles and behaviors, resulting in a focused immersion in an alternative, often radically different, lifestyle. We are not talking here about the conversion to an addict identity which is characteristic of many treatment programs. The kind of conversion that many of the self-remitters we interviewed experienced was not to an addict identity, but rather to a new identity that was part of their natural communities.

For instance, many former addicts and alcoholics join religious groups where they become engaged in religious activities such as praying, reading the Bible, attending church services, and becoming personally active in other organized religious activities. These naturally occurring conversion experiences are often all-encompassing and can promote many of the natural recovery strategies that we have discussed above. For example, it is well known that many American males of African ancestry have resolved these kinds of problems by joining the Nation of Islam—the most well-known case being that of Malcolm X. Those who join and remain loyal to the principles and teachings of such a group create new social support networks, find new forms of leisure, modify their diets, assume meaningful responsibilities, and generally integrate into their lives much of what has been discussed above.

However, conversion experiences need not be religious in nature. For some, a complete immersion in the student role could mean that the former substance user who has become a college student directs most of his or her energies toward activities that result in being an excellent student. The student attends all his or her classes; reads and studies all class assignments, including many of the suggested additional readings; develops an in-depth understanding of the content of his or her courses; takes on leadership roles on campus; and through devotion to learning, earns the respect of his or her fellow students and professors. Immersion in such newly found roles can serve to create a new set of values and opportunities that are totally inconsistent with heavy, chronic intoxicant use. Thus, you may not need to "convert" to an addict identity, but you may need to experience a natural conversion that allows you to develop a strong belief structure.

IDENTITY

The majority of the self-remitters we interviewed had abandoned their addict identities and had taken on more conventional roles. During the interviews most took pride in telling us that they did not see themselves as addicts. Instead, their identities centered on the new roles they were performing as students, parents, or workers. Ultimately, those attempting to recover naturally from their addictions need to discover new selves and new ways of being that are deeply rewarding. Discovering "who you are" and becoming attached to social and community groups that support this emerging identity is perhaps the most important thing you can do to promote a natural recovery from addiction. In fact, people often discover "who they are" in the context of their lives in established institutions and social relationships. People are more than their addictions. Everyone is capable of accepting and expressing love, of offering and receiving community, and of creating meaningful social roles. Creating and nurturing new and more positive identities, while at times difficult, is almost always worth the effort.

Conclusion

The strategies we have discussed above are by no means an exhaustive listing of the options available to those who overcome substance use problems without treatment. They are simply those that were common among the self-remitters we interviewed.

One of the things that struck us in the process of writing this book was that successful recovery without treatment in many ways resembles what transpires in effective treatment and even in self-help groups. Recall that in chapter 6 we talked about the value of examining self-recovery for the treatment of substance-dependent clients. Hence, although the approaches we have identified above are directed toward those interested in self-recovery, they could also benefit those who are undergoing treatment, are in aftercare programs, or have completed treatment. In fact, most of this information would be especially useful to those who have completed an inpatient treatment program and are returning to their natural environments.

We also realize that people reading this material who have had direct experience with or otherwise know of the pleasurable sensations that accompany the ingestion of these substances, might have reservations about the efficacy of some of our suggestions. Some might not accept that improved nutrition and health can result in a state of well-being that counters the appeal of using drugs or alcohol. Others might feel that simply severing relationships with using friends and creating new, healthier relationships would not necessarily prevent a return to destructive substance use. In a sense, they would be correct. No single suggestion alone will likely lead to a successful natural recovery. Only through a combination of strategies are addicted individuals likely to realize fundamental changes in their addictive behaviors and in their overall sense of physical and mental wellbeing.

Equally important, the kinds of core changes that we have discussed generally occur gradually, slowly becoming established routines in a person's life. We have no optimal time frame to propose, as each situation and each person is, of course, different. We know of successful cases where former alcoholics and drug addicts realized a relatively comfortable, appealing, and stable state within a few months. We know of other self-recovery attempts that have wavered back and forth, including the return to problematic substance use, for several years before the person finally enjoyed a state of comfort and contentment that was independent of intoxicants. We also know of cases where self-recovery efforts have resulted in a return to use, but at much lower and nondestructive levels that endured for many years. Controlled use or moderation after a period of chronic use does occur. But, like natural recovery, controlled use is likely to be underestimated.

Finally, regardless of whether a person pursues self-recovery or enters treatment, we know that quitting drugs and alcohol after many years of dependence on these substances is an arduous process for most. We are not oblivious to the sheer difficulty and torment that some experience in their genuine attempts to change their lives. However, among the self-remitters that we interviewed, various combinations of these strategies did result in victories over the destructive addictive use of intoxicants by making their wearisome journeys less uncomfortable, more appealing, more meaningful, and more productive. And, because of their decision to quit alcohol and drug addiction on their own rather than by entering the established treatment system, their addict identities are insignificant parts of who they *were* rather than large parts of who they *are*.

NOTES

Notes to Chapter 1

1. See, for example, William Miller and Nick Heather (eds.), *Treating Addictive Behaviors: Processes and Change* (New York: Plenum Press, 1986); Harold Mulford, "Rethinking the Alcohol Problem: A Natural Processes Model," *Journal of Drug Issues* 14 (1984): 31; George Vaillant, *The Natural History of Alcoholism: Causes, Patterns, and Paths to Recovery* (Cambridge: Harvard University Press, 1983); Howard Shaffer and Stephanie Jones, *Quitting Cocaine: The Struggle against Impulse* (Lexington, Mass.: Lexington Books, 1989); Linda Sobell, Mark Sobell, and Tony Toneatto, "Recovery from Alcohol Problems without Treatment," in Nick Heather, William Miller, and J. Greely (eds.), *Self Control and the Addictive Behaviors* (New York: Macmillan, 1992); Robert Granfield and William Cloud, "The Elephant That No One Sees: Natural Recovery among Middle-Class Addicts," *Journal of Drug Issues* 26 (1996): 45–61. Deborah Finfgeld, "Resolution of Drinking Problems without Formal Treatment," *Perspectives in*

Psychiatric Care 33 (July 1997): 14–35; Keith Humphreys, Rudolf Moos, and John Finney, "Two Pathways out of Drinking Problems without Professional Treatment," *Addictive Behaviors* 20 (1995): 427–41.

2. David Lewis, "Spontaneous Remission: A Current Study and the Views of Benjamin Rush," *Brown University Digest of Addiction Theory and Application* 10 (October 1991): 10.

3. Bill Moyers, *Moyers on Addiction. Copyright © 1998 Thirteen/ WNET and Public Affairs Television, Inc.* For an insightful discussion of the hegemony of a disease model of alcoholism in Hollywood films, see Norman Denzin, *Hollywood Shot by Shot: Alcoholism in American Cinema* (Hawthorne, N.Y.: Aldine, 1991).

4. Stanton Peele, "Addiction as a Cultural Concept," *Annals of the New York Academy of Sciences* 602 (1990): 205–20, argues that, based on public opinion polls, 90 percent of Americans view alcoholism as an illness that must be treated.

5. Donald Goodwin, J. Bruce Crane, and Samuel B. Guze, "Felons Who Drink: An Eight-Year Follow-up," *Quarterly Journal of Studies on Alcohol* 32 (1971): 136–147.

6. See generally, R. Hingson, N. Scotch, N. Day, and A. Culbert, "Recognizing and Seeking Help for Drinking Problems," *Journal of Studies on Alcohol* 11 (1980): 1102–17. Ron Roizen, Dan Cahalan, and Patricia Shanks, "'Spontaneous Remission' among Untreated Problem Drinkers," in Denise Kandel (ed.), *Longitudinal Research on Drug Use: Empirical Findings and Methodological Issues* (Washington, D.C.: Hemisphere Publishing, 1978); Linda Sobell, J. Cunningham, Mark Sobell, and Tony Toneatto, "A Life-Span Perspective on Natural Recovery from Alcohol Problems," in John Baer, G. Alan Marlatt, and R. McMahon (eds.), *Addiction Behaviors across the Life Span: Prevention, Treatment, and Policy Issues* (Newbury Park, Calif.: Sage, 1993).

7. E. Lambert, *The Collection and Interpretation of Data from Hidden Populations* (Rockville, Md.: National Institute on Drug Abuse, 1990); Raymond Lee, *Doing Research on Sensitive Topics* (Newbury Park, Calif.: Sage, 1993).

8. Granfield and Cloud, "The Elephant That No One Sees" (1996).

9. Caryle Hirshberg and Marc Ian Barasch, *Remarkable Recovery: What Extraordinary Healings Tell Us about Getting Well and Staying Well* (New York: Riverhead Books, 1995).

10. Henry Dreher, "Remarkable Recovery: Book Reviews," *Natural Health* 25 (July 1995): 148.

11. Ibid.

12. Norman Cousins, *Anatomy of an Illness as Perceived by the Patient* (New York: Doubleday, 1991).

13. Andrew Weil, *Spontaneous Healing* (New York: Fawcett Columbine, 1995).

14. See generally, Sobell et al. "A Life-Span Perspective on Natural Recovery from Alcohol Problems" (1993); Dan Waldorf, "Natural Recovery from Opiate Addiction: Some Social-Psychological Processes of Untreated Recovery," *Journal of Drug Issues* 13 (Spring 1983): 237–80; Patrick Biernacki, *Pathways from Heroin Addiction: Recovery without Treatment* (Philadelphia: Temple University Press, 1986).

15. Charles Winick, "Maturing Out of Narcotic Addiction," *Bulletin on Narcotics* 14 (1962): 1–7; Linda Sobell, John Cunningham, Mark Sobell, Sangeeta Agrawal, Douglas Gavin, Gloria Leo, and Karen Singh, "Fostering Self-Change among Problem Drinkers: A Proactive Community Intervention," *Addictive Behaviors* 21 (1996): 817–33.

16. Harold Klingemann, "Coping and Maintenance Strategies of Spontaneous Remitters from Problem Use of Alcohol and Heroin in Switzerland," *International Journal of the Addictions* 27 (1992): 1359–88.

17. Ronald Stall and Patrick Biernacki, "Spontaneous Remission from the Problematic Use of Substances: An Inductive Model Derived from a Comparative Analysis of Alcohol, Opiates, Tobacco, and Food/Obesity Literatures," *International Journal of the Addictions* 21 (1986): 1–23; Ronald Stall, "An Examination of Spontaneous Remission from Problem Drinking in the Bluegrass Region of Kentucky," *Journal of Drug Issues* 13 (1983): 191–206; Glenn Walters, "Spontaneous Remission from Alcohol, Tobacco, and Other Drug Abuse: Seeking Quantitative Answers to Qualitative Questions" (in press).

18. Arnold Ludwig, "Cognitive Processes Associated with "'Spontaneous' Recovery from Alcoholism," *Journal of Studies on Alcohol* 46 (1985): 53–58; Reginald Smart, "Spontaneous Recovery in Alcoholics: A Review and Analysis of the Available Research," *Drug and Alcohol Dependence* 1 (1975/1976): 277–85.

19. Rossana Mariezcurrena, "Recovery from Addictions without

Treatment: Literature Review," *Scandinavian Journal of Behavior Therapy* 23 (1994): 131–54.

20. Benjamin Rush, *An Inquiry into the Effects of Ardent Spirits Upon the Human Body and Mind*, 1785. Cited in Lewis, "Spontaneous Remission" (1991).

21. Anthony Giddens, *Modernity and Self-Identity: Self and Society in the Late Modern Age* (Stanford: Stanford University Press, 1991).

22. Pierre Bourdieu, *Distinction: A Social Critique of the Judgment of Taste* (Cambridge: Harvard University Press, 1984).

23. J. David Brown, "Preprofessional Socialization and Identity Transformation: The Case of the Professional Ex.," *Journal of Contemporary Ethnography* 20 (1991): 157–78.

24. Constructivist perspectives in sociology hold that social problems emerge out of the subjective reactions of interested parties to particular types of social behavior. For constructivists, the analysis of social problems should focus more on the subjective dimensions of public alarm than on its actual objective conditions, which are often neither necessary nor sufficient. For general constructivist views in sociology, see Malcolm Spector and John Kitsuse, *Constructing Social Problems* (Menlo Park, Calif.: Cummings, 1977); Joel Best, *Threatened Children* (Chicago: University of Chicago Press, 1990); Theodore Sasson, *Crime Talk: How Citizens Construct a Social Problem* (Hawthorne, N.Y.: Aldine De Gruyter, 1995). Joseph Gusfield, *The Culture of Public Problems* (Chicago: University of Chicago Press, 1981). For a constructivist analysis of drug scares, see Craig Reinarman and Harry Levine, "The Crack Attack: Politics and Media in the Crack Scare," in Craig Reinarman and Harry Levine (eds.), *Crack in America: Demon Drugs and Social Justice* (Berkeley: University of California Press, 1997); Laura Gomez, *Misconceiving Mothers* (Philadelphia: Temple University Press, 1997).

25. Enoch Gordis, "Accessible and Affordable Health Care for Alcoholism and Related Problems: Strategies for Cost Containment," *Journal of Studies on Alcohol* 28 (1987): 582.

26. See Joel Best (ed.), *Images of Issues: Typifying Contemporary Social Problems* (Hawthorne, N.Y.: Aldine De Gruyter, 1995).

27. Craig Reinarman, "The Social Construction of Alcohol Problems: The Case of Mothers against Drunk Drivers and Social Control in

the 1980s," *Theory and Society* 17 (1988): 91–119. For an insightful discussion of the problematization of alcohol problems, see Ron Roizen and Kaye Middleton Fillmore, "Natural Remission as Symbolic Property in Alcohol Research," paper presented at the International Conference on Natural History of Addictions, Les Diablerets, Switzerland, March 5–12, 1999.

28. Peele, "Addiction as a Cultural Concept" (1990).

29. Stanton Peele, "Can We Treat Away Our Alcohol and Drug Problems or Is the Current Treatment Binge Doing More Harm than Good?" *Journal of Psychoactive Drugs* 20 (1988): 375–83.

30. Stanton Peele and Archie Brodsky, "AA Abuse," *Reason* (November 1991): 34–39.

31. Joseph Schneider, "Deviant Drinking as Disease: Alcoholism as a Social Accomplishment," *Social Problems* 25 (1978): 361–72.

32. Harry Levine, "The Discovery of Addiction: Changing Conceptions of Habitual Drunkenness in America," *Journal of Studies on Alcohol* 39 (1978): 143–74; Harry Levine, "The Alcohol Problem in America: From Temperance to Alcoholism," *British Journal of Addiction* 79 (1984): 109–19.

33. Peele, "Addiction as a Cultural Concept" (1990): 207.

34. Ansley Hamid, *Drugs in America: Sociology, Economics, and Politics* (Gaithersburg, Md.: Aspen Publishing, 1998).

35. Carolyn Weisner and Robin Room, "Financing and Ideology in Alcohol Treatment," *Social Problems* 32 (1978): 157–84.

36. The authors would like to thank Craig Reinarman for suggesting this phrase.

37. Finfgeld, "Resolution of Drinking Problems" (1997).

38. Harvard Medical School Health Publishing Group, "Treatment of Drug Abuse and Addiction—Part III," *Harvard Mental Health Letter* 12 (October 1995).

39. Linda Sobell, John Cunningham, and Mark Sobell, "Recovery from Alcohol Problems with and without Treatment: Prevalence in Two Population Surveys," *American Journal of Public Health* 96 (1996): 966–72.

40. Vaillant, *The Natural History of Alcoholism* (1983).

41. Dan Waldorf, Craig Reinarman, and Sheigla Murphy, *Cocaine Changes: The Experience of Using and Quitting* (Philadelphia: Temple University Press, 1991).

42. Glenn Walters, "The Natural History of Substance Abuse in an Incarcerated Criminal Population," *Journal of Drug Issues* 26 (Fall 1996): 943–59.

43. Victor Gecas and Michael Schwalbe, "Beyond the Looking Glass Self: Social Structure and Efficacy-Based Self-Esteem," *Social Psychology Quarterly* 46 (1983): 77–88; Anna Riley, "The Ghetto Underclass Experience: A Social Psychological Analysis," paper presented at the annual meeting of the American Sociological Association, San Francisco: August 1998.

44. Walters, "The Natural History" (1996).

45. James Maddux and David Desmond, "New Light on the Maturing Out Hypothesis in Opioid Dependence," *Bulletin on Narcotics* 32 (1980): 15–25.

46. Waldorf, Reinarman, and Murphy, *Cocaine Changes* (1991).

47. Sobell, Cummingham, and Sobell, "Recovery from Alcohol Problems" (1996).

48. Waldorf, "Natural Recovery from Opiate Addiction" (1983).

49. Waldorf, Reinarman, and Murphy, *Cocaine Changes* (1991).

50. Klingemann, "Coping and Maintenance Strategies" (1992).

51. W. Saunders and P. Kershaw, "Spontaneous Remission from Alcoholism: A Community Study," *British Journal of Addiction* 74 (1979): 251–66.

52. Waldorf, "Natural Recovery from Opiate Addiction," (1983); Biernacki, *Pathways from Heroin Addiction* (1986).

53. Walters, "Spontaneous Remission from Alcohol, Tobacco, and Other Drug Abuse" (in press).

54. Sobell et al., "Fostering Self-Change among Problem Drinkers" (1996). For sociological research on self-change, see K. Jill Kiecolt, "Stress and the Decision to Change Oneself: A Theoretical Model," *Social Psychological Quarterly* 57 (1994): 49–63; Peter Burke, "Identity Processes and Social Stress," *American Sociological Review* 56 (1991): 836–49.

55. Ludwig, "Cognitive Processes Associated with 'Spontaneous' Recovery from Alcoholism" (1985): 57.

56. Stall and Biernacki, "Spontaneous Remission from the Problematic Use of Substances" (1986).

57. Sobell, Cunningham, and Sobell, "Recovery from Alcohol Problems" (1996); Barry Tuchfeld, "Spontaneous Remission in Alcoholics: Empirical Observations and Theoretical Implications," *Journal of Stud-*

ies on Alcohol 42 (1981): 626–41; Jalie Tucker, Rudy Vuchinich, and Julie Gladsjo, "Environmental Events Surrounding Natural Recovery from Alcohol-Related Problems," *Journal of Studies on Alcohol* 55 (1994): 401–11.

58. See Arlie Hochschild, *The Managed Heart* (Berkeley: University of California Press, 1983) for a discussion of emotion work.

59. Biernacki, *Pathways from Heroin Addiction* (1986).

60. Stephan Mugford and Phil Cohen, *Drug Use, Social Relations, and Commodity Consumption: A Study of Recreational Cocaine Users in Sydney, Canberra and Melbourne*. Report to the National Campaign against Drug Abuse (Canberra: Australia National University, 1988).

61. For a discussion of the "vocabulary of motive," see C. Wright Mills, "Situated Actions and Vocabularies of Motive," *American Sociological Review* 5 (1940): 904–13.

62. Philippe Bourgois, *In Search of Respect: Selling Crack in El Barrio* (Cambridge: Cambridge University Press, 1995). Mitchell Ratner, *Crack Pipe as Pimp: An Ethnographic Investigation of Sex-for-Crack Exchanges* (New York: Lexington Books, 1993). Patricia Adler, *Wheeling and Dealing: An Ethnography of an Upper-Level Drug Dealing and Smuggling Community* (New York: Columbia University Press, 1985).

63. Stuart Hills and Ron Santiago, *Tragic Magic: The Life and Crimes of a Heroin Addict* (Chicago: Nelson-Hall, 1992).

64. Waldorf, "Natural Recovery from Opiate Addiction" (1983); Sobell, Sobell, and Toneatto, "Recovery from Alcohol Problems without Treatment" (1992).

65. Project MATCH Group, "Matching Alcoholism Treatments to Client Heterogeneity: Project MATCH Posttreatment Drinking Outcomes," *Journal of Studies on Alcohol* 58 (January 1997): 7–29.

66. Klingemann, "Coping and Maintenance Strategies" (1992); Tucker, Vuchinich, and Gladsjo, "Environmental Events Surrounding Natural Recovery" (1994).

67. Clifford Geertz, *The Interpretation of Cultures: Selected Essays* (New York: Basic Books, 1973).

68. John Lofland and Lyn Lofland, *Analyzing Social Settings: A Guide to Qualitative Observation and Analysis* (Belmont, Calif.: Wadsworth Press, 1984).

69. Yvonne Lincoln and Egon Guba, *Naturalistic Inquiry* (Newbury Park, Calif.: Sage, 1985).

70. Institute of Medicine, *Broadening the Base of Treatment for*

Alcohol Problems (Washington, D.C.: National Academy Press, 1990). See also Chad Emrick, J. Scott Tonigan, Henry Montgomery, and Laura Little, "Alcoholics Anonymous: What Is Currently Known?" in Barbara McCrady and William Miller (eds.), *Research on Alcoholics Anonymous: Opportunities and Alternatives* (New Brunswick, N.J.: Rutgers Center of Alcohol Studies, 1993).

71. Deborah Dawson, "Correlates of Past-Year Status among Treated and Untreated Persons with Former Alcohol Dependence: United States, 1992," *Alcoholism: Clinical and Experimental Research* 20 (1996): 771–79.

72. Project MATCH Group, "Matching Alcoholism Treatments" (1997).

73. Ibid., 25.

Notes to Chapter 2

1. Alisse Waterston, *Street Addicts in the Political Economy* (Philadelphia: Temple University Press, 1993).

2. Pertti Alasuutari, *Desire and Craving: A Cultural Theory of Alcoholism* (Albany: State University of New York Press, 1992).

3. John Kobler, *Ardent Spirits: The Rise and Fall of Prohibition* (New York: Putnam, 1973).

4. Victor Turner, *The Ritual Process: Structure and Anti-Structure* (Ithaca, N.Y.: Cornell University Press, 1969).

5. Max Weber, *From Max Weber: Essays in Sociology,* edited by H. H. Gerth and C. Wright Mills (New York: Oxford University Press, 1958).

6. John Rumbarger, *Profits, Power, and Prohibition: Alcohol Reform and the Industrializing of America, 1800–1930* (Albany: State University of New York Press, 1989).

7. Wolfgang Schivelbusch, *Tastes of Paradise: A Social History of Spices, Stimulants, and Intoxicants* (New York: Vintage, 1993).

8. Craig Reinarman and Harry Levine (eds.), *Crack in America: Demon Drugs and Social Justice* (Berkeley: University of California Press, 1997), 5.

9. Rumbarger, *Profits, Power, and Prohibition* (1989).

10. See Joel Best, *Threatened Children* (Chicago: University of Chicago Press, 1990) for a discussion of "typification."

11. Rick Fantasia, *Cultures of Solidarity: Consciousness, Action and Contemporary American Workers* (Berkeley: University of California Press, 1988), 20.

12. David Musto, *The American Disease: Origins of Narcotic Control* (New Haven, Conn.: Yale University Press, [1973] 1987).

13. Edward Brecher, *Licit and Illicit Drugs* (Boston: Little, Brown, 1972).

14. Eva Bertram, Morris Blachman, Kenneth Sharpe, and Peter Andreas, *Drug War Politics: The Price of Denial* (Berkeley: University of California Press, 1996). Robert Granfield and Kevin Ryan, "Professional Conflict and Ethical Dilemmas in American Drug Policy" (in press).

15. See E.M. Jellinek, *The Disease Concept of Alcoholism* (Highland Park, N.J.: Hillhouse, 1960).

16. Joseph Schneider, "Deviant Drinking as Disease: Alcoholism as a Social Accomplishment," *Social Problems* 25 (1978): 361–72. See also Robin Room, "Drinking and Disease: Comments on 'The Alcohologist's Addiction,'" *Quarterly Journal of Studies on Alcohol* 33 (1972): 1049–59.

17. David Rosenhan, "On Being Sane in Insane Places," *Science* 179 (1973): 250–58; Thomas Szasz, *The Myth of Mental Illness: Foundations of a Theory of Personal Conduct* (New York: Hoeber-Harper, 1961).

18. Antonio Gramsci, *Selections from Prison Notebooks* (New York: International Publishers, 1971).

19. Alasuutari, *Desire and Craving* (1992).

20. Ibid., 160.

21. Philippe Bourgois, *In Search of Respect: Selling Crack in El Barrio* (Cambridge: Cambridge University Press, 1995). Alasuutari, *Desire and Craving* (1992).

22. Norman Zinberg, *Drug, Set, and Setting: The Basis for Controlled Intoxicant Use* (New Haven, Conn.: Yale University Press, 1984).

23. Lee Robins, Darlene Davis, and Donald Goodwin, "Drug Use in U.S. Army Enlisted Men in Vietnam: A Follow-Up on Their Return Home," *American Journal of Epidemiology* 99 (1974): 235–49.

24. Richard Klein, *Cigarettes Are Sublime* (Durham, N.C.: Duke University Press, 1996), 184.

25. Stanton Peele, *The Diseasing of America: Addiction Treatment Out of Control* (Lexington, Mass.: Lexington Books, 1989).

26. Luigi Zoja, *Drugs, Addiction and Initiation: The Modern Search for Ritual* (Boston: Sigo Press, 1989), 93.

27. Dan Waldorf, Craig Reinarman, and Sheigla Murphy, *Cocaine Changes: The Experience of Using and Quitting* (Philadelphia: Temple University Press, 1991).

28. For a discussion of drug use in the inner cities, see Bourgois, *In Search of Respect* (1995); and Terry Williams, *The Cocaine Kids: The Inside Story of a Teenage Drug Ring* (Reading, Mass.: Addison-Wesley, 1989).

29. This term is commonly used to describe the social ties and resources that ultimately affect a person's quality of life chances in society. We explore the social capital of our respondents and its relation to natural recovery in greater depth later in this book. For general discussions of the concept of "social capital," see James Coleman, *Foundations of Social Theory* (Cambridge: Harvard University Press, 1990); Robert Putnam, *Making Democracy Work: Civic Traditions in Modern Italy* (Princeton: Princeton University Press, 1993); Pierre Bourdieu, *Distinction: A Social Critique of the Judgment of Taste* (Cambridge: Harvard University Press, 1984).

30. Waldorf, Reinarman, and Murphy, *Cocaine Changes* (1991).

31. See Bourgois, *In Search of Respect* (1995); and Waterston, *Street Addicts* (1993).

32. Alfred Lindesmith, *Opiate Addiction* (Evanston, Ill.: Principia Press, 1947).

33. Bryan Wilson, *Magic and the Millennium* (London: Heineman, 1973), 422.

34. Andrew Weil, *The Natural Mind* (Boston: Houghton Mifflin, 1972).

35. See Denise Brissett, "Denial in Alcoholism: A Sociological Interpretation," *Journal of Drug Issues* 18 (1988): 385–402.

36. For a discussion of the consumerist tendencies produced by capitalism, see Daniel Bell, *The Cultural Contradictions of Capitalism* (New York: Basic Books, 1976); and Herbert Marcuse, *One-Dimensional Man: Studies in the Ideology of Advanced Industrial Societies* (Boston: Beacon Press, 1964).

37. Max Weber, *The Protestant Ethic and the Spirit of Capitalism* (London: Unwin, [1920] 1985).

38. David Karp, *Speaking of Sadness* (New York: Oxford University Press, 1996), 54.

39. American Psychiatric Association, *Diagnostic and Statistical Manual of Mental Disorders: DSM-IV,* (Washington, D.C.: American Psychiatric Association, 1994).

40. Dianne Vaughan, *Uncoupling* (New York: Oxford University Press, 1986).

41. Richard Gelles and Murray Straus, *Intimate Violence* (New York: Simon and Schuster, 1988).

42. Charles Faupel, *Shooting Dope: Career Patterns of Hard-Core Heroin Users* (Gainsville, Fla.: University of Florida Press, 1991).

43. Richard Jenkins, *Social Identity* (London: Routledge, 1996).

Notes to Chapter 3

1. For a discussion of how using, experiencing, and quitting drugs is a learned experience, see Howard Becker, "Becoming a Marijuana User," *American Journal of Sociology* 59 (1953): 235–42, which argues that neophyte users must learn the technique, learn to perceive the effects, and learn to interpret these effects as pleasurable. Also see Arnold Ludwig, "Cognitive Processes Associated with 'Spontaneous' Recovery from Alcoholism," *Journal of Studies on Alcohol* 46 (1985): 53–58, which argues that those who spontaneously recover from alcoholism form negative associations to the notion of drinking.

2. Patrick Biernacki, *Pathways from Heroin Addiction: Recovery without Treatment* (Philadelphia: Temple University Press, 1986); Howard Shaffer and Stephanie Jones, *Quitting Cocaine: The Struggle against Impulse* (Lexington, Mass.: Lexington Books, 1989); Dan Waldorf, Craig Reinarman, and Sheigla Murphy, *Cocaine Changes: The Experience of Using and Quitting* (Philadelphia: Temple University Press, 1991).

3. Biernacki, *Pathways from Heroin Addiction* (1986).

4. For a discussion of the difficulties associated with recovery, see Marsh Ray, "The Cycle of Abstinence and Relapse among Heroin Addicts," in Howard Becker (ed.), *The Other Side* (New York: Free Press, 1964).

5. Shaffer and Jones, *Quitting Cocaine* (1989).

6. There is an abundance of ethnographic research on the subculture of drug use. See generally, Marsha Rosenbaum, *Women on Heroin*

(New Brunswick, N.J.: Rutgers University Press, 1981); Bill Hanson, George Beschner, James Walters, Elliott Bovelle (eds.), *Life with Heroin: Voices from the Inner City* (Lexington, Mass.: D. C. Heath, 1985); Edward Preble and John Casey, "Taking Care of Business—The Heroin User's Life on the Street," *International Journal of Addictions* 4 (1969): 1–24; Dan Waldorf, *Careers in Dope* (Englewood Cliffs, N.J.: Prentice Hall, 1973); Richard Stephens, *The Street Addict Role: A Theory of Heroin Addiction* (Albany: State University of New York Press, 1991).

7. Biernacki, *Pathways from Heroin Addiction* (1986), 76.

8. Stanton Peele, *The Meaning of Addiction: Compulsive Experience and Its Interpretation* (Lexington, Mass.: D. C. Heath, 1985).

9. Biernacki, *Pathways from Heroin Addiction* (1986), 97. Also see Norman Denzin, *The Recovering Alcoholic* (Thousand Oaks, Calif.: Sage, 1987).

10. Helen Rose Fuchs Ebaugh, *Becoming an EX: The Process of Role Exit* (Chicago: University of Chicago Press, 1988).

11. For personal transformations based on religious conversion, see John Lofland and Rodney Stark, "Becoming a World Saver: A Theory of Conversion to a Deviant Perspective," in John Lofland (ed.), *Protest: Studies of Collective Behavior and Social Movements* (New Brunswick, N.J.: Transaction Books, 1988); and Richard Travisano, "Alternation and Conversion as Qualitatively Different Transformations," in Gregory Stone and H. Farberman (eds.), *Social Psychology through Symbolic Interaction* (Waltham, Mass.: Ginn-Blaisdell, 1981).

12. Biernacki, *Pathways from Heroin Addiction* (1986), 97.

13. Gregory Bateson, "The Cybernetics of 'Self': A Theory of Alcoholism," in Gregory Bateson (ed.), *Steps to an Ecology of Mind* (New York: Ballantine Books, 1972).

14. Biernacki, *Pathways from Heroin Addiction* (1986); Dan Waldorf, "Natural Recovery from Opiate Addiction: Some Social-Psychological Processes of Untreated Recovery," *Journal of Drug Issues* 13 (Spring 1983): 237–80.

15. E. O'Reilly, *Sobering Tales: Narratives of Alcoholism and Recovery* (Amherst, Mass.: University of Massachusetts Press, 1997).

16. Norman Denzin, *The Alcoholic Society* (New Brunswick, N.J.: Transaction Books, 1993).

17. Patricia Adler and Peter Adler, *Backboards and Blackboards: College Athletes and Role Engulfment* (New York: Columbia University Press, 1991).

18. Denzin, *The Alcoholic Society* (1993); J. David Brown, "Preprofessional Socialization and Identity Transformation: The Case of the Professional Ex.," *Journal of Contemporary Ethnography* 20 (1991): 157–78.

19. Edwin Schur, *Labeling Deviant Behavior: Its Sociological Implications* (New York: Harper and Row, 1971).

20. Ebaugh, *Becoming an EX* (1988).

21. Adler and Adler, *Backboards and Blackboards* (1991).

22. Denzin, *The Recovering Alcoholic* (1987); O'Reilly, *Sobering Tales* (1997); Brown, "Preprofessional Socialization and Identity Transformation" (1991).

23. David Rudy, *Becoming Alcoholic: Alcoholics Anonymous and the Reality of Alcoholism* (Carbondale, Ill.: Southern Illinois University Press, 1986).

24. Travisano, "Alternation and Conversion" (1981), 535.

25. Max Heirich, "Change of Heart: A Test of Some Widely Held Theories about Religious Conversion," *American Sociological Review* 83 (1977): 674.

26. Roger Straus, "Changing Oneself: Seekers and the Creative Transformation of Life Experience," in J. Lofland (ed.), *Doing Social Life: The Qualitative Study of Human Interaction in Natural Settings* (New York: Wiley and Sons, 1976).

27. Lofland and Stark, "Becoming a World Saver" (1988).

28. Ibid., 139.

29. Biernacki, *Pathways from Heroin Addiction* (1986), 88–89.

30. James Christopher, *Unhooked: Staying Sober and Drug Free* (Buffalo, N.Y.: Prometheus Books, 1989).

31. John Lofland (ed.), *Protest: Studies of Collective Behavior and Social Movements.* (New Brunswick, N.J.: Transaction Books, 1988).

32. Becker, "Becoming a Marijuana User" (1953).

33. Ebaugh, *Becoming an EX* (1988).

34. Richard Jessor and Shirley Jessor, *Problem Behavior and Psychosocial Development: A Longitudinal Study of Youth* (New York: Academic Press, 1977); James Jorguez, "The Retirement Phase of the Heroin-Using Career," *Journal of Drug Issues* 13 (1983): 343.

35. Ebaugh, *Becoming an EX* (1988).

36. Patricia Erikson, E. M. Adlaf, Glenn Murray, and Reginald Smart, *The Steel Drug: Cocaine in Perspective* (Lexington, Mass.: Lexington Books, 1987); Waldorf, Reinarman, and Murphy, *Cocaine Changes* (1991).

37. Ebaugh, *Becoming an EX* (1988), 86.

38. Lofland and Stark, "Becoming a World Saver" (1988), 138.

39. Anselm Strauss, *Mirrors and Masks* (New York: Free Press, 1958).

40. Louis Zurcher, *The Mutable Self* (Beverly Hills, Calif.: Sage, 1977).

41. George Herbert Mead, *Mind, Self and Society* (Chicago: University of Chicago Press, 1934).

42. Harrison Trice and Paul Roman, "Delabeling, Relabeling, and Alcoholics Anonymous," *Social Problems* 17 (1970): 538–46; Brown, "Preprofessional Socialization and Identity Transformation" (1991).

43. Denzin, *The Alcoholic Society* (1993).

44. Peele, *The Meaning of Addiction* (1985), 154.

45. Norman Zinberg, *Drug, Set, and Setting: The Basis for Controlled Intoxicant Use* (New Haven, Conn.: Yale University Press, 1984). See also Craig MacAndrew and Robert Edgerton, *Drunken Comportment: A Social Explanation* (Chicago: Aldine, 1969); Howard Becker, "History, Culture, and Subjective Experience: An Exploration of the Bases of Drug-Induced Experiences," *Journal of Health and Social Behavior* 8 (1967): 162–76; Alfred Lindesmith, *Opiate Addiction* (Evanston, Ill.: Principia Press, 1947); Lee Robins, Darlene Davis, and Donald Goodwin, "Drug Use in U.S. Army Enlisted Men in Vietnam: A Follow-Up on Their Return Home," *American Journal of Epidemiology* 99 (1974).

46. Sheigla Murphy and Marsha Rosenbaum, "Two Women Who Used Cocaine Too Much: Class, Race, Gender, Crack, and Coke," in Craig Reinarman and Harry Levine (eds.), *Crack in America: Demon Drugs and Social Justice* (Berkeley: University of California Press, 1997), 109.

47. Robert Simmonds, "Conversion or Addiction: Consequences of Joining a Jesus Movement Group," in J. Richardson (ed.) *Conversion Careers: In and out of the New Religions* (Beverly Hills, Calif.: Sage 1977).

48. E. Burke Rochford, *Hare Krishna in America* (New Brunswick, N.J.: Rutgers University Press, 1986).

49. A. L. Mauss and D. W. Peterson, "Les 'Jesus freaks' et le retour à la respectabilité," *Social Compass* 21 (1974): 269.

50. Trice and Roman, "Delabeling, Relabeling" (1970); Talcott Parsons, *The Social System* (Chicago: Free Press, 1951).

51. For discussion of stigma reduction, see Erving Goffman, *Stigma: Notes on the Sociology of Deviance* (Englewood Cliffs, N.J.: Prentice-Hall, 1963).

52. Brown, "Preprofessional Socialization and Identity Transformation" (1991).

53. Biernacki, *Pathways from Heroin Addiction* (1986).

54. Lofland and Stark, "Becoming a World Saver" (1988).

55. For an insightful discussion on this point, see Craig Reinarman. "The 12-Step Movement and Advanced Capitalist Culture: Notes on the Politics of Self-Control in Postmodernity," in M. Darnovsky, B. Epstein, and R. Flacks (eds.), *Cultural Politics and Social Movements* (Philadelphia: Temple University Press, 1995).

56. Graham Allan, *Friendship: Developing a Sociological Perspective* (Boulder, Colo.: Westview, 1989).

57. Rosenbaum, *Women on Heroin* (1981); Waldorf, Reinarman, and Murphy, *Cocaine Changes* (1991); William Cloud, "From Down Under: A Qualitative Study on Heroin Addiction Recovery," (Ph.D. dissertation, University of Denver (1987).

58. Murphy and Rosenbaum, "Two Women Who Used Cocaine Too Much" (1997).

59. Mitchell Ratner, *Crack Pipe as Pimp: An Ethnographic Investigation of Sex-for-Crack Exchanges* (New York: Lexington Books, 1993).

60. Biernacki, *Pathways from Heroin Addiction* (1986); James Maddux and David Desmond, "New Light on the Maturing Out Hypothesis in Opioid Dependence," *Bulletin on Narcotics* 32 (1980).

61. Dick Anthony, Thomas Robbins, Madeline Doucas, and Thomas Curtis, "Patients and Pilgrims: Changing Attitudes towards Psychotherapy of Converts to Eastern Mysticism," in James Richardson (ed.), *Conversion Careers: In and out of the New Religions* (Beverly Hills, Calif.: Sage, 1977).

62. Waldorf, Reinarman, and Murphy, *Cocaine Changes* (1991);

Zinberg, *Drug, Set, and Setting* (1984); Andrew Weil, *The Natural Mind* (Boston: Houghton Mifflin, 1972).

63. See Philippe Bourgois, *In Search of Respect: Selling Crack in El Barrio* (Cambridge: Cambridge University Press, 1995); Alisse Waterston, *Street Addicts in the Political Economy* (Philadelphia: Temple University Press, 1993).

64. Peele, *The Meaning of Addiction* (1985), 129.

65. Craig Reinarman and Harry Levine (eds.), *Crack in America: Demon Drugs and Social Justice* (Berkeley: University of California Press, 1997).

66. Ibid., 9.

67. Denzin, *The Recovering Alcoholic* (1987).

Notes to Chapter 4

1. Erving Goffman, *Asylums* (Garden City, N.J.: Anchor Books, 1961).

2. Stanton Peele, *The Diseasing of America: Addiction Treatment Out of Control* (Lexington, Mass.: Lexington Books, 1989).

3. Pertti Alasuutari, *Desire and Craving: A Cultural Theory of Alcoholism* (Albany: State University of New York Press, 1992); Stanton Peele, "Addiction as a Cultural Concept," *Annals of the New York Academy of Sciences* 602 (1990): 205–20.

4. Harry Levine, "The Discovery of Addiction: Changing Conceptions of Habitual Drunkenness in America," *Journal of Studies on Alcohol* 39 (1978): 143–74.

5. Wolfgang Schivelbusch, *Tastes of Paradise: A Social History of Spices, Stimulants, and Intoxicants* (New York: Vintage, 1993).

6. Gary Albrecht, *The Disability Business: Rehabilitation in America* (Newbury Park, Calif.: Sage, 1992); Irving Zola, "Self, Identity, and the Naming Question: Reflections on the Language of Disability," *Social Science and Medicine* 36 (1993): 167–73.

7. David Rosenhan, "On Being Sane in Insane Places," *Science* 179 (1973): 250–58.

8. Robert Granfield, "Constructing Disability: Organizational Practice and Community Response," *Journal of Applied Sociology* 13 (1996): 44–59; Robert Scott, The *Making of Blind Men* (New York: Russell Sage Foundation, 1969).

9. Zola, "Self, Identity, and the Naming Question" (1993).

10. Edwin Lemert, *Social Pathology* (New York: McGraw-Hill, 1951); Howard Becker, *The Outsiders: Studies in the Sociology of Deviance* (Glencoe, Ill.: Free Press, 1963).

11. Goffman, *Asylums* (1961).

12. Geoffrey Skoll, *Walk the Walk and Talk the Talk: An Ethnography of a Drug Abuse Treatment Facility* (Philadelphia: Temple University Press, 1992).

13. Patricia Adler and Peter Adler, *Backboards and Blackboards: College Athletes and Role Engulfment* (New York: Columbia University Press, 1991).

14. Thomas Szasz, *The Myth of Mental Illness: Foundations of a Theory of Personal Conduct* (New York: Hoeber-Harper, 1961).

15. Granfield, "Constructing Disability" (1996); Rosanne Darling, "Parental Entrepreneurship: A Consumerist Response to Professional Dominance," *Journal of Social Issues* 44 (1988): 141–58; Joe Shapiro, *No Pity* (New York: Times Books, 1994).

16. Nicholas Fox, *Postmodernism, Sociology and Health* (Toronto: University of Toronto Press, 1994).

17. See Michel Foucault, *Discipline and Punish* (Harmondsworth: Penguin, 1976); *Madness and Civilization* (London: Tavistock, 1967); *Power/Knowledge: Selected Interviews and Other Writings 1972–1977* (New York: Pantheon Books, 1980).

18. Robert Wuthnow, James Davidson Hunter, Albert Bergesen, and Edith Kursweil, *Cultural Analysis* (New York: Routledge, Chapman and Hall, 1984).

19. Fox, *Postmodernism, Sociology and Health* (1994), 24.

20. Michel Foucault, "Technologies of the Self," in Luther Martin, Huck Gutman, and Patrick Hutton (eds.), *Technologies of the Self* (London: Tavistock, 1988).

21. Ibid., 18.

22. Nikolas Rose, *Governing the Soul* (London: Routledge, 1989).

23. Paul Hutton, "Foucault, Freud and the Technologies of the Self," in Luther Martin, Huck Gutman, and Patrick Hutton (eds.), *Technologies of the Self* (London: Tavistock, 1988); Fox, *Postmodernism, Sociology and Health* (1994).

24. David Karp, *Speaking of Sadness* (New York: Oxford University Press, 1996).

25. Albrecht, *The Disability Business* (1992).

26. Barry Glassner, "Fitness and the Postmodern Self," *Journal of Health and Social Behavior* 30 (1989): 180–91.

27. Eliot Freidson, *Professional Power* (Chicago: University of Chicago Press, 1986).

28. Darling, "Parental Entrepreneurship" (1988); David Engel, "Origin Myths: Narratives of Authority, Resistance, Disability and Law," *Law and Society* 27 (1991): 785–826.

29. Fox, *Postmodernism, Sociology and Health* (1994).

30. Irving Zola, "Toward Independent Living: Goals and Dilemmas," in Nancy Crewe and Irving Zola (eds.), *Independent Living for Physically Disabled People* (San Francisco: Jossey-Bass, 1983).

31. Granfield, "Constructing Disability" (1996).

32. Gareth Williams, "The Genesis of Chronic Illness: Narrative Reconstruction," in Lewis Hinchman and Sandra Hinchman (eds.), *Memory, Identity, Community: The Idea of Narrative in the Human Sciences* (Albany: State University of New York Press, 1997).

33. Fox, *Postmodernism, Sociology and Health* (1994), 71. See also Arthur Kleinman, *The Illness Narratives: Suffering, Healing and the Human Condition* (New York: Basic Books, 1988).

34. R. Hugman, *Power in Caring Professions* (Basingstoke: Macmillan, 1991); Jeffry Galper, *The Politics of Social Services* (Englewood Cliffs, N.J.: Prentice-Hall, 1975).

35. The remaining 15 percent offered a variety of reasons such as the stigma associated with treatment, limited availability, and inability to share problems with others.

36. Patrick Biernacki, *Pathways from Heroin Addiction: Recovery without Treatment* (Philadelphia: Temple University Press, 1986).

37. Charles Bufe, *Alcoholics Anonymous: Cult or Cure* (San Francisco: Sharp Press, 1991).

38. Criticism of essentialist views emerged from feminist scholarship which maintained that arguments about the characteristics assumed to be natural of men and women are specious. For instance, women aren't naturally or essentially more cooperative or submissive as a group. See Angela Harris, "Race and Essentialism in Feminist Legal Theory," *Stanford Law Review* 42 (1990): 581–616. Cynthia Fuchs Epstein, *Deceptive Distinctions: Sex, Gender, and the Social Order* (New Haven, Conn.: Yale University Press, 1988); Robert Granfield, "Con-

textualizing the Different Voice: Women, Occupational Goals, and Legal Education," *Law and Policy* 16 (1994): 1–26. Similarly, what has come to be known as "queer theory" takes exception to essentialist forms of reasoning. See Ruthann Robson, *Sappho Goes to Law School* (New York: Columbia University Press, 1998).

39. Joseph Schneider, "Deviant Drinking as Disease: Alcoholism as a Social Accomplishment," *Social Problems* 25 (1978): 361–72.

40. Glenn Walters, *The Addiction Concept: Working Hypothesis or Self-Fulfilling Prophesy* (Boston: Allyn and Bacon, 1999).

41. See Joel Best, *Threatened Children* (Chicago: University of Chicago Press, 1990) for a discussion of urban myths.

42. Peele, *The Diseasing of America* (1989); Wendy Kaminer, *I'm Dysfunctional, You're Dysfunctional: The Recovery Movement and Other Self-Help Fashions* (New York: Vintage, 1993).

43. The recognition of natural recovery may be the kind of politically inconvenient scientific knowledge that will improve treatment and public policy regarding addiction. See Dan Waldorf, Craig Reinarman, and Sheigla Murphy, *Cocaine Changes: The Experience of Using and Quitting* (Philadelphia: Temple University Press, 1991).

44. Adler and Adler, *Backboards and Blackboards* (1991), 28.

45. There is a voluminous sociological literature on roles and the self. For a discussion of role hierarchies, see Sheldon Stryker, *Symbolic Interactionism: A Social Structural Version* (Menlo Park, Calif.: Cummings, 1980); Peter Burke and Donald Reitzes, "An Identity Theory Approach to Commitment," *Social Psychology Quarterly* 54 (1991): 280–86.

46. Everett Hughes, "Dilemmas and Contradictions in Status," *American Journal of Sociology* 50 (1945): 353–59.

47. Adler and Adler, *Backboards and Blackboards* (1991), 225.

48. Ralph Turner, "The Real Self: From Institution to Impulse," *American Sociological Review* 81 (1976): 989–1016, which argues that people find their real selves through conventional institutions or through expressive outlets.

49. David Snow and Leon Anderson, *Down on Their Luck: A Study of Homeless Street People* (Berkeley: University of California Press, 1993).

50. Alan Klein, *Baseball on the Border: A Tale of Two Laredos* (Princeton: Princeton University Press, 1997).

51. Stephen Holden, "Rock Kings, Drag Queens: A Common Strut," *New York Times,* June 14, 1998, Section 2:1.

52. Robert Granfield, *Making Elite Lawyers: Visions of Law at Harvard and Beyond* (New York: Routledge, 1992).

53. Alfred Lindesmith, *Opiate Addiction* (Evanston, Ill.: Principia Press, 1947).

54. J. David Brown, "Preprofessional Socialization and Identity Transformation: The Case of the Professional Ex.," *Journal of Contemporary Ethnography* 20 (1991): 157–78; Peele, *The Diseasing of America* (1989).

55. Snow and Anderson, *Down on Their Luck* (1993).

56. See Erving Goffman, *Stigma: Notes on the Sociology of Deviance* (Englewood Cliffs, N.J.: Prentice-Hall, 1963).

57. Fred Davis, "Deviance Disavowal: The Management of Strained Interaction by the Visibly Handicapped," *Social Problems* 9 (1961): 120–32.

58. David Robertson, "The Alcohologist's Addiction," *Quarterly Journal of Studies on Alcohol* 33 (1972): 1028–42.

59. Talcott Parsons, *The Social System* (Chicago: Free Press, 1951).

60. See Peele, *The Diseasing of America* (1989). Also, Herbert Fingerette, *Heavy Drinking: The Myth of Alcoholism as a Disease* (Berkeley: University of California Press, 1988); John Seeley, "Alcoholism as a Disease: Implications for Social Policy," in David Pittman and Charles Snyder (eds.), *Society, Culture, and Drinking Patterns* (New York: Wiley and Sons, 1962); Robin Room, "Sociological Aspects of the Disease Concept of Alcoholism," in *Research Advances in Alcohol and Drug Problems,* vol. 7 (New York: Plenum Press, 1983).

Notes to Chapter 5

1. Anthony Giddens, *The Constitution of Society* (Cambridge: Polity Press, 1984).

2. Ira Cohen, "Structuration Theory and Social Praxis," in Anthony Giddens and Jonathan Turner, *Social Theory Today* (Stanford: Stanford University Press, 1987).

3. For an overview of the theoretical debates in symbolic interactionism, see Larry Reynolds, *Interactionism: Exposition and Critique* (Dix Hills, N.Y.: General Hall, 1993).

4. Anthony Giddens, *Central Problems in Social Theory* (Berkeley: University of California Press, 1979).

5. Anthony Giddens, *Modernity and Self-Identity: Self and Society in the Late Modern Age* (Stanford: Stanford University Press, 1991), 9.

6. David Karp, *Speaking of Sadness* (New York: Oxford University Press, 1996), 186.

7. Christopher Lasch, *Haven in a Heartless World: The Family Besieged* (New York: W. W. Norton, 1995).

8. Stanley Aronowitz, *The Politics of Identity: Class, Culture, Social Movements* (New York: Routledge, 1992); Todd Gitlin, *The Twilight of Common Dreams: Why America Is Wracked by Culture Wars* (New York: Henry Holt, 1995).

9. Giddens, *Modernity and Self-Identity* (1991).

10. Anthony Giddens, *The Transformation of Intimacy* (Stanford: Stanford University Press, 1992), 74.

11. David Forbes, *False Fixes: The Cultural Politics of Drugs, Alcohol, and Addictive Relations* (Albany: State University of New York Press, 1994), 15.

12. Giddens, *Modernity and Self-Identity* (1991).

13. Ibid., 142.

14. Ibid., 143.

15. See Herbert Marcuse, *Eros and Civilization* (Boston: Beacon Press, 1955); Ralph Turner, "The Real Self: From Institution to Impulse," *American Sociological Review* 81 (1976): 989–1016.

16. Giddens, *Modernity and Self-Identity* (1991), 228.

17. Dan Waldorf, Craig Reinarman, and Sheigla Murphy, *Cocaine Changes: The Experience of Using and Quitting* (Philadelphia: Temple University Press, 1991). Sheigla Murphy and Marsha Rosenbaum, "Two Women Who Used Cocaine Too Much: Class, Race, Gender, Crack, and Coke," in Craig Reinarman and Harry Levine (eds.), *Crack in America: Demon Drugs and Social Justice* (Berkeley: University of California Press, 1997).

18. K. Jill Kiecolt, "Stress and the Decision to Change Oneself: A Theoretical Model," *Social Psychology Quarterly* 57 (1994): 61.

19. Victor Gecas and Michael Schwalbe, "Beyond the Looking Glass Self: Social Structure and Efficacy-Based Self-Esteem," *Social Psychology Quarterly* 46 (1983): 77–88.

20. James Coleman, *Foundations of Social Theory* (Cambridge: Harvard University Press, 1990), 302.

21. Pierre Bourdieu and Loic J. D. Wacquant, *An Invitation to Reflexive Sociology* (Chicago: University of Chicago Press, 1992), 119.

22. For discussions of "social capital," see Robert Putnam, *Making Democracy Work: Civic Traditions in Modern Italy* (Princeton: Princeton University Press, 1993); Francis Fukuyama, *Trust: The Social Virtues and the Creation of Prosperity* (New York: Free Press, 1995); and Coleman, *Foundations* (1990).

23. Mark Granovetter, *Getting a Job: A Study of Contacts and Careers* (Cambridge: Harvard University Press, 1974).

24. Mark Granovetter, "The Myth of Social Network Analysis as a Special Method in the Social Sciences," *Connections* 13 (1991): 13–16.

25. Mark Granovetter and Charles Tilly, "Inequality and Labor Processes," in Neal Smelser (ed.), *Handbook of Sociology* (Newbury Hills, Calif.: Sage, 1988), 192.

26. Granovetter, *Getting a Job* (1974); Robert Granfield and Thomas Koenig, "Pathways to Elite Law Firms: Professional Stratification and Social Networks," in Gwen Moore and Alan Whitt (eds.), *Research on Politics and Society* (Greenwich, Conn.: JAI Press, 1992).

27. Putnam, *Making Democracy Work* (1993); Robert Putnam, "Bowling Alone: America's Declining Social Capital," *Journal of Democracy* 6 (1995): 65–78.

28. Coleman, *Foundations* (1990); Fukuyama, *Trust* (1995).

29. Murphy and Rosenbaum, "Two Women Who Used Cocaine Too Much" (1997); Philippe Bourgois, *In Search of Respect: Selling Crack in El Barrio* (Cambridge: Cambridge University Press, 1995).

30. Kiecolt, "Stress and the Decision to Change Oneself," (1994); Gecas and Schwalbe, "Beyond the Looking Glass Self," (1983).

31. Chris Tilly and Charles Tilly, *Work under Capitalism* (Boulder, Colo.: Westview Press, 1998), 172.

32. Michael Piore and Charles Sabel, *The Second Industrial Divide: Possibilities for Prosperity* (New York: Basic Books, 1984).

33. William Julius Wilson, *When Work Disappears: The World of the New Urban Poor* (New York: Alfred A. Knopf, 1996).

34. Coleman, *Foundations* (1990), 320.

35. Ibid.

36. Fukuyama, *Trust* (1995).

37. Karp, *Speaking of Sadness* (1996).

38. Candace Clark, "Sympathy Biography and Sympathy Margin," *American Journal of Sociology* 93 (1987): 290–321.

39. Karp, *Speaking of Sadness* (1996).

40. Granovetter, *Getting a Job* (1974); Granfield and Koenig, "Pathways to Elite Law Firms" (1992). See also Mark Granovetter, "The Strength of Weak Ties," *American Journal of Sociology* 78 (1973): 1460–80.

41. Paul Goldstein, Henry Brownstein, Patrick Ryan, and Patricia Bellucci, "Crack and Homicide in New York City: A Case Study in the Epidemiology of Violence," in Craig Reinarman and Harry Levine (eds.), *Crack in America: Demon Drugs and Social Justice* (Berkeley, CA: University of California Press, 1997).

42. Isidor Chein, Donald Gerard, Robert Lee, and Eva Rosenberg, *The Road to H* (New York: Basic Books, 1964); Elliott Currie, *Reckoning: Drugs, the Cities, and the American Future* (New York: Hill and Wang, 1993).

43. Giddens, *The Transformation of Intimacy* (1992); Forbes, *False Fixes* (1994).

44. Giddens, *The Constitution of Society* (1984).

45. For a lucid discussion of the social reproduction of inequality, see Jay MacLeod, *Ain't No Makin' It* (Boulder, Colo.: Westview Press, 1995).

46. Paul Willis, *Learning to Labor* (New York: Columbia University Press, 1977).

47. Dorothy Holland and Margaret Eisenhart, *Educated in Romance* (Chicago: University of Chicago Press, 1990).

48. Mercer Sullivan, *"Getting Paid": Youth Crime and Work in the Inner City* (Ithaca, N.Y.: Cornell University Press, 1990); Elijah Anderson, *Streetwise: Race, Class, and Change in an Urban Community* (Chicago: University of Chicago Press, 1990).

49. See Karl Marx, *The Eighteenth Brumaire of Louis Bonaparte* (New York: International Publishing, 1969).

50. Giddens, *The Transformation of Intimacy* (1992), 94.

51. Ibid., 93.

Notes to Chapter 6

1. See Roberto Unger, *Social Theory: Its Situation and Its Task* (Cambridge: Cambridge University Press, 1987). Unger uses the term

"false necessity" as a way of dispelling the illusions associated with institutionalized thought and action. For Unger, liberation from "false necessity" does not eradicate the consuming power of illusions, but does allow for "antinecessitarian" possibilities. Because of this, overcoming false necessity is a radical project.

2. Glenn Walters, "Spontaneous Remission from Alcohol, Tobacco, and Other Drug Abuse: Seeking Quantitative Answers to Qualitative Questions" (in press).

3. Arnold Ludwig, "Cognitive Processes Associated with `Spontaneous' Recovery from Alcoholism," *Journal of Studies on Alcohol* 46 (1985): 53–58; Mark Sobell, Linda Sobell, Tony Toneatto, and Gloria Leo, "What Triggers the Resolution of Alcohol Problems without Treatment?" *Alcoholism: Clinical and Experimental Research* 17 (1993): 217–24; Jalie Tucker, Rudy Vuchinich, and Julie Gladsjo, "Environmental Events Surrounding Natural Recovery from Alcohol-Related Problems," *Addictions Nursing* 6 (1994): 117–28; Dan Waldorf, Craig Reinarman, and Sheigla Murphy, *Cocaine Changes: The Experience of Using and Quitting* (Philadelphia: Temple University Press, 1991).

4. David Armor and Jan Meshkoff, "Remission among Treated and Untreated Alcoholics," in Nancy Mello (ed.), *Advances in Substance Abuse: Behavioral and Biological Research* (Greenwich, Conn.: JAI Press, 1983); Ludwig, "Cognitive Processes Associated with `Spontaneous' Recovery from Alcoholism" (1985); Linda Sobell, Mark Sobell, and Tony Toneatto, "Recovery from Alcohol Problems without Treatment," in Nick Heather, William Miller, and J. Greely (eds.), *Self Control and the Addictive Behaviors,* (New York: Macmillan, 1992); Tucker, Vuchinich, and Gladsjo, "Environmental Events Surrounding Natural Recovery" (1994); George Vaillant and E. S. Milofsky, "Natural History of Male Alcoholism: IV. Paths to Recovery," *Archives of General Psychiatry* 39 (1982): 127–33; Walters, "Spontaneous Remission from Alcohol, Tobacco, and Other Drug Abuse" (in press).

5. William Cloud and Robert Granfield, "Natural Recovery from Addictions: Treatment Implications," *Addictions Nursing* 6 (1994): 112–16; Robert Granfield and William Cloud, "The Elephant That No One Sees: Natural Recovery among Middle-Class Addicts," *Journal of Drug Issues* 26 (1996): 45–61; Ludwig, "Cognitive Processes Associated with 'Spontaneous' Recovery from Alcoholism" (1985).

6. Linda Sobell, John Cunningham, Mark Sobell, Sangeeta Agrawal, Douglas Gavin, Gloria Leo, and Karen Singh, "Fostering Self-Change among Problem Drinkers: A Proactive Community Intervention," *Addictive Behaviors* 21 (1996): 817–33; Stanton Peele, *The Diseasing of America: Addiction Treatment Out of Control* (Lexington, Mass.: Lexington Books, 1989), 177.

7. Sobell et al., "Fostering Self-Change among Problem Drinkers" (1996).

8. Donald Goodwin, J. Bruce Crane, and Samuel B. Guze, "Felons Who Drink: An Eight-Year Follow-Up," *Quarterly Journal of Studies on Alcohol* 32 (1971): 136–47.

9. Peter Nathan, "Treatment Outcomes for Alcoholism in the U.S.: Current Research," in T. Lorberg, William Miller, Peter Nathan, and G. Alan Marlatt (eds.), *Addictive Behaviours: Prevention and Early Intervention* (Amsterdam: Swets and Zeitlinger, 1989), 87; Ron Roizen, Don Calahan, and Patricia Shanks, "'Spontaneous Remission' among Untreated Problem Drinkers," in Denise Kandel (ed.), *Longitudinal Research on Drug Use: Empirical Findings and Methodological Issues* (Washington, D.C.: Hemisphere Publishing, 1978), 197.

10. Barry Tuchfeld, "Spontaneous Remission in Alcoholics: Empirical Observations and Theoretical Implications," *Journal of Studies on Alcohol* 42 (1981): 626–41.

11. Waldorf, Reinarman, and Murphy, *Cocaine Changes* (1991).

12. James Maddux and David Desmond, "New Light on the Maturing Out Hypothesis in Opioid Dependence," *Bulletin on Narcotics* 32 (1980): 15–25.

13. Walters, "Spontaneous Remission from Alcohol, Tobacco, and Other Drug Abuse" (in press).

14. Sobell et al., "Fostering Self-Change among Problem Drinkers" (1996).

15. See, for example, William Cloud and Robert Granfield, "Terminating Addiction Naturally: Post-Addict Identity and the Avoidance of Treatment," *Clinical Sociological Review* 12 (1994): 159–74.

16. Michael Mueller and June Wyman, "Study Sheds New Light on the State of Drug Abuse Treatment Nationwide," National Institute on Drug Abuse, *NIDA Notes* 12 (1997): 1.

17. Victor Gecas and Michael Schwalbe, "Beyond the Looking Glass Self: Social Structure and Efficacy-Based Self-Esteem," *Social*

Psychology Quarterly 46 (1983): 77–88; Marsha Rosenbaum, *Women on Heroin* (New Brunswick, N.J.: Rutgers University Press, 1981).

18. Philippe Bourgois, *In Search of Respect: Selling Crack in El Barrio* (Cambridge: Cambridge University Press, 1995); Sheigla Murphy and Marsha Rosenbaum, "Two Women Who Used Cocaine Too Much: Class, Race, Gender, Crack, and Coke," in Craig Reinarman and Harry Levine (eds.), *Crack in America: Demon Drugs and Social Justice* (Berkeley: University of California Press, 1997), 109.

19. Rosenbaum, *Women on Heroin* (1981). See also Craig Reinarman, "The 12-Step Movement and Advanced Capitalist Culture: Notes on the Politics of Self-Control in Postmodernity," in M. Darnovsky, B. Epstein, and R. Flacks (eds.), *Cultural Politics and Social Movements* (Philadelphia: Temple University Press, 1995).

20. Waldorf, Reinarman, and Murphy, *Cocaine Changes* (1991).

21. Granfield and Cloud, "The Elephant That No One Sees," (1996); Sobell et al., "What Triggers the Resolution of Alcohol Problems without Treatment?" (1993).

22. Personal correspondence with the Betty Ford Clinic in California, the Hazelden Foundation in Minnesota, and the Cottonwood De Tucson Treatment Facility in Tucson, Arizona (November 1998).

23. Personal correspondence with four inpatient drug and alcohol treatment facilities in Denver, Colorado (November 1998).

24. Lani Nelson-Zlupko, Eda Kauffman, and Martha Morrison Dore, "Gender Differences in Drug Addiction and Treatment: Implications for Social Work Intervention with Substance-Abusing Women," *Social Work* 40 (January 1995): 45.

25. Maureen Norton-Hawk, "Unintended Consequences: The Prosecution of Maternal Substance Abuse," in Peter Venturelli (ed.), *Drug Use in America: Social, Cultural, and Political Perspectives* (Boston: Jones and Bartlett, 1994); Laura Gomez, *Misconceiving Mothers* (Philadelphia: Temple University Press, 1997).

26. George DeLeon, "Therapeutic Communities," in Marc Galanter and Herbert Kebler (eds.), *Textbook of Substance Abuse Treatment* (Washington, D.C.: American Psychiatric Press, 1994).

27. Peele, *The Diseasing of America* (1989).

28. Ibid.

29. Cloud and Granfield, "Terminating Addiction Naturally (1994).

30. Peter Burke, "Identity Processes and Social Stress," *American Sociological Review* 56 (1991): 836–49.

31. Ibid., 847.

32. Marsh Ray, "The Cycle of Abstinence and Relapse among Heroin Addicts," in Howard Becker (ed.), *The Other Side* (New York: Free Press, 1964).

33. Douglas Cameron, *Liberating Solutions to Alcohol Problems: Treating Problem Drinkers without Saying No* (Northvale, N.J.: Jason Aronson, 1995).

34. Peele, *The Diseasing of America* (1989).

35. Harrison Trice and Paul Roman, "Delabeling, Relabeling, and Alcoholics Anonymous," *Social Problems* 17 (1970): 538–46.

36. Howard Becker, *The Outsiders: Studies in the Sociology of Deviance* (Glencoe, Ill.: Free Press, 1963); Edwin Lemert, *Social Pathology* (New York: McGraw-Hill, 1951).

37. Peele, *The Diseasing of America* (1989).

38. Albert Bandura, *Social Foundations of Thought and Action: A Social Cognitive Theory* (Englewood Cliffs, N.J.: Prentice-Hall, 1986).

39. Albert Bandura, "Human Agency in Social Cognitive Theory," *American Psychologist* 44 (1989): 1176.

40. Ibid.

41. Martin Bloom, *Primary Prevention Practices* (Thousand Oaks, Calif.: Sage, 1996).

42. Lorraine Gutierrez, Ruth Parsons, and Enid Cox, *Empowerment in Social Work Practice: A Sourcebook* (Pacific Grove, Calif.: Brooks/Cole Publishing, 1998), xix.

43. Douglas Perkins and Marc Zimmerman, "Empowerment Theory, Research, and Application," *American Journal of Community Psychology* 23 (1995): 569–78.

44. Marc Zimmerman, "Psychological Empowerment: Issues and Illustrations," *American Journal of Community Psychology* 23 (1995): 581–99.

45. Perkins and Zimmerman, "Empowerment Theory, Research, and Application" (1995).

46. Ibid. See also Ruth Parsons, "Empowerment Based Social Work Practice: A Study of Process and Outcomes," paper presented at the Annual Program Meeting of the Council on Social Work Education, San Diego, Calif., 1995.

47. Francis Fukuyama, *Trust: The Social Virtues and the Creation of Prosperity* (New York: Free Press, 1995).

48. Perkins and Zimmerman, "Empowerment Theory, Research, and Application" (1995).

49. Henry Giroux, *Border Crossings: Cultural Workers and the Politics of Education* (New York: Routledge, 1992).

50. Jeffry Galper, *The Politics of Social Services* (Englewood Cliffs, N.J.: Prentice-Hall, 1975); Steven Wineman, *The Politics of Human Services* (Boston: South End Press, 1984).

51. Zimmerman, "Psychological Empowerment" (1995); Marc Zimmerman, B. Israel, A. Schulz, and B. Checkoway, "Further Explorations in Empowerment Theory: An Empirical Analysis of Psychological Empowerment," *American Journal of Community Psychology* 20 (1992): 707–27.

52. William Cloud, "From Down Under: A Qualitative Study on Heroin Addiction Recovery," Ph.D. dissertation, University of Denver (1987); Granfield and Cloud, "The Elephant That No One Sees" (1996); Sobell et al., "What Triggers the Resolution of Alcohol Problems without Treatment?" (1993); Tucker, Vuchinich, and Gladsjo, "Environmental Events Surrounding Natural Recovery" (1994); Dan Waldorf, "Natural Recovery from Opiate Addiction: Some Social-Psychological Processes of Untreated Recovery," *Journal of Drug Issues* 13 (Spring 1983): 237–80; Walters, "Spontaneous Remission from Alcohol, Tobacco, and Other Drug Abuse" (in press).

53. Nick Heather, "The Public Health and Brief Interventions for Excessive Alcohol Consumption: The British Experience," *Addictive Behaviors* 21 (1996): 857–68.

54. Thomas Bien, William Miller, and J. Scott Tonigan, "Brief Interventions for Alcohol Problems: A Review," *Addiction* 88 (1993): 315–36; Cameron, *Liberating Solutions* (1995).

55. Cloud and Granfield, "Natural Recovery from Addictions" (1994); Judith Lewis, Robert Dana, and Gregory Blevins, *Substance Abuse Counseling: An Individualized Approach*, 2nd ed. (Pacific Grove, Calif.: Brooks/Cole Publishing, 1994): 15; Sobell et al., "What Triggers the Resolution of Alcohol Problems without Treatment?" (1993); Arnold Washton, *Cocaine Addiction: Treatment, Recovery, and Relapse Prevention* (New York: Norton, 1989), 75.

56. William Miller and Richard Hester, "Inpatient Alcoholism Treat-

ment: Who Benefits?" *American Psychologist* 41 (1986): 794–805. See also Stanton Peele and Archie Brodsky, with Mary Arnold, *The Truth about Addiction and Recovery: The Life Process Program for Outgrowing Destructive Habits* (New York: Simon and Schuster, 1991).

57. Bien, Miller, and Tonigan, "Brief Interventions for Alcohol Problems" (1993). This point is also made in the recent Project MATCH findings. See Project MATCH Group, "Matching Alcoholism Treatments to Client Heterogeneity: Project MATCH Posttreatment Drinking Outcomes," *Journal of Studies on Alcohol* 58 (January 1997): 7–29.

58. Heather, "The Public Health and Brief Interventions for Excessive Alcohol Consumption" (1996).

59. Sobell et al., "Fostering Self-Change among Problem Drinkers" (1996).

60. Heather, "The Public Health and Brief Interventions for Excessive Alcohol Consumption" (1996); William Miller, R. Gayle Benefield, and J. Scott Tonigan, "Enhancing Motivation for Change in Problem Drinking: A Controlled Comparison of Two Therapist Styles," *Journal of Consulting and Clinical Psychology* 93 (1993): 455–61; Thiagarajan Sithartan, David Kavanagh, and Geoffrey Sayer, "Moderating Drinking by Correspondence: An Evaluation of a New Method of Intervention," *Addiction* 91 (1996): 345–53.

61. Linda Sobell, John Cunningham, and Mark Sobell, "Recovery from Alcohol Problems with and without Treatment: Prevalence in Two Population Surveys," *American Journal of Public Health* 96 (1996): 966–72.

62. Heather, "The Public Health and Brief Interventions for Excessive Alcohol Consumption" (1996).

63. James Coleman, *Foundations of Social Theory* (Cambridge: Harvard University Press, 1990); Robert Putnam, *Making Democracy Work: Civic Traditions in Modern Italy* (Princeton: Princeton University Press, 1993).

64. Coleman, *Foundations* (1990), 304.

65. Ibid.

66. Ibid.

67. John Hagan and Bill McCarthy, *Mean Streets: Youth, Crime, and Homelessness* (Cambridge: Cambridge University Press, 1997).

68. Coleman, *Foundations* (1990).

69. Rosenbaum, *Women on Heroin* (1981).

70. Charles Faupel, *Shooting Dope: Career Patterns of Hard-Core Heroin Users* (Gainesville, Fla.: University of Florida Press, 1991).

71. William Julius Wilson, *When Work Disappears: The World of the New Urban Poor* (New York: Alfred A. Knopf, 1996).

72. Harold Dowieko, *Concepts of Chemical Dependency*, 4th ed. (Pacific Grove, Calif.: Brooks/Cole Publishing, 1999); Paul Mulinski, "Dual Diagnosis in Alcoholic Clients: Clinical Applications," *Social Casework* 70 (1989): 333–39.

73. Dowieko, *Concepts of Chemical Dependency* (1999).

74. Granfield and Cloud, "The Elephant That No One Sees," (1996); Sobell, Cunningham, and Sobell, "Recovery from Alcohol Problems" (1996); Patrick Biernacki, *Pathways from Heroin Addiction: Recovery without Treatment* (Philadelphia: Temple University Press, 1986).

75. Cloud and Granfield, "Natural Recovery from Addictions" (1994); Lewis, Dana, and Blevins, *Substance Abuse Counseling* (1994), 4; Mark Sobell and Linda Sobell, *Problem Drinking: Guided Self-Change Treatment* (New York: Guilford Press, 1993), 6.

76. Burke, "Identity Processes and Social Stress" (1991).

77. Helen Annis, "Relapse to Substance Abuse: Empirical Findings within a Cognitive Learning Approach," *Journal of Psychoactive Drugs* 22 (1990): 117–24; Dennis Daley, *Kicking Addictive Habits Once and for All: A Relapse Prevention Guide* (San Francisco: Jossey-Bass, 1991); Terence Gorski, "Relapse Prevention: A State of the Art Overview," *Addiction and Recovery* (March/April 1993): 25; G. Alan Marlatt and Judith Gordon (eds.), *Relapse Prevention: Maintenance Strategies in the Treatment of Addictive Behaviors* (New York: Guilford Press, 1985).

78. Steven Stocker, "Drug Addiction Treatment Conference Emphasizes Combining Therapies," *NIDA Notes*, National Institute on Drug Abuse 13 (1998): 1.

79. Gary Fisher and Thomas Harrison, *Substance Abuse: Information for Social Workers, Therapists, and Counselors* (Needham Heights, Mass.: Allyn and Bacon, 1997), 256.

80. C. Cummings, Judith Gordon, and G. Alan Marlatt, "Relapse: Strategies of Prevention and Prediction," in William Miller (ed.), *The Addictive Behaviors* (Oxford: Permagon, 1980); Marlatt and Gordon, *Relapse Prevention* (1985).

81. Daley, *Kicking Addictive Habits Once and for All* (1991).

82. Terence Gorski, "The CENAPS Model of Relapse Prevention: Basic Principles and Procedures," *Journal of Psychoactive Drugs* 22 (1990): 125–33.

83. Annis, "Relapse to Substance Abuse" (1990).

84. Helen Annis, *Inventory of Drinking Situations* (Toronto: Addiction Research Foundation of Ontario, 1982).

85. Hagan and McCarthy, *Mean Streets* (1997).

86. Ibid.

87. Robert Prus, *Symbolic Interaction and Ethnographic Research: Intersubjectivity and the Study of Human Lived Experience* (Albany: State University of New York Press, 1996); David Karp, *Speaking of Sadness* (New York: Oxford University Press, 1996).

88. Murphy and Rosenbaum, "Two Women Who Used Cocaine Too Much (1997).

89. Hagan and McCarthy, *Mean Streets* (1997).

90. Biernacki, *Pathways from Heroin Addiction* (1986).

91. Ibid.

92. Ibid.

Notes to Chapter 7

1. Howard Shaffer and Stephanie Jones, *Quitting Cocaine: The Struggle against Impulse* (Lexington, Mass.: Lexington Books, 1989); Patrick Biernacki, *Pathways from Heroin Addiction: Recovery without Treatment* (Philadelphia: Temple University Press, 1986).

2. Ralph Turner, "Role Change," *Annual Review of Sociology* 16 (1990): 887.

3. Biernacki, *Pathways from Heroin Addiction* (1986).

4. Charles Cooley, *Human Nature and Social Order* (New York: Scribner's 1902); George Herbert Mead, *Mind, Self and Society* (Chicago: University of Chicago Press, 1934).

5. Norman Denzin, *Symbolic Interactionism and Cultural Studies: The Politics of Interpretation* (Cambridge: Blackwell, 1992).

6. See Peter Burke and Donald Reitzes, "An Identity Theory Approach to Commitment," *Social Psychology Quarterly* 54 (1991): 280–86, and D. L. Morgan and Michael Schwalbe, "Mind and Self in Society: Linking Social Structure and Social Cognition," *Social Psychology Quarterly* 53 (1990): 148.

7. Harry Stack Sullivan, *The Interpersonal Theory of Psychiatry* (New York: W. W. Norton, 1953).

8. Erving Goffman, *The Presentation of Self in Society* (New York: Doubleday, 1959).

9. Sheldon Stryker, *Symbolic Interactionism: A Social Structural Version* (Menlo Park, Calif.: Cummings, 1980). See also Sheldon Stryker and Richard Serpe, "Commitment, Identity Salience, and Role Behavior: Theory and Research Example," in W. Ickes and E. Knowles (eds.), *Personality, Roles, and Social Behavior* (New York: Springer-Verlag, 1982).

10. Burke and Reitzes, "An Identity Theory Approach to Commitment" (1991).

11. Peter Callero, "Role-Identity Salience," *Social Psychology Quarterly* 48 (1985): 203–15.

12. Sheldon Stryker, "Identity Salience and Role Performance: The Importance of Symbolic Interaction Theory for Family Research," *Journal of Marriage and the Family* 30 (1968): 558–64.

13. Arlie Hochschild, *The Time Bind: When Work Becomes Home and Home Becomes Work* (New York: Owl Books, 1997).

14. John Hoelter, "The Effects of Role Evaluation and Commitment on Identity Salience," *Social Psychology Quarterly* 46 (1983): 14–47.

15. Michael Hogg, Deborah Terry, and Katherine White, "A Tale of Two Theories: A Critical Comparison of Identity Theory with Social Identity Theory," *Social Psychology Quarterly* 58 (1995): 255–68.

16. Burke and Reitzes, "An Identity Theory Approach to Commitment" (1991).

17. Richard Stephens, *The Street Addict Role: A Theory of Heroin Addiction* (Albany: State University of New York Press, 1991): 42.

18. Ibid., 58–59.

19. See James Prochaska and Carlo DiClemente, "Toward a Comprehensive Model of Change," in William Miller and Richard Hester (eds.), *Treating Addictive Behaviors: Processes of Change* (New York: Plenum Press, 1986). See also James Prochaska, Carlo DiClemente, and John Norcross, "In Search of How People Change: Applications to Addictive Behaviors," *American Psychologist* 47 (1992): 1102–14.

20. Stanton Peele, "Recovering from an All-or-Nothing Approach to Alcohol," *Psychology Today* (September/October 1996): 35–43, 68–70.

21. Robert Prus, *Symbolic Interaction and Ethnographic Research:*

Intersubjectivity and the Study of Human Lived Experience (Albany: State University of New York Press, 1996), 174.

22. Peele, "Recovering from an All-or-Nothing Approach to Alcohol" (1996).

23. Norman Zinberg, *Drug, Set, and Setting: The Basis for Controlled Intoxicant Use* (New Haven, Conn.: Yale University Press, 1984).

24. Dan Waldorf, Craig Reinarman, and Sheigla Murphy, *Cocaine Changes: The Experience of Using and Quitting* (Philadelphia: Temple University Press, 1991).

25. David Forbes, *False Fixes: The Cultural Politics of Drugs, Alcohol, and Addictive Relations* (Albany: State University of New York Press, 1994).

26. See Robert Granfield, "Converting the Converted: Differentials in Adolescent Receptivity to Alcohol Education," in Brenda Forester and Jeffrey Salloway (eds.), *Preventions and Treatments of Alcohol and Drug Abuse* (Lewiston, N.Y.: Edwin Mullen Press, 1991).

27. Earl Wysong, Richard Aniskiewicz, and David Wright, "Truth and DARE: Tracking Drug Education to Graduation and as Symbolic Politics," *Social Problems* 41 (1994): 448–72.

28. Dirk Johnson, "Second Thoughts on Cops in the Class," *New York Times* (September 27, 1998): sec. 4, p. 3.

29. For a review of research studies on DARE, see Susan Ennett, Nancy Tobler, Christopher Ringwalt, and Robert Flewelling, "How Effective Is Drug Abuse Resistance Education? A Meta-Analysis of Project DARE Outcome Evaluations," *American Journal of Public Health* 84 (1994): 1394–1401. It should be pointed out that DARE officials sought to interfere with the publication of this study's results. See Dennis Cauchon, "Study Critical of DARE Rejected," *USA Today* (October 4, 1994): 2A.

30. Steven Schinke, Gilbert Botvin, and Mario Orlando, *Substance Abuse in Children and Adolescents: Evaluation and Intervention* (Newbury Park, Calif.: Sage, 1991); Gilbert Botvin, "Substance Abuse Prevention: Theory, Practice, and Effectiveness," in Michael Tonry and James Q. Wilson (eds.), *Drugs and Crime* (Chicago: University of Chicago Press, 1990).

31. Karen Auge, "Cities Take DARE—and Drop It," *Denver Post* (December 7, 1998): A1.

32. David Duncan and Rick Petosa, "Social and Community Factors Associated with Drug Use and Abuse among Adolescents," in Thomas Gullotta, Gerald Adams, and Raymond Montemayor (eds.), *Substance Misuse in Adolescence* (Thousand Oaks, Calif.: Sage, 1995).

33. J. David Hawkins, Richard F. Catalano, and Janet Y. Miller, "Risk and Protective Factors for Alcohol and Other Drug Problems in Adolescence and Early Childhood: Implications for Substance Abuse Prevention," *Psychological Bulletin* 112 (1992): 64–105.

34. Albert Bandura, *Social Foundations of Thought and Action: A Social Cognitive Theory* (Englewood Cliffs, N.J.: Prentice-Hall, 1986); Ronald Akers, Marvin Krohn, L. Lanza-Kaduce, and M. Radosevich, "Social Learning and Deviant Behavior: A Specific Test of a General Theory," *American Sociological Review* 44 (1979): 636–55.

35. Travis Hirschi, *Causes of Delinquency* (Berkeley: University of California Press, 1969).

36. Stanton Peele, "What Can We Expect from Treatment of Adolescent Drug and Alcohol Abuse?" *Pediatrician* 14 (1987): 67.

37. Ibid.

38. Doug Easterling, Kaia Gallagher, Jodi Drisko, and Tracy Johnson, *Promoting Health by Building Community Capacity: Evidence and Implications for Grantmakers* (Denver: Colorado Trust, 1998).

39. Robert Putnam, "Bowling Alone: America's Declining Social Capital," *Journal of Democracy* 6 (1995): 65.

40. See Alan Wolfe, *Whose Keeper? Social Science and Moral Obligation* (Berkeley: University of California Press, 1989), which argues that government subsidies to the poor may undermine collective action.

41. John McKnight, *The Careless Society: Community and Its Counterfeits* (New York: Basic Books, 1995), xi.

42. Craig Reinarman and Harry Levine (eds.), *Crack in America: Demon Drugs and Social Justice* (Berkeley: University of California Press, 1997), 319.

43. Eva Bertram, Morris Blachman, Kenneth Sharpe, and Peter Andreas, *Drug War Politics: The Price of Denial* (Berkeley: University of California Press, 1996); Steven Witosky, *Beyond the War on Drugs: Overcoming a Failed Public Policy* (Buffalo, N.Y.: Prometheus Books, 1990); Dan Baum, *Smoke and Mirrors: The War on Drugs and the Politics of Failure* (Boston: Little Brown, 1996); Mike Grey, *Drug Crazy:*

How We Got into This Mess and How We Can Get Out (New York: Random House, 1998); Richard Miller, *Drug Warriors and Their Prey: From Police Power to Police State* (Westport, Conn.: Praeger, 1996).

44. See Jeffrey A. Fagan, "Do Criminal Sanctions Deter Drug Crimes?" in Doris Layton MacKenzie and Craig Uchida (eds.), *Drugs and Crime: Evaluating Public Policy Initiatives* (Thousand Oaks, Calif.: Sage, 1994).

45. James Inciardi and Anne Pottieger, "Kids, Crack, and Crime," *Journal of Drug Issues* 21 (1991): 266–67.

46. William McColl, "Baltimore City's Drug Treatment Court: Theory and Practice in an Emerging Field," *Maryland Law Review* 55 (1996): 478.

47. Elliott Currie, *Reckoning: Drugs, the Cities, and the American Future* (New York: Hill and Wang, 1993), 199.

48. Ibid., 201.

49. Jeffry Tauber, *The Importance of Immediate and Intensive Intervention in a Court-Ordered Drug Rehabilitation Program: An Evaluation of the F.I.R.S.T. Diversion Project after Two Years* (Oakland, Calif.: Municipal Court, Oakland-Piedmont-Emeryville Judicial District, 1993).

50. Robert Granfield, Cynthia Eby, and Thomas Brewster, "An Examination of the Denver Drug Court: The Impact of a Treatment-Oriented Drug-Offender-System," *Law and Policy* 20 (1998): 183–202.

51. Peter Reuter, "Hawks Ascendant: The Punitive Trend of American Drug Policy," *Daedalus* 121 (1992): 15–52.

52. McColl, "Baltimore City's Drug Treatment Court" (1996), 514.

53. Tauber, *The Importance of Immediate and Intensive Intervention* (1993), 29.

54. Janet Reno, "The Criminal Justice System: Toward the 21st Century," *Duke Journal of Gender Law and Policy* 1 (1994): 39–50.

55. Eva Bertram and Kenneth Sharpe, "Resisters Say We're Fighting the Wrong Battles," *Nation* (January 6, 1997): 11.

56. Carrie Menkel-Meadow, "The Trouble with the Adversary System in a Post-Modern, Multi-Cultural World," *William and Mary Law Review* 38 (1996): 5–44.

57. Bertram et al., *Drug War Politics* (1996), 256.

58. Bertram and Sharpe, "Resisters Say" (1997).

59. Ethan Nadelmann, "Drug Prohibition in the United States:

Costs, Consequences, and Alternatives," in James Inciardi and Karen McElrath (eds.), *The American Drug Scene: An Anthology* (Los Angeles: Roxbury Publishing, 1995).

60. Tracy Meares, "Rethinking Federal Criminal Law: Charting Race and Class Differences in Attitudes toward Drug Legalization and Law Enforcement: Lessons for Federal Criminal Law," *Buffalo Criminal Law Review* 1 (1997): 165. See also Tracy Meares, "Social Organization and Drug Law Enforcement," *American Criminal Law Review* 35 (1998): 191–227, for a further discussion of how punitive drug policies break down social organization and social networks.

61. Reinarman and Levine, *Crack in America* (1997), 341.

62. Robert Bales, "Attitudes toward Drinking in the Irish Culture," in David Pittman and Charles Synder (eds.), *Society, Culture, and Drinking Patterns* (New York: John Wiley, 1962).

63. Zinberg, *Drug, Set, and Setting* (1984).

64. Wolfgang Schivelbusch, *Tastes of Paradise: A Social History of Spices, Stimulants, and Intoxicants* (New York: Vintage, 1993).

65. Lee Robins, Darlene Davis, and Donald Goodwin, "Drug Use in U.S. Army Enlisted Men in Vietnam: A Follow-Up on Their Return Home," *American Journal of Epidemiology* 99 (1974): 235–49.

66. Howard Becker, "History, Culture, and Subjective Experience: An Exploration of the Bases of Drug-Induced Experiences," *Journal of Health and Social Behavior* 8 (1967): 162–76.

67. Zinberg, *Drug, Set, and Setting* (1984).

68. Waldorf, Reinarman, and Murphy, *Cocaine Changes* (1991), 279.

69. Frederic Jameson, *Postmodernism or, The Cultural Logic of Late Capitalism* (Durham, N.C.: Duke University Press, 1991).

70. Alan Wolfe, "Out of the Frying Pan, into… What?," in Alan Wolfe (ed.), *America at Century's End* (Berkeley: University of California Press, 1991).

71. See C. Wright Mills, *The Sociological Imagination* (London: Oxford University Press, 1959).

72. David Harvey, *The Condition of Postmodernity* (Cambridge: Blackwell, 1989), 65.

73. Kenneth Gerson, *The Saturated Self: Dilemmas of Identity in Modern Life* (New York: Basic Books, 1991), 7.

74. See James Davidson Hunter, *Culture Wars: The Struggle to Define America* (New York: Basic Books, 1995).

75. Francis Fukuyama, *Trust: The Social Virtues and the Creation of Prosperity* (New York: Free Press, 1995), 312.

76. Todd Gitlin, *The Twilight of Common Dreams: Why America Is Wracked by Culture Wars* (New York: Henry Holt, 1995).

77. Norman Denzin, *The Alcoholic Society* (New Brunswick, N.J.: Transaction Books, 1993), 369.

78. R. J. Sampson, S. W. Raudenbush, and F. Earls, "Neighborhoods and Violent Crime: A Multilevel Study of Collective Efficacy," *Science* 277 (1997): 918.

79. Anthony Giddens, *Modernity and Self-Identity: Self and Society in the Late Modern Age* (Stanford: Stanford University Press, 1991), 28.

80. Amitai Etzioni, *The Moral Dimension: Toward a New Economics* (New York: Free Press, 1988). Etzioni, a leader in the "communitarian movement," argues that a responsive community is one in which "the individual and the community make each other and require each other." For Etzioni, a balance between these two dimensions of life is necessary to develop a moral society. As Etzioni writes, "While it is possible to think abstractly about individuals apart from community, if individuals were actually without community they would have very few of the attributes commonly associated with the notion of an individual person. Such individuals typically are mentally unstable, impulsive, prone to suicide, and otherwise mentally and psychosomatically ill. . . . The I's need a We to be." *The Moral Dimension* (1988), 9.

81. Elijah Anderson, *Streetwise: Race, Class, and Change in an Urban Community* (Chicago: University of Chicago Press, 1990).

82. William Julius Wilson, *When Work Disappears: The World of the New Urban Poor* (New York: Alfred A Knopf, 1996).

83. Jay MacLeod, *Ain't No Makin' It* (Boulder, Colo.: Westview Press, 1995).

84. Loïc Wacquant, "The Ghetto, the State, and the New Capitalist Economy," *Dissent* (Fall 1989): 508–20.

INDEX

ABOUT THE AUTHORS

Robert Granfield is an associate professor of sociology at the University of Denver. His primary scholarly interests lie in the areas of drugs and society and the sociology of law. He is the author of *Making Elite Lawyers: Visions of Law at Harvard and Beyond*, as well as several articles on the subjects of legal ethics, law school socialization, drug courts, drug policy, disabilities, and social theory. He was formerly a director of an adolescent alcohol and drug abuse program outside Boston. He is also a professional percussionist with the Kusagea Nobi Drum Ensemble, which performs and records traditional rhythms from West Africa.

William Cloud is an associate professor at the Graduate School of Social Work at the University of Denver, where he developed and has been chair of the Drug Dependency

Concentration in the M.S.W. program. His extensive research and practice experience in addictions began over two decades ago.

Stanton Peele is a psychologist and attorney in Morristown, New Jersey. His highly influential publications on the nature and treatment of addiction include such books as *Love and Addiction, The Meaning of Addiction, Diseasing of America,* and *The Truth about Addiction and Recovery.* He is a winner of the Mark Keller Award, given by the Rutgers Center of Alcohol Studies, and the Lindesmith Award for lifetime achievement in scholarship from the Drug Policy Foundation.